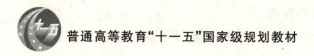
普通高等教育"十一五"国家级规划教材

Selected Articles from American & British
Newspapers & Magazines
Volume II

美英报刊文章选读

下册

（第五版）

主　编	周学艺	郭丽萍			
副主编	马　兴	艾久红			
编　委	袁宪军	杨小凤	艾久红	陈文玉	丁剑仪
	高天增	葛　红	郭丽萍	李素杰	李　欣
	刘满贵	刘雪燕	罗国华	马　兴	石　芸
	江学磊	韦毅民	徐　威	杨　博	叶慧瑛
	张慧宇	赵　林	周建萍	周学艺	左　进

北京大学出版社
PEKING UNIVERSITY PRESS

图书在版编目(CIP)数据

美英报刊文章选读. 下册/周学艺,郭丽萍主编. —5 版. —北京:北京大学出版社,2014.5
(大学美英报刊教材系列)
ISBN 978-7-301-24100-4

Ⅰ.①美… Ⅱ.①周…②郭… Ⅲ.①英语—阅读教学—高等学校—自学参考资料 Ⅳ.①H319.4

中国版本图书馆 CIP 数据核字(2014)第 068360 号

书　　　名:	美英报刊文章选读(下册)(第五版)
著作责任者:	周学艺　郭丽萍　主编
责 任 编 辑:	李　颖
标 准 书 号:	ISBN 978-7-301-24100-4/H・3502
出 版 发 行:	北京大学出版社
地　　　址:	北京市海淀区成府路 205 号　100871
网　　　址:	http://www.pup.cn　新浪官方微博:@北京大学出版社
电 子 信 箱:	zpup@pup.cn
电　　　话:	邮购部 62752015　发行部 62750672　编辑部 62754382
	出版部 62754962
印　　　刷　者:	三河市博文印刷有限公司
经　　　销　者:	新华书店
	730 毫米×980 毫米　16 开本　13.5 印张　400 千字
	1996 年 4 月第 1 版　2001 年 10 月第 2 版
	2007 年 1 月第 3 版　2010 年 8 月第 4 版
	2014 年 5 月第 5 版　2023 年 1 月第 6 次印刷
定　　　价:	32.00 元

未经许可,不得以任何方式复制或抄袭本书之部分或全部内容。
版权所有,侵权必究
举报电话: 010−62752024　电子信箱: fd@pup.pku.edu.cn

Contents

Unit Eight
The World

Lesson Twenty-four
    Text   Greece as Victim
           （希腊危机，孰之过?）
           (*The New York Times*, June 17, 2012) ················ 2
    语言解说 借喻词和提喻词（Ⅰ）················ 8

Lesson Twenty-five
    Text   The Coming Conflict in the Arctic
           （世界列强北冰洋争霸）
           (*Global Research*, July 17, 2007) ················ 11
    语言解说 借喻词和提喻词（Ⅱ）················ 19

Lesson Twenty-six
    Text   Rethinking the Welfare State: Asia's Next Revolution
           （亚洲国家福利制度改革需慎行）
           (*The Economist*, September 8, 2012) ················ 22
    语言解说 委婉语 ················ 33

Lesson Twenty-seven
    Text   The Hopeful Continent: Africa Rising
           （充满希望的大陆——非洲正在崛起）
           (*The Economist*, December 3, 2011) ················ 35
    读报知识 报刊的政治倾向性 ················ 42

Unit Nine
Society

Lesson Twenty-eight
    Text   Does Online Dating Make It Harder to Find 'the One'

　　　　　（交友网站能找到意中人吗？）
　　　　　(*Time*, February 7, 2012) ················· 44
　　新闻写作　句法上的简约 ················· 52

Lesson Twenty-nine
　　Text　Yawns: A generation of the young, rich and frugal
　　　　　（年轻而富有、节俭而朴实的一代）
　　　　　(The Associated Press, May 4, 2008) ············· 55
　　语言解说　Generation 何其多？ ················· 65

Lesson Thirty
　　Text　Ahead-of-the-Curve Careers
　　　　　（领先于潮流的新职业）
　　　　　(*U.S. News & World Report*, December 19, 2007) ········· 66
　　语言解说　Administration 和 Government ············· 74

Unit Ten
Business

Lesson Thirty-one
　　Text　Model economics: The beauty business
　　　　　（模特经济学：美女产业）
　　　　　(*The Economist*, February 11, 2012) ············· 76
　　新闻写作　报刊常用套语 ················· 87

Lesson Thirty-two
　　Text　Free talking and fast results
　　　　　（美国商人的谈判之道）
　　　　　(*Financial Times*, August 2, 2000) ············· 89
　　学习方法　勤上网和查词典 ················· 95

Lesson Thirty-three
　　Text　A Bountiful Undersea Find, Sure to Invite Debate
　　　　　（海底宝藏打捞引争议）
　　　　　(*The New York Times*, May 19, 2007) ············· 98
　　语言解说　Community ················· 105

Unit Eleven
Science

Lesson Thirty-four
 Text Google's zero-carbon quest
   （谷歌的零碳计划）
   (*Fortune*, July 12, 2012) ·············· 106
 语言解说 科技旧词引申出新义 ·············· 118

Lesson Thirty-five
 Text Nanospheres leave cancer no place to hide
   （纳米球使癌细胞无处藏身）
   (*New Scientist*, June 21, 2007) ·············· 121
 语言解说 Nano/Virtual/Cyber ·············· 126

Lesson Thirty-six
 Text Why Bilinguals Are Smarter
   （掌握外语使你更聪明）
   (*The New York Times*, Mar 18, 2012) ·············· 128
 广告与漫画 内容和语言特色 ·············· 134

Lesson Thirty-seven
 Text The Evolution Wars
   （进化论与上帝造人说之争）
   (*Time*, August 15, 2005) ·············· 137
 读报知识 宗教 ·············· 150

Unit Twelve
Sports and Entertainment

Lesson Thirty-eight
 Text Basketball: The incredible story of Jeremy Lin,
   the new superstar of the NBA
   （林书豪：NBA 传奇新星）
   (*The Independent*, February 16, 2012) ·············· 154
 学习方法 英语为何生词多而难记 ·············· 160

Lesson Thirty-nine
 Text Kaka: Brazil's Mr. Perfect

　　　　（卡卡：巴西人的偶象）
　　　　（FIFA.com, November 30, 2007）……………… 162
　　学习方法　名师指点词语记忆法……………………………… 171
Lesson Forty
　　Text　The reality-television business: Entertainers to the world
　　　　（电视真人秀娱乐全球）
　　　　（*The Economist*, November 5, 2011）……………… 173
　　学习方法　词根的重要性………………………………………… 181

附　录

I　报刊标题常用词汇 ……………………………………… 184
II　标题自我测试 …………………………………………… 189
III　报刊课考试的若干建议 ………………………………… 194
IV　考试样题 ………………………………………………… 196

Unit Eight
The World

Lesson Twenty-four

课文导读

  2009 年发端于希腊的欧洲主权债务危机曾显现出向欧元区核心国家蔓延的态势,西班牙、爱尔兰、葡萄牙等国虽然与希腊病情各异,但都要求欧盟、IMF 等救助。这严重阻碍欧洲乃至全球经济复苏的脚步。在作者看来,欧盟不是一个统一的国家,却在多国发行同一货币并实施统一的货币政策,一旦出事就难以调解。虽然希腊在加入欧元区之前,就已经出现腐败、偷漏税、高失业率等问题,但依靠其旅游和造船业仍可"维持生计"。在加入欧元区之后,希腊一度被认为是安全的投资之地。事实上,希腊经济表面繁荣,但国债高,通胀上升快。巨大的财政赤字和滞涨的经济状况使其变得日益缺乏竞争力。追根溯源,究竟是希腊导致了这场灾难还是欧盟及欧元体系的弊端将希腊卷入这场危机之中,使之成了牺牲品?希腊及整个欧元区经济的脱困之路又在何方?2008 年诺贝尔经济学奖得主 Paul Krugman 主张扩大政府开支,而欧盟却与之相反,主张紧缩。这是自希腊经济危机以来一直在欧盟乃至全球争论的问题。
  本文是一篇典型的经济评论,其观点只代表作者一家之言。同学们可以分析一下标题下方插图的含义。右边的球形代表哪个国家?它为何被欧元拴着?这与"Greece as Victim"标题有何联系?

Pre-reading Questions

1. How much do you know about Greece, and its culture?
2. What are some of the important industries in the Greek economy?

Text

Greece as Victim
By Paul Krugman

1 Ever since Greece hit the skids[1], we've heard a lot about what's wrong with everything Greek. Some of the accusations are true, some are false—but all of them are beside the point[2]. Yes, there are big failings in Greece's economy, its politics and no doubt its society. But those failings aren't what caused the crisis that is tearing Greece apart, and threatens to spread across Europe.

2 No, the origins of this disaster lie farther north, in Brussels, Frankfurt and Berlin, where officials created a deeply—perhaps fatally—flawed monetary system, then compounded the problems of that system by substituting moralizing for analysis.[3] And the solution to the crisis, if there is one, will have to come from the same places.

3 So, about those Greek failings: Greece does indeed have a lot of corruption and a lot of tax evasion, and the Greek government has had a habit of living beyond its means. Beyond that, Greek labor productivity[4] is low by European standards—about 25 percent below the European Union[5] average. It's worth noting, however, that labor productivity in, say, Mississippi is similarly low by American standards—and by about the same margin.

4 On the other hand, many things you hear about Greece just aren't true. The Greeks aren't lazy—on the contrary, they work longer hours than almost anyone else in Europe, and much longer hours than the Germans in particular. Nor does Greece have a runaway welfare state, as conservatives like to claim; social expenditure as a percentage of G.D.P., the standard measure of the size of the welfare state, is substantially lower in Greece than in, say, Sweden or Germany, countries that have so far weathered the European crisis pretty well.

5 So how did Greece get into so much trouble? Blame the euro[6].

6 Fifteen years ago Greece was no paradise, but it wasn't in crisis either.

Unemployment was high but not catastrophic, and the nation more or less paid its way on world markets, earning enough from exports, tourism, shipping and other sources to more or less pay for its imports.

7   Then Greece joined the euro, and a terrible thing happened: people started believing that it was a safe place to invest. Foreign money poured into Greece, some but not all of it financing government deficits[7]; the economy boomed; inflation rose; and Greece became increasingly uncompetitive. To be sure, the Greeks squandered much if not most of the money that came flooding in, but then so did everyone else who got caught up in the euro bubble.

8   And then the bubble burst, at which point the fundamental flaws in the whole euro system became all too apparent.

9   Ask yourself, why does the dollar area—also known as the United States of America—more or less work, without the kind of severe regional crises now afflicting Europe? The answer is that we have a strong central government, and the activities of this government in effect provide automatic bailouts to states that get in trouble.

10   Consider, for example, what would be happening to Florida right now, in the aftermath of its huge housing bubble[8], if the state had to come up with the money for Social Security and Medicare[9] out of its own suddenly reduced revenues. Luckily for Florida, Washington rather than Tallahassee is picking up the tab, which means that Florida is in effect receiving a bailout on a scale no European nation could dream of[10].

11   So Greece, although not without sin, is mainly in trouble thanks to the arrogance of European officials, mostly from richer countries, who convinced themselves that they could make a single currency work without a single government. And these same officials have made the situation even worse by insisting, in the teeth of [11] the evidence, that all the currency's troubles were caused by irresponsible behavior on the part of those Southern Europeans, and that everything would work out if only people were willing to suffer some more.

12   Which brings us to Sunday's Greek election[12], which ended up settling nothing. The governing coalition[13] may have managed to stay in power[14], although even that's not clear (the junior partner in the coalition is threatening to defect). But the Greeks can't solve this crisis anyway.

13   The only way the euro might—might—be saved is if the Germans and the European Central Bank[15] realize that they're the ones who need to change their behavior, spending more and, yes, accepting higher inflation. If not—well, Greece will basically go down in history as the victim of other people's hubris. (From *The New York Times*, June 17, 2012)

New Words

afflict /əˈflɪkt/ *v.* to affect sb/sth in an unpleasant or harmful way

aftermath /ˈɑːftəmæθ/ *n.* the period of time after sth such as a war, storm, or accident when people are still dealing with the results

arrogance /ˈærəɡəns/ *n.* a feeling or an impression of superiority; pride; haughtiness 傲慢 (*cf* hubris)

catastrophic /ˌkætəˈstrɒfɪk/ *adj.* causing a lot of destruction, suffering, or death; disastrous;

compound /ˈkɒmpaʊnd/ *v.* to make a difficult situation worse by adding more problems 使严重

conservative /kənˈsɜːvətɪv/ *n.* sb who likes old and established ways and doesn't like change, esp. sudden change 保守派人士

defect /dɪˈfekt/ *v.* to desert a political party, group, or country, esp. in order to join an opposing one 变节, 叛变, 脱离

deficit /ˈdefɪsɪt/ *n.* the amount by which money spent or owed is greater than money earned in a particular period of time 赤字

evasion /ɪˈveɪʒn/ *n.* the act of avoiding sb or sth that you are supposed to do

flawed /flɔːd/ *adj.* spoiled by having mistakes, weaknesses 有缺陷的

Florida /ˈflɒrɪdə/ *n.* a state in the southeast U.S.

hubris /ˈhjuːbrɪs/ *n. fml* too much pride (*cf* arrogance)

inflation /ɪnˈfleɪʃn/ *n.* (the rate of) a continuing rise in prices 通货膨胀

monetary /ˈmʌnɪtri/ *adj.* of or about money, esp. all the money in a country

moralize /ˈmɒrəlaɪz/ *v.* to tell other people your ideas about right and wrong behaviour, esp. when they have not asked for your opinion 说教

revenue /ˈrevənjuː/ *n.* money that the government receives from tax 税收

runaway /ˈrʌnəweɪ/ *adj.* out of control

squander /ˈskwɒndə(r)/ *v.* to waste money, time, etc., in a stupid or careless way 挥霍, 浪费

substantially /səbˈstænʃəli/ *adv.* considerably; a lot

weather /ˈweðə(r)/ *v.* to come through (something) safely; survive

Notes

1. hit the skids—*AmE sl.* to decline; decrease in value or status; (*fig.*) go downhill
2. beside the point—has nothing to do with the main subject
3. No, the origins of this disaster ... for analysis.—The origin of the Greek crisis lies in the EU, whose officials created a completely wrong and fatal monetary system, i. e. the euro system. And they made the problems of the euro system more complicated because they don't want to analyze the reasons for those problems, instead, they tried to convince people that there is no problem in their system. 此处 Brussels, Frankfurt 和 Berlin 都是欧盟重要机构所在地，用作指代，是新闻用语修辞格的一个特点。

    a. Brussels—It is not only the capital of Belgium（比利时）but also serves as capital of the European Union（欧盟总部所在地）, hosting the major political institutions of the Union. It is called the capital of Europe. At the same time, the headquarters of NATO（北大西洋公约组织）is also set up in Brussels. 布鲁塞尔

    b. Frankfurt—Germany's commercial, industrial, financial and transportation center, and the largest financial centre in the Eurozone（欧元区）. The European Central Bank (ECB, 欧洲央行) is also headquartered there. In 19th of October 2011, "Frankfurt Group"（法兰克福集团）was born. The inner circle comprises of the leaders of Germany and France, the presidents of the European Commission（欧委会主席）and the European Council of EU leaders（欧盟理事会主席）, the heads of the ECB（欧洲央行）and IMF（世界货币基金组织）, the chairman of Eurogroup finance ministers（欧元区财长会议主席）, and the European commissioner for economic and financial affairs（欧盟经济及货币事务委员）.

    c. Berlin—the capital and largest city of Germany. According to a Reuters report on Nov. 19, 2011, Berlin (here referring to the government of Germany) is the biggest contributor to Greek emergency lending programs, which wants Greece to buy back half of its outstanding bonds（债券）from private investors at 25 percent of their value as one way to reduce its unsustainable debt.

4. labor productivity—A measurement of economic growth of a country. Labor productivity measures the amount of goods and services produced by one hour of labor. More specifically, it measures the amount of real GDP produced by an hour of labor. Growing labor productivity depends on three main factors: investment and saving in physical capital(实物资本), new technology and human capital(人力资本). 劳动生产率

5. European Union (EU)—with its headquarters in Brussels, is an international organization comprising 28 European countries and governing common economic, social, and security policies. The EU was created by the Maastricht Treaty(《马斯特里赫特条约》,简称《马约》), which entered into force on November 1, 1993. Institutions of the EU include the European Commission(欧盟委员会), the Council of the European Union(欧盟理事会), the Court of Justice of the European Union(欧盟法院), the European Central Bank(欧洲中央银行), the Court of Auditors(欧盟审计院), and the European Parliament(欧洲议会). With a combined population of over 500 million inhabitants, or 7.3% of the world population, the EU in 2012 generated a nominal gross domestic product (GDP) of 16.584 trillion US dollars, representing the largest nominal GDP in the world.

6. euro—Introduced in 1999, it is now the currency used by the Institutions of the EU and is the official currency of the eurozone, which consists of 17 of the 27 member states of the European Union. The euro is the second largest reserve currency(储备货币)as well as the second most traded currency in the world after the U.S. dollar. As of March 2013, with almost 920 billion in circulation, the euro has the highest combined value of banknotes and coins in circulation in the world, having surpassed the U.S. dollar.

7. financing government deficits—supplying money to fill the gap of government deficits. It was reported that the Greek government budget deficits was equal to 10 percent of the country's GDP in 2012. 政府赤字

8. housing bubble—The U.S. housing bubble is an economic bubble affecting many parts of the United States housing market in over half of American states. Housing prices peaked in early 2006, started to decline in 2006 and 2007, and reached new lows in 2012.

In 2008, when the subprime mortgage crisis(次贷危机)began, the home price index reported its largest price drop in its history. Florida is one of the states most strongly affected. The credit crisis resulting from the bursting of the housing bubble is the primary cause of the 2007—2009 recession in the U.S.

9. Social Security and Medicare

   a. Social Security—a U.S. social insurance program funded through dedicated payroll taxes called FICA(联邦保险捐助条例). It is used to refer to the benefits for retirement, disability, survivorship, and death—the four main benefits provided by traditional private-sector pension plans. The U.S. Social Security program is the largest government program in the world. 社会保障计划

   b. Medicare—here referring to U.S. Medicare Insurance Plans for Seniors. 扶老医疗保健计划(cf. Medicaid 济贫助残医疗计划)

10. Luckily for Florida...no European nation could dream of. —对佛罗里达州来说幸运的是,为此买单的是华盛顿而不是塔拉哈西。这意味着佛州得到的是一次欧洲国家根本无法企及的大规模财政援助。

    a. Tallahassee—the state capital of Florida, USA. (塔拉哈西,佛州首府,此处借指佛州政府)

    b. pick up the tab—to pay the bill

    c. bailout—a rescue from financial difficulties 注资救助

11. in the teeth of—against the strength of; in spite of opposition from (对抗;不顾)

12. Which brings us to Sunday's Greek election... —Sunday's Greek election is held in this context. (句首的"Which"用作代词,相当于"this"或"that"。)

    Sunday's Greek election—the Greek legislative election(国会选举)that took place on June 17, 2012.

13. The governing coalition—希腊在2012年5月议会选举后无法形成联合政府,遂按照宪法于6月再举行大选。希腊总统召集党派领袖商讨,但无法达成共识,遂根据宪法解散新当选的议会,并举行新一届国会选举。最终新民主党获得129席位居第一,左翼联盟获得71席位列第二。由于支持紧缩政策的两个政党——新民主党与泛希腊社会运动党共取得162席,刚好过半数,在联合了民主左派后,组成三党执政联盟。

14. in power—holding the position of having political control of a country or government (cf in office, out of power/office)
15. the European Central Bank (ECB)—It is the central bank for the euro and manages the monetary policy（货币政策）of the 17 EU member states which constitute the Eurozone. Its primary objective is to maintain price stability within the Eurozone, which is the same as keeping inflation（通货膨胀）low and preventing deflation（通货紧缩）. 欧洲央行

Questions

1. Are there any failings in Greece's economy? What are they?
2. What happened after Greece became a member of the euro zone?
3. Why is the Florida housing bubble mentioned in the text?
4. Is it possible for the euro to be saved? How?
5. According to the author, what are the causes of the Greek debt crisis?

语 言 解 说

借喻词和提喻词（I）

报刊中多借喻词和提喻词，与委婉语、竞选用语和法律语言等相比较易理解，不过得具有较广泛的文化背景知识。

凡世界各国首都均可指代所在国及其政府，凡战争地、协议签订地和重要机构的总部所在地也均可用来喻指此战争、协议和该机构。地名是这两种修辞格里用得较多的。如本文的 Berlin, Washington, Tallahassee, Brussels, Frankfurt 就是典型的例子。

一、借喻法

1. 常见借喻法

借一事物的名称指代另一事物，称为借喻或借代法（metonymy），如以 the Crown 喻指"皇室事务"，Pentagon 指代"美国防部"，the blue helmets 喻"联合国维和部队"等。英语中往往用一个词代表整个事件或

背景。在现代英美报刊语言中常见到以地名或国名代表整个事件。① 如 Vietnam/Viet Nam 指"越南战争",Bosnia 是"波黑"的简称,喻"波黑战争",Hungary 指"匈牙利事件",the Gulf "海湾战争",Dayton "代顿协议"或代顿和平协议,Post-Soviet 苏联解体后,等等。见例句：

(1) Yet in the years since **Vietnam**, critics in and out of uniform have repeatedly charged that too many officers have become cautious bureaucrats, adept at Pentagon politics perhaps, but interested more in advancing their careers than in preparing for the brutal exigencies of combat. (*Time*)

然而,自从**越南战争**开始以来的年代中,军内外批评家一再指责道……

(2) Once the political chaff is dusted away, the minidebate over **Bosnia** is instructive. Both Bush and Clinton were saying the same thing. (*Time*)

这是《时代》周刊报道1992年美国大选时,老布什代表共和党总统候选人与民主党候选人克林顿进行电视总统候选人的辩论,此例中的Bosnia 指的就是借喻"波黑战争"。political chaff 指的是"竞选废话"。

(3) Washington concluded after **Dayton**, when NATO bombers seemed to bring him [Milosevic] to the negotiating table… (*Time*)

Dayton 为美国俄亥俄州一城市,是波黑和平协议签订地。此例不能说"代顿后美国断定……"。这里的 Dayton 是指 1995 年关于结束波黑内战和版图划分等而达成的协议,称为 the Dayton (Peace) accords, "代顿(和平)协议"。这样就好理解了。其正式名称应是"Bosnia and Herzegovina Peace Agreements"。

2. 另类借喻法

陆国强先生在论及借代曾举 November 等词语为例说明："在涉及美国初选或大选时,报刊常以词代事的方式进行报道。"②

现在用年份(缩略词)可指代选举及经济情况,如"The Economy Sucks. But Is It '92 Redux?"(2008/1/21 *Newsweek*)(经济不振,是否这是1992年大选时经济情况和大选形势的翻版? 当时因老布什执政时经济衰退,竞选连任败给了克林顿)。此外,还可借喻战争。如：

The decisive step toward victory in Iraq, say military officials, will be to crush Saddam's elite Republican Guard. At least three Guard

---

① 陆国强:现代英语词汇学,上海外语教育出版社,1983年,第66页。
② 同上,第67页。

divisions are massed outside Baghdad, facing the American invaders. In '91, the Americans used air power and their superior armor to badly maul some of these same Republican Guard divisions. But it is often overlooked that several of the Guard battalions stood and fought and then made an orderly retreat, living to fight again another day. (2003/4/7 *Newsweek*)

此例中的"'91"指1991年以美国为首的联军发动的第一次伊拉克战争。这种以年份或日期指代战争或事件如英文里用 9/11 指 2001 年"9·11"恐怖袭击事件,也是报刊中常用的一种形式,正如 since 1949 指代新中国成立。

二、提喻法

以局部代表全体,或以全体喻指部分,称为提喻或举隅法(synecdoche synecdoche),报刊中较普遍,例如:Bosnia 代表"波黑",London 代表英国,Kremlin(克里姆林宫)代表苏联、(现)俄罗斯,Washington 代表美国,还可代表东部,如 Washington mafia,喻指东部权势集团,cutthroat 代表 assassin(暗杀)或 murder。

三、一词数义

为避免用词重复、使读者产生联想等原因,作者常使用这两种修辞手段。在报刊文章中,为简约、换词等目的,这两种喻词用得尤其多。如 Foggy Bottom(雾谷),是美国首都华盛顿一地名,国务院所在地,喻"国务院",在修辞格里称借代法。又因其外交政策像雾蒙蒙的深山低谷一样模糊不清,令人难以捉摸,颇像"'雾'底洞",因此又用做隐喻(metaphor)来比喻"国务院的政策"。再如 Washington 做借喻指"美国或联邦政府",做提喻指"美国",做隐语可比喻为"贪污腐败(corruption)、尔虞我诈(fraud)和铺张浪费(waste)的官场"。

Lesson Twenty-five

课文导读

冷战从二次大战结束后开始,止于1989年柏林墙(Berlin Wall)的拆除或1991年苏联解体。有的学者认为,美俄新的冷战战场已经转移到了终年冰封的北冰洋。那里蕴藏着丰富的油气煤资源,有第二个中东之称,将是未来世界巨大的能源宝库。在已非完全是枪炮坦克称霸世界的年代,谁控制了经济,谁就掌握了世界,而谁占有能源,谁就扼住了经济命脉。在20世纪的中东,美苏两国不择手段,甚至不惜发动代理人的战争,现在的北冰洋,俄、加等国相继声称拥有主权并大力进行科技研发,勘测地形,归纳版图,政治交锋,甚至武力威胁,目的就是想将丰富的能源据为己有。

现代工业的发展使得能源日益枯竭,能源危机越发显得紧迫,美俄欧等国对能源的抢夺也势必随之升级。随着时间的推移,一场新世纪的战争或许会在寒冷的北冰洋拉开帷幕。

Pre-reading Questions

1. Do you know anything about the Arctic Ocean?
2. Which are the countries located in or near the Arctic?

Text

The Coming Conflict in the Arctic
Russia and US to Square Off[1] Over Arctic Energy Reserves
By Vladimir Frolov

1   Russian President Vladimir Putin[2] and U. S. President George W. Bush spent most of their time at the "lobster summit" at Kennebunkport[3], Maine, discussing how to prevent the growing tensions between their two countries from getting out of hand. The media and international affairs experts have been portraying missile

defense in Europe and the final status of Kosovo[4] as the two most contentious issues between Russia and the United States, with mutual recriminations over "democracy standards" providing the background for the much anticipated onset of a new Cold War. But while this may well be true for today, the stage has been quietly set for a much more serious confrontation in the non-too-distant future between Russia and the United States—along with Canada, Norway and Denmark.

2 Russia has recently laid claim to[5] a vast 1,191,000 sq km (460,800 sq miles) chunk of the ice-covered Arctic seabed. The claim is not really about territory, but rather about the huge hydrocarbon reserves[6] that are hidden on the seabed under the Arctic ice cap. These newly discovered energy reserves will play a crucial role in the global energy balance as the existing reserves of oil and gas are depleted over the next 20 years.

3 Russia has the world's largest gas reserves and is the second largest exporter of oil after Saudi Arabia, but its oil and gas production is slated to decline after 2010 as currently operational reserves dwindle. Russia's Natural Resources Ministry estimates that the country's existing oil reserves will be depleted by 2030.

4 The 2005 BP World Energy Survey[7] projects that U.S. oil reserves will last another 10 years if the Arctic National Wildlife Refuge[8] is not opened for oil exploration, Norway's reserves are good for about seven years and British North Sea reserves[9] will last no more than five years—which is why the Arctic reserves, which are still largely unexplored, will be of such crucial importance to the world's energy future. Scientists estimate that the territory contains more than 10 billion tons of gas and oil deposits. The shelf is about 200 meters (650 feet) deep and the challenges of extracting oil and gas there appear to be surmountable, particularly if the oil prices stay where they are now—over $70 a barrel.

5 The Kremlin[10] wants to secure Russia's long-term dominance over global energy markets. To ensure this, Russia needs to find new sources of fuel and the Arctic seems like the only place left to go. But there is a problem: International law does not recognize Russia's right to the entire Arctic seabed north of the Russian coastline.

6 The 1982 International Convention on the Law of the Sea establishes a

12 mile zone for territorial waters and a larger 200 mile economic zone in which a country has exclusive drilling rights for hydrocarbon and other resources.[11]

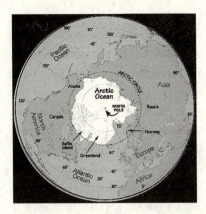

7   Russia claims that the entire swath of Arctic seabed in the triangle that ends at the North Pole belongs to Russia, but the United Nations Committee that administers the Law of the Sea Convention has so far refused to recognize Russia's claim to the entire Arctic seabed.

8   In order to legally claim that Russia's economic zone in the Arctic extends far beyond the 200 mile zone, it is necessary to present viable scientific evidence showing that the Arctic Ocean's sea shelf to the north of Russian shores is a continuation of the Siberian continental platform[12]. In 2001, Russia submitted documents to the UN commission on the limits of the continental shelf seeking to push Russia's maritime borders beyond the 200 mile zone. It was rejected.

9   Now Russian scientists assert there is new evidence that Russia's northern Arctic region is directly linked to the North Pole via an underwater shelf. Last week a group of Russian geologists returned from a six-week voyage to the Lomonosov Ridge[13], an underwater shelf in Russia's remote eastern Arctic Ocean. They claimed the ridge was linked to Russian Federation[14] territory, boosting Russia's claim over the oil-and gas-rich triangle.

10   The latest findings are likely to prompt Russia to lodge another bid at the UN to secure its rights over the Arctic sea shelf. If no other power challenges Russia's claim, it will likely go through unchallenged.

11   But Washington seems to have a different view and is seeking to block the anticipated Russian bid. On May 16, 2007, Senator Richard Lugar (R-Indiana), the ranking Republican on the Senate Foreign Relations Committee, made a statement encouraging the Senate to ratify the Law of the Sea Convention, as the Bush Administration wants. The Reagan administration[15] negotiated the Convention, but the Senate refused to ratify it for fear that it would unduly limit the U.S. freedom

of action on the high seas[16].

12   The United States has been jealous of Russia's attempts to project its dominance in the energy sector and has sought to limit opportunities for Russia to control export routes and energy deposits outside Russia's territory. But the Arctic shelf is something that Russia has traditionally regarded as its own. For decades, international powers have pressed no claims to Russia's Arctic sector for obvious reasons of remoteness and inhospitability, but no longer.

13   Now, as the world's major economic powers brace for the battle for the last barrel of oil, it is not surprising that the United States would seek to intrude on Russia's home turf. It is obvious that Moscow would try to resist this U.S. intrusion and would view any U.S. efforts to block Russia's claim to its Arctic sector as unfriendly and overtly provocative. Furthermore, such a policy would actually help the Kremlin justify its hard-line position[17]. It would certainly prove right Moscow's assertion that U.S. policy towards Russia is really driven by the desire to get guaranteed and privileged access to Russia's energy resources.

14   It promises to be a tough fight. (From *Global Research*[18], July 17, 2007)

New Words

administer /əd'mɪnɪstə/ *v.* to be responsible for making certain that sth is done according to the rules 负责(法规的)实施

assert /ə'sɛːt/ *v.* to state a fact or belief firmly 坚持说；断言

Arctic /'ɑːktɪk/ *n.* the area of the world around the North Pole. It is extremely cold and there is very little light in winter and very little darkness in summer. 北极地区

bid /bɪd/ *n.* an attempt to do sth or to obtain, win, or attract sth; effort; endeavour 努力；尝试；要求

boost /buːst/ *v.* to increase or improve sth and make it more successful 增加……的分量；加重……的砝码

brace /breɪs/ *v.* to prepare for sth difficult, dangerous, or unpleasant that is about to happen 准备迎接(困难等)

chunk /tʃʌŋk/ *n.* a large part or amount of sth

commission /kə'mɪʃən/ *n.* a group of people who have been appointed to find out about sth or to control sth 委员会（被指派去查究某事或者主管某事的一班人）

democracy standard /dɪˈmɒkrəsɪ ˈstændəd/ sth that you use in order to judge the quality of democracy 民主标准

deplete /dɪˈpliːt/ v. to use up or remove all the contents of sth 用光；耗尽

deposit /dɪˈpɒzɪt/ n. an amount of a substance that has been left somewhere as a result of a chemical or geological process 矿藏量（由于地质变化或化学变化而生成的一定量的物质）

dominance /ˈdɒmɪnəns/ n. the fact of being more powerful, more important, or more noticeable than other people or things （压倒一切的）优势地位

dwindle /ˈdwɪndl/ v. to gradually become less and less or smaller and smaller 日益减少；日益枯竭

exploration /ˌekspləˈreɪʃən/ n. the act of traveling through a place in order to find out about sth or find sth such as oil or gold 勘探

extract /ɪksˈtrækt/ v. to obtain a raw material from the ground or from another substance by using machines or industrial processes 采掘；提取

geologist /dʒɪˈɒlədʒɪst/ n. a scientist who studies the rocks, soil etc that make up the Earth, and the way they have changed since the Earth was formed 地质学家

hydrocarbon /ˈhaɪdrəʊkɑːbən/ n. a chemical compound of hydrogen and carbon, such as petrol 碳氢化合物

inhospitability /ɪnˌhɒspɪˈtælɪtɪ/ n. (of a place) having the qualities which make it not suitable to live in or stay in, esp. because of severe weather conditions, lack of shelter etc（因气候条件等生活环境恶劣而使某地）无法居住

lodge /lɒdʒ/ v. to formally make sth such as a complaint, protest or claim 正式提出（申诉、要求或主张）

onset /ˈɒnset/ n. the beginning of sth, esp. sth bad

operational /ˌɒpəˈreɪʃənəl/ adj. ready to be used 即可使用的

plea /pliː/ n. a request that is urgent or full of emotion 恳求；吁请

project /prəˈdʒekt/ v. 1. to express or represent (oneself or one's qualities) outwardly, esp. in a way that has a favourable effect on others 使自己的特点呈现，表现（自己）；张扬 2. to judge, calculate, estimate, or predict (sth in the future), based on present data or trends 设想，估计

promise /ˈprɒmɪs/ v. to make you expect that sth will happen

prompt /prɒmpt/ v. to make sb decide to do sth 促使（某人决定做某事）

provocative /prəˈvɒkətɪv/ adj. intended to make people react angrily or argue against it 挑衅性的

ranking /ˈræŋkɪŋ/ adj. of high, or the highest, rank or position in an organization or is one of the best at an activity

ratify /ˈrætɪfaɪ/ v. to make a treaty or written agreement official by giving formal approval to it, usu. by signing it or voting for it 批准；认可（条约、协议等）

recede /rɪˈsiːd/ v. to move back from a high point or level 后退；跌落

recrimination /rɪˌkrɪmɪˈneɪʃən/ n. a situation in which people are accusing or criticizing one another 互相指责

reserve /rɪˈzɜːv/ n. a supply of sth that is available for use when it is needed 蕴藏

Saudi Arabia /ˈsaʊdɪ əˈreɪbjə/ an oil-producing country in the Middle East, ruled by a king. The city of Mecca, the holiest place in the religion of Islam, is in Saudi Arabia. 沙特阿拉伯

seabed /ˈsiːbed/ n. the land at the bottom of the sea 海床，海底

sector /ˈsektə/ n. one of the parts into which an area is divided, esp. for military purposes 部分（为军事等目的而划分的地域）

secure /sɪˈkjʊə/ v. to get sth, sometimes with difficulty

shelf /ʃelf/ n. the gently sloping undersea area surrounding a continent at depths of up to 200 m, at the edge of which the continental slope drops steeply to the ocean floor 大陆架（大陆向水下延伸的一段缓坡，水深不超过200米，再往前就是大陆坡，坡势陡峭，直落洋底）

Siberian /saɪˈbɪrɪən/ adj. of or relating to or characteristic of Siberia or the Siberians 西伯利亚的；西伯利亚人的

slate /sleɪt/ v. to expect or plan to happen in the future, esp. at a particular time[常用被动语态]预计会（发生或进行）

submit /səbˈmɪt/ v. to formally send a proposal, report, or request to sb so that they can consider it or decide about it 呈报

summit /ˈsʌmɪt/ n. an important formal meeting between leaders of governments from two or more countries 首脑会议，峰会

surmountable /səˈmaʊntəbl/ adj. (of a difficulty or problem) able to be overcome or dealt with successfully 可以克服的；可以战胜的

swath /swɔːθ/ n. a large area of a particular type 大片区域

unduly /ʌnˈdjuːlɪ/ *adv.* to an excessive, improper, or unjustifiable degree; excessively; too much 过分地，不合适地

viable /ˈvaɪəbl/ *adj.* able to work successfully; feasible 可望成功的；切实可行的

Notes

1. square off—to get ready for a fight
2. Vladimir Putin—1952—   , President of Russia(1999—2008; 2012—)
3. lobster summit at Kennebunkport—Lobster is the seafood of choice at Kennebunkport, the small town on the Maine coast that is home to President Bush senior's (老布什的) summer retreat and is now the place for talks between his son and Vladimir Putin. It is a meeting that mixes fishing and dining with serious talks. 在肯尼邦克港镇举行的"龙虾高峰会"

    Kennebunkport—a town in York County, Maine, US
4. the final status of Kosovo—Kosovo is an area in southern Serbia, where people of Albanian origin wanted independence. During and after the breakup of Yugoslavia there were increasing conflicts, culminating in the Kosovo War of 1999. The result of that war was Yugoslavia's acceptance of UN Security Council Resolution 1244, which led to the initiation of a Kosovo status process in 2005. Encouraged by the USA and the EU, the Kosovo government in 2008 declared independence from Serbia. Some Western countries have recognized its independence, while the majority of UN member states have not. 科索沃最终的地位问题。科索沃是前南联盟塞尔维亚共和国的一个自治省，南部与阿尔巴尼亚和马其顿毗邻，阿尔巴尼亚族人占90%以上，其余多为塞族和黑山族人。1999年科索沃战争结束后由联合国托管。塞尔维亚希望保持对科索沃的主权，而阿族则要求"完全独立"。
5. lay claim to—say that sth that you don't have belongs to you 声称……理当是自己的
6. hydrocarbon reserves—油气煤储量（Hydrocarbons, which are combustible, are the main components of fossil fuels, which include petroleum, coal, and natural gas. 因油、气、煤的主要成分是碳氢化合物，故以碳氢化合物代之。）
7. BP World Energy Survey—英国石油公司世界能源预测

BP—British Petroleum
8. Arctic National Wildlife Refuge—国家北极野生动植物保护区
9. British North Sea reserves—英国北海油气储量

    the North Sea—part of the Atlantic Ocean, between Britain and NW Europe. It's economically important because of its fish, and also for oil and gas discovered in the 1960s.

10. the Kremlin—the group of buildings in Moscow which was the centre of the government of the former Soviet Union, and which is now the centre of the Russian government; here referring to the Russian government 克里姆林宫；此处指代俄罗斯政府

11. The 1982 International Convention on the Law of the Sea... for hydrocarbon and other resources.—1982年海洋法国际公约规定一国可对距其海岸线12海里以内的海域拥有主权，对200海里（约370公里）的海域拥有经济专属权，在该范围内拥有对油气煤和其他资源的独家开采权。

    The 1982 International Convention on the Law of the Sea—The UN Convention on Law of the Sea, passed in 1982, refers to several UN events and one treaty. The treaty provides new universal legal controls for the management of marine natural resources and the control of pollution.

12. continental platform—the zone that includes both the continental shelf or continental borderland and the continental slope 大陆台地（包括大陆架、大陆边缘和大陆坡）

13. Lomonosov Ridge—an underwater oceanic ridge in the Arctic Ocean. It spans for 1800 km from the New Siberian Islands over the central part of the ocean to the Ellesmere Island of the Canadian Arctic islands. Slopes of the ridge are relatively steep, broken up by canyons, and covered with layers of silt. 罗蒙诺索夫海岭是北冰洋中部的海底山脉，起自俄罗斯北冰洋岸的新西伯利亚群岛附近，沿东经140度线通过北极，延伸到加拿大北部的埃尔斯米尔岛东北侧，长1,800公里，宽60—200公里。北冰洋的北极海就是以这条海岭分界为欧亚海盆和美亚海盆。

14. Russian Federation—简称Russia

15. The Reagan administration—里根政府 (See Note 17 of Lesson Ten)

16. the high seas—the open ocean, esp. that not within any country's jurisdiction 公海（通航无限制的海，尤指不在任何国家管辖范围之内的海）

17. hard-line position—a strict way of dealing with sb or sth 强硬立场 (*cf*. hawk/dove 鹰派/鸽派)
18. Global Research—环球研究是全球化研究中心（The Centre for Research on Globalisation）的官方网站。全球化研究中心是总部设于加拿大蒙特利尔的一家非营利性独立研究机构。该网站自2001年9月创办以来，发表了大量关于全球化方面的文章和书籍，其研究成果还包括世界经济和政治地理等领域。

Questions

1. What issues would the two heads of states discuss at the Lobster Summit at Kennebunkport?
2. What's the real purpose of Russia's claim to the vast area of the ice-covered Arctic seabed?
3. Why are the Arctic reserves so attractive to Arctic-rim countries?
4. Why doesn't International law recognize Russia's right to the entire Arctic seabed north of the Russian coastline?
5. What is the viable scientific evidence supporting Russia's claim? What has boosted Russia's claim over the oil-and-gas-rich triangle?
6. What is the US government's attitude to the Russian claim? Why did President Bush urge the Senate to ratify the Law of the Sea Convention?
7. Why did the author say that it promises to be a tough fight?

语言解说

借喻词和提喻词（Ⅱ）

以下是主编经年累月在读报和编书过程中积累的两种喻词，这对初读报者扩大知识和词汇面是极其有益的。

Word	Meaning	Metonymical/Synecdochical Meaning
Broadway	百老汇大街（纽约一街名）	纽约戏剧业，美国戏剧业
The capitol	美国州议会或政府大厦	美国州议会，州政府
The Capitol	美国国会大厦，州议会大厦	美国国会，州议会
Capitol Hill	国会山（国会大厦所在地）	美国国会

续表

Word	Meaning	Metonymical/Synecdochical Meaning
Donkey	驴	美国民主党
Elephant	象	美国共和党
ends of Pennsylvania Street	宾夕法尼亚大街（首都华盛顿一街名）两端	美国国会和行政当局,白宫和国会大厦,美国行政和立法部门
green berets	绿色贝雷帽	（美国）特种部队
The Hill	＝ Capitol Hill	美国国会
Hollywood	好莱坞（洛杉矶一地名）	美国电影业、电影界或娱乐业
John	约翰（美国人一常用名）	美国人
J Street	华盛顿一街名	美国特工处
K Street	华盛顿一街名	美国游说界
Langley	兰利（弗吉尼亚州一地名）	中央情报局
Madison Avenue	麦迪逊大街（纽约一街名）	美国广告业
Oval Office	椭圆形办公室	美国总统办公室,总统（职务）
Pentagon	五角大楼	美国国防部
Silicon Valley	硅谷（美国加州一地名）	美国高科技集中地
1600 Pennsylvania Street	宾夕法尼亚大街（华盛顿一街名）1600号	（美国）白宫,总统府
Uncle Sam	山姆大叔	美国政府；美国人
Wall Street	华尔街（纽约一街名）	美国金融界
White House	白宫	总统府,行政部门
Buckingham Palace	（英国）白金汉宫	英国王宫
The City (of London)	伦敦城	英国金融界；英国商业界
Downing Street	唐宁街（伦敦一街名）	英国首相府或首相；英国政府或内阁
Fleet Street	舰队街（伦敦一街名）	英国新闻界或报业
Lion	狮	英国
London	伦敦	英国或政府
New Scotland Yard	新苏格兰场（伦敦一地名）	伦敦警察局,该局刑事调查（侦缉）处

续表

Word	Meaning	Metonymical/Synecdochical Meaning
Ulster	阿尔斯特（在爱尔岛北部）	北爱尔兰
Westminster	威斯敏斯特（伦敦西部一住宅区）	英国议会或政府
Windsor	温莎（英格兰东南部一城市）	英国王室
Whitehall	白厅（伦敦一街名）	英国政府
Brussels	布鲁塞尔（比利时首都）	欧洲联盟；北大西洋公约组织
blue helmet	蓝盔	联合国维和人员
blue helmets	蓝盔帽	蓝盔部队，联合国维和部队
Horn of Africa	非洲之角	索马里和埃塞俄比亚
Elysée Palace	爱丽舍宫	法国总统府，法国总统职位
Quai d'Orsay	凯道赛（巴黎一码头名）	法国外交部
Kremlin	克里姆林宫	前苏联；前苏联政府；俄罗斯；俄罗斯政府
Moscow	莫斯科	前苏联；俄罗斯；俄罗斯政府
Gulag	古拉格群岛	（前苏联）劳改营，劳动改造管理总局
Evan	伊凡（前苏联和俄罗斯人常用名）	前苏联人；俄罗斯人
Beijing	北京	中国；中国政府

Lesson Twenty-six

课 文 导 读

近年来亚洲国家经济发展强劲而举世瞩目。越来越多的亚洲国家脱离赤贫状态,民众对国家福利制度的诉求越来越高。于是乎,亚洲大国诸如中国和印度的福利制度出现了高歌猛进式的发展。福利制度应跨越式发展,一蹴而就,还是应稳步推进呢?本文根据欧美国家福利制度的发展过程,指出了亚洲国家政府中决策人物在福利制度的制定与实施过程中值得反思的问题和难点,提出了可资借鉴的经验教训和建议。亚洲国家如何能既保持强劲的经济发展势头,又能真正实现向福利国家的转变,这的确需要一场社会革命。

Pre-reading Questions

1. What do you think of China's social welfare? What benefits has it brought to the people?
2. How much do you know about the social welfare programs of other countries?

Text

Rethinking the Welfare State: Asia's Next Revolution
By Tweet

1   Countries across the continent are building welfare states[1]—with a chance to learn from the West's mistakes.

2   Asia's economies have long wowed the world with their dynamism. Thanks to years of spectacular growth, more people have been pulled from abject poverty in modern Asia than at any other time in history. But as they become more affluent, the region's citizens want more from their governments. Across the continent pressure is growing for public pensions, national health insurance, unemployment benefits and other

hallmarks of social protection. As a result, the world's most vibrant economies are shifting gear, away from simply building wealth towards building a welfare state.

3   The speed and scale of this shift are mind-boggling. Last October Indonesia's government promised to provide all its citizens with health insurance by 2014. It is building the biggest "single-payer" national health scheme[2]—where one government outfit collects the contributions and foots the bills—in the world. In just two years China has extended pension coverage to an additional 240 million rural folk, far more than the total number of people covered by Social Security, America's public-pension system[3]. A few years ago about 80% of people in rural China had no health insurance. Now virtually everyone does. In India some 40 million households benefit from a government scheme[4] to provide up to 100 days' work a year at the minimum wage, and the state has extended health insurance to some 110 million poor people, more than double the number of uninsured in America.

4   If you take Germany's introduction of pensions in the 1880s as the beginning and Britain's launch of its National Health Service[5] in 1948 as the apogee, the creation of Europe's welfare states took more than half a century. Some Asian countries will build theirs in a decade. If they get things wrong, especially through unaffordable promises, they could wreck the world's most dynamic economies. But if they create affordable safety nets, they will not just improve life for their own citizens but also become role models themselves. At a time when governments in the rich world are failing to redesign states to cope with ageing populations and gaping budget deficits, this could be another area where Asia leapfrogs the West.

Beyond Bismarck and Beveridge[6]

5   History offers many lessons for the Asians on what to avoid. Europe's welfare states began as basic safety nets. But over time they turned into cushions. That was partly because, after wars and the Depression[7], European societies made redistribution their priority, but also because the recipients of welfare spending became powerful interest groups. The eventual result, all too often, was economic sclerosis with an ever-bigger state. America has kept its safety net less generous, but has made mistakes in creating its entitlements system[8]—including making unaffordable pension and health-care promises, and tying people's health insurance to their employment.

6   The record in other parts of the emerging world, especially Latin America, is even worse. Governments have tended to collect insufficient tax revenue to cover their spending promises. Social protection often aggravated inequalities, because pensions and health care flowed to affluent urban workers but not the really poor. Brazil famously has a first-world rate of government spending but third-world public services.

7   Asia's governments are acutely conscious of all this. They have little desire to replace traditions of hard work and thrift with a flabby welfare dependency. The region's giants can seek inspiration not from Greece but from tiny Singapore, where government spending is only a fifth of GDP[9] but schools and hospitals are among the best in the world. So far, the safety nets in big Asian countries have generally been minimalist: basic health insurance and pensions which replace a small fraction of workers' former income. Even now, the region's social spending relative to the size of its economies is only about 30% of the rich-country average and lower than any part of the emerging world except sub-Saharan Africa[10].

8   That leaves a fair amount of room for expansion. But Asia also faces a number of peculiarly tricky problems. One is demography. Although a few countries, notably India, are relatively youthful, the region includes some of the world's most rapidly ageing populations. Today China has five workers for every old person. By 2035 the ratio will have fallen to two. In America, by contrast, the baby-boom[11] generation meant that the Social Security system had five contributors

per beneficiary in 1960, a quarter of a century after its introduction. It still has three workers for every retired person.

9   Another problem is size, which makes welfare especially hard. The three giants—China, India and Indonesia—are vast places with huge regional income disparities within their borders. Building a welfare state in any one of them is a bit like creating a single welfare state across the European Union. Lastly, many Asian workers (in India it is about 90%) are in the "informal" economy[12], making it harder to verify their incomes or reach them with transfers.

Cuddly tigers, not flabby cats[13]

10   How should these challenges be overcome? There is no single solution that applies from India to South Korea. Different countries will, and should, experiment with different welfare models. But there are three broad principles that all Asian governments could usefully keep in mind.

11   The first is to pay even more attention to the affordability over time of any promises. The size of most Asian pensions may be modest, but people collect them at an early age. In China, for example, women retire at 55; in Thailand many employees are obliged to stop work at 60 and can withdraw their pension funds at 55. That is patently unsustainable. Across Asia, retirement ages need to rise, and should be indexed to life expectancy.

12   Second, Asian governments need to target their social spending more carefully. Crudely put, social provision should be about protecting the poor more than subsidizing the rich. In fast-ageing societies, especially, handouts to the old must not squeeze out investment in the young. Too many Asian governments still waste oodles of public money on regressive universal subsidies. Indonesia, for instance, last year spent nine times as much on fuel subsidies as it did on health care, and the lion's share[14] of those subsidies flows to the country's most affluent. As they promise a broader welfare state, Asia's politicians have the political opportunity, and the economic responsibility, to get rid of this kind of wasteful spending.

13   Third, Asia's reformers should concentrate on being both flexible and innovative. Don't stifle labor markets with rigid severance rules[15] or

over-generous minimum wages. Make sure pensions are portable, between jobs and regions. Don't equate a publicly funded safety net with government provision of services (a single public payer may be the cheapest way to provide basic health care, but that does not have to mean every nurse needs to be a government employee). And use technology to avoid the inefficiencies that hobble the rich world's public sector. From making electronic health records ubiquitous to organizing transfer payments through mobile phones, Asian countries can create new and efficient delivery systems with modern technology.

14 In the end, the success of Asia's great leap towards welfare provision will be determined by politics as much as economics. The continent's citizens will have to show a willingness to plan ahead, work longer and eschew handouts based on piling up debt for future generations; virtues that have so far eluded their rich-world counterparts. Achieving that political maturity will require the biggest leap of all. (From *The Economist*, September 8, 2012)

New Words

abject /ˈæbdʒekt/ *adj.* the state of being extremely poor, unhappy, unsuccessful, pitiful etc 不幸的, 悲惨的

affluent /ˈæfluənt/ *adj.* having plenty of money, nice houses, expensive things etc; wealthy 富足的

aggravate /ˈæɡrəveɪt/ *v.* to make a bad situation, an illness, or an injury worse 雪上加霜

apogee /ˈæpədʒiː/ *n.* the most successful part of sth 最高点, 顶峰

beneficiary /ˌbenɪˈfɪʃəri/ *n.* someone who gets advantages from an action or change (遗嘱, 保险等的) 受益人; (退休金等的) 领受人

contributor /kənˈtrɪbjətə(r)/ *n.* someone who gives money, help, ideas etc to sth that a lot of other people are also involved in 贡献者

coverage /ˈkʌvərɪdʒ/ *n.* the protection an insurance company gives you, so that it pays you money if you are injured, or sth is stolen etc 费用的承担

crudely /ˈkruːdli/ *adv.* expressed in a simple way 简单表达

cuddly /ˈkʌdli/ *adj.* lovable; suitable for cuddling 可爱的, 想抱的

cushion /ˈkʊʃn/ *n.* sth esp. money, that prevents you from being immediately affected by a bad situation 缓冲, 解难

demography /dɪˈmɒrəfi/ *n.* the study of human populations and the ways in which they change, for example the study of how many births, marriages and deaths happen in a particular place at a particular time 人口学

disparity /dɪˈspærəti/ *n.* a difference between two or more things, esp. an unfair one 差距，悬殊

dynamism /ˈdaɪnəmɪzəm/ *n.* energy and determination to succeed 劲头，魄力

elude /ɪˈluːd/ *v.* (of a fact, answer etc.) to be difficult for (sb) to find or remember 把……难倒，记不起

entitlement /ɪnˈtaɪtlmənt/ *n.* the official right to have or do sth or the amount that you have a right to receive 应得的东西

eschew /ɪsˈtʃuː/ *v.* to deliberately avoid doing or using sth 避开；戒绝

expectancy /ɪkˈspektənsi/ *n.* the length of time that a person or animal is expected to live 生命预期

flabby /ˈflæbi/ *adj.* weak or not effective 无力的；软弱的

foot /fʊt/ *v.* to pay for sth esp. sth expensive that you do not want to pay for 结(账)，付(款)

gear /ɡɪə(r)/ *n.* an apparatus, esp. one consisting of a set of toothed wheels, that allows power to be passed from one part of a machine to another so as to control power, speed, or direction of movement 档位(汽车变速)

hallmark /ˈhɔːlmɑːk/ *n.* an idea, method, or quality that is typical of a particular person or thing 标志，特点

hobble /ˈhɒbl/ *v.* to deliberately make sure that a plan, system etc cannot work successfully 阻碍，阻挠

index /ˈɪndeks/ *v.* to arrange for the level of wages, pensions etc to increase or decrease according to the level of prices 〈美口〉按生活指数调整

insured /ɪnˈʃʊəd/ *n.* an insured person 被保险人

leapfrog /ˈliːpfrɒɡ/ *v.* to suddenly become better, more advanced etc than people or organizations that were previously better than you 跨越

mind-boggling /ˈmaɪndˌbɒɡlɪŋ/ *adj.* difficult to imagine and very big, strange, or complicated

minimalist /ˈmɪnɪməlɪst/ *adj.* deliberately designed to be as simple as possible; used esp. to describe the inside of someone's house where there is little furniture and very few patterns or decorations 简朴的

oodles /ˈuːdlz/ *n.* a large amount of sth 大量的

outfit /ˈaʊtfɪt/ *n.* a group of people who work together as a team or organization 群体

patently /ˈpeɪtntlɪ/ *adv.* very clearly 清晰的

portable pension pension that workers can keep when they move from one job to another 可转移的退休金

provision /prəˈvɪʒn/ *n.* the act of providing 供给，服务

ratio /ˈreɪʃɪəʊ/ *n.* a relationship between two amounts, represented by a pair of numbers showing how much bigger one amount is than the other 比率

regressive /rɪˈgresɪv/ *adj.* returning to an earlier, less advanced state, or causing sth to do this

sclerosis /skləˈrəʊsɪs/ *n.* a disease that causes an organ or soft part of your body to become hard 僵化，硬化

severance /ˈsevərəns/ *n.* money paid by a company to one of their workers losing their job through no fault of their own, esp. when the job is no longer necessary because of reorganization in the company 离职补偿金

stifle /ˈstaɪfl/ *v.* to stop sth from happening or developing 遏制，抑制

subsidy /ˈsʌbsədɪ/ *n.* money paid, esp. by a government or an organization to make prices lower, reduce the cost of producing goods etc 津贴；补贴；补助金

transfer /trænsˈfɜː(r)/ *v. & n.* to move money from one account or institution to another 转账

ubiquitous /juːˈbɪkwɪtəs/ *adj.* seeming to be everywhere

unsustainable /ˌʌnsəˈsteɪnəbl/ *adj.* unable to continue at the same rate or in the same way 不可持续的

verify /ˈverɪfaɪ/ *v.* to discover whether sth is correct or true

vibrant /ˈvaɪbrənt/ *adj.* full of activity or energy in a way that is exciting and attractive; lively 充满活力的

wow /waʊ/ *v. slang* to cause surprise or admiration 使人惊喜的，发出感叹

wreck /rek/ *v.* to completely spoil sth. so that it cannot continue in a successful way; ruin 致残，毁坏

Notes

1. welfare state—a concept of government in which the state plays a key role in the protection and promotion of the economic and social well-being of its citizens. It is based on the principles of equality of

opportunity, equitable distribution（机会平等、公平分配）of wealth, and public responsibility for those unable to avail(有助于)themselves of the minimal provisions for a good life. The general term may cover a variety of forms of economic and social organization. 福利国家。福利制度指的是国家或政府在立法或政策范围内为所有对象普遍提供在一定的生活水平上尽可能提高生活质量的资金和服务的社会保障制度。

2. "single-payer" national health scheme—a system in which the government pays for all health care costs. But the term "single-payer" only describes the funding mechanism—referring to health care financed by a single public body from a single fund. The healthcare services may be offered by either the government or private organizations. Usually, the fund holder is the state, but some forms of single-payer use a mixed public-private system. 单一支付方医疗体系是一种由政府作为唯一支付方,负责筹资和购买医疗服务的体系。在这种体系下,来自雇主、个人和政府的资金会由政府筹集起来统一管理,并用于支付每个公民的医疗开支。现在世界上很多国家都采用这种单一支付方体系,比如加拿大的医疗保险、英国的国民医疗保健制度等。

3. social security, America's public-pension system—社会保障印美国公共保险制度。起先由美国联邦政府于1935年实施,其中有退休、失业、残废等保险。后来,其中部分职能已转交或下放给地方政府,并在克林顿执政时期进行了大胆改革。它是一种公共福利措施。

   pension—a fixed sum paid regularly to a person

4. government scheme—It refers to the Mahatma Gandhi National Rural Employment Guarantee Act (MGNREGA), an Indian job guarantee scheme, enacted by legislation on 25 August 2005. The scheme provides a legal guarantee for at least one hundred days of employment in every financial year to adult members of any rural household willing to do public work-related unskilled manual work at the statutory minimum wage（法定最低工资）of 120 rupees (US＄2.20) per day in 2009 prices. If they fail to do so the government has to pay the salary at their homes. 指印度议会2005年8月23日以口头表决的方式批准的政府提交的《全国农村就业保障法案》。根据此法案,印度政府今后将每年斥资4000亿卢比(1美元约合43卢比),以确保印度7.2亿农村人口中每个家庭每年都能获得

100天的就业机会，并领取政府发放的最低日工资120卢比的报酬。

5. National Health Service—It may refer to one or more of the four publicly funded healthcare systems within the UK. The systems are primarily funded through general taxation rather than requiring private insurance payments. The services provide a comprehensive range of health services, the vast majority of which are free at the point of use for residents of the UK. The four systems are quite independent, and operate under different management, rules, and political authority. 英国医疗保健制度，1948年建立，基本上是公费，并覆盖全民。

6. Beyond Bismarck and Beveridge—Here it means that the development of Asian countries' welfare states is beyond the imagination of Bismarck and Beveridge, both are authorities in this field. 小标题中提到这两个人正是照应了上一段的"If you take Germany's introduction of pensions in the 1880s as the beginning and Britain's launch of its National Health Service in 1948 as the apogee". 他们的时代与此对应。

    a. Bismarck, Otto von—1815 – 1898, was a conservative German statesman who dominated European affairs from the 1860s to his dismissal in 1890. In 1871, he unified most of the German states into a powerful German Empire under Prussian leadership, which created a balance of power that preserved peace in Europe from 1871 until 1914. He designed and introduced social insurance in Germany to promote the well-being of workers in order to keep the German economy operating at maximum efficiency, thus creating a new nation-state and leading the way to the first welfare state. 俾斯麦是19世纪德国政治家，担任普鲁士首相期间通过一系列铁血战争统一德国，并成为德意志帝国第一任宰相。俾斯麦以保守专制主义者的身份，镇压了19世纪80年代的社会民主运动，但他通过立法建立了世界上最早的工人养老金、健康和医疗保险及社会保险制度。

    b. Beveridge, William—1879 – 1963, was a British economist and social reformer. As one of the theoretical founders of the welfare states, he is best known for his 1942 report "Social Insurance and Allied Services" (known as the Beveridge Report) which served as the basis for the post-World War II welfare state. He was an authority on unemployment insurance from early in his career, served under Winston Churchill on the Board of Trade as Director of the newly created labor exchanges and later as Permanent Secretary of the Ministry of Food. 威廉·贝弗里奇是福利国家的理论建构者之一,他于1942年发表《社会保险报告书》,也称《威廉·贝弗里奇报告》,提出建立"社会权利"新制度,包括失业及无生活能力之公民权、退休金、教育及健康保障等理念。他是自由主义者,主张市场经济。他于1944年发表《自由社会的全面就业》一书,主张有国家及市场导向的私人企业来联合运作,对当代社会福利政策及保健制度具有深远影响。

7. The Depression—also "The Great Depression," a severe worldwide economic depression in the 1930s. It was marked by the Wall Street Crash of October 1929, wiping out 40 percent of the paper values of common stock. The market crash marked the beginning of a decade of high unemployment, poverty, low profits, deflation, plunging farm incomes, and lost opportunities for economic growth and personal advancement. The core of the problem was the immense disparity between the country's productive capacity and the ability of people to consume. The Depression caused huge political and economic changes in America and the world and was believed to be a direct contributor to World War II. 20世纪30年代的经济大萧条

8. entitlements system—the social security system or program(见"语言解说")

9. GDP—*abbrev.* gross domestic product, the total value of all goods and services produced in a country in one year, except for income received from abroad. GDP per capita(人均GDP) is often considered an indicator of a country's standard of living. 国内生产总值

10. Sub-Saharan Africa—Geographically it refers to the area of the continent of Africa that lies south of the Sahara. Politically, it consists of all African countries that are fully or partially located south of the Sahara (excluding Sudan). It contrasts with North Africa, which is considered a part of the Arab world. 撒哈拉以南非洲,俗称黑非洲

11. baby-boom—a big increase in the number of babies being born within a certain period of time. Here it refers to the famous post-World War II baby boom in the US between about 1946 and 1964. Here in the article, the author means that thanks to this baby-boom which brought demographic bonus (人口红利) to America's

economy, there are still enough workers to support the retired people and the Social Security System. 美国第二次世界大战后出现的婴儿潮

12. informal economy—economic activities organized without government approval, outside mainstream industry and commerce, including barter of goods and services(易物交换), mutual self-help, odd jobs, street trading(沿街摆摊), and other such direct sale activities. Income generated by the informal economy is usually not recorded for taxation purposes, and is often unavailable for GDP computations. Informal employment are lack of protection in the event of non-payment of wages(拖欠工资), compulsory overtime or extra shifts(强制超时或加班), lay-offs without notice or compensation(无通知或补偿的辞退), unsafe working conditions and the absence of social benefits such as pensions, sick pay and health insurance. 非正规经济;零散的经济活动

13. Cuddly tigers, not flabby cats—是幼虎而不是病猫,暗喻亚洲国家有很大的发展潜力

14. the lion's share—the largest portion

15. severance rules—解聘规则(cf. severance pay 遣散费,解雇费)

Questions

1. What was the most important mission of the major Asian countries in the past decades? And what do their people concentrate on in recent years?
2. In building their welfare states, what achievements have the big giants of Asia accomplished and what problems have they got?
3. What lessons should the Asian countries learn from the western countries and what suggestions does the author offer?
4. Why does the author say that social protection often aggravated inequalities?
5. Do you agree with the author's opinion that different countries will and should experiment with various welfare models?

Lesson Twenty-six

语言解说

委婉语

委婉语多是报刊语言的一个特点,也是读报者理解上的一大难题。委婉语(euphemism)修辞格原本用来谈论生理、疾病、死、卖淫、同性恋等令人尴尬、不快或禁忌的话题,有的较文雅礼貌,有的含糊其辞,以使听者顺耳,读者舒服。各界都用委婉语,用多了即成弊病。见本课第5段用的委婉语例句:

America has kept its safety net less generous, but has made mistakes in creating its **entitlements system**—including making unaffordable pension and health-care promises, and tying people's health insurance to their employment.

这句话的意思很清楚,社会安全网(safely net)不如应得权利制度覆盖的面广,但何谓这个拗口的制度或计划(program)? 它包括 1. Social Security 和扶老医疗计划;2. 济贫医疗计划和生活费用、津贴等在内的 Public Welfare Programs。但多数情况下只指 Social Security(社会保障制度)。用 entitlement 这个字意为只要你够条件,就有权利得到联邦政府的津贴和补助,并非政府的施舍。1996 年《福利改革法》生效后,这些福利或大打折扣或无权得到了。句中的 entitlements system 指 Social Security System or Program,词义是不恰当的。

1. 社会领域委婉语

2007 年 10 月 2 日至 11 日,上海举办了一届智残者奥林匹克夏季运动会,根据 2007 年 10 月 1 日出版的 *Newsweek* 上一篇"Shanghai Soften Up"文章里用的"the Special Olympics World Summer Games"。"the Special Olympics"就是委婉语,在这篇文章中的其他委婉语还有:the less fortunate, special-needs pupils 以及:

Four years ago the city began setting up a network of "Sunshine Homes" to provide activities and vocational training for **mentally challenged** students aged 16 to 35.

(上海在四年前就开始为 16 岁至 35 岁的智残学生提供活动和职业训练而建立了一系列充满温暖的智残人场所。)

对于残疾人,报刊为不得罪任何一方读者,一般不会或不应该用 the retarded/disabled/deaf/crippled/deformed/disabled/handicapped 等,但可以用 people with mental retardation/disabilities 等。不过最受青睐的委婉用法是:physically/mentally/visually/vertically/challenged(身

体、智力、视力有缺陷及个子不高的)。此外,还有 physically inconvenienced(身体不便的),partially sighted(只有部分视力的),visually impaired(视力受损的)和 the otherly abled(有其他方面能力的人)等等。

2. 政治领域

委婉语成了政客歪曲事实、掩盖丑行、欺世盗名,奸商蒙骗消费者,记者追求语言新奇的手段,因而泛滥成灾,不少令受众不知所云。如老布什总统出尔反尔,承诺不增税,后来不明说"tax increase",而用了遭人讥讽的"revenue enhancement"(岁入增加),人称 Bushisms。

战争不用 war 而用"future unpleasantness"。为掩盖平民伤亡,政府不明言 civilian casualties/death 而用"附带性损伤",媒体将 terrorists 称之为"insurgents"。美国对战俘施酷刑或严刑拷打称之为"physical persuasion"(或许是仿花钱打点的"currency persuasion")。

以上有些是说话兜圈子(circumlocution syndrome)。难怪 2005 年 *U.S. News & World Report* 在一篇文章的漫画里讽刺说:"能用拗口的委婉语,何必直说呢?"(Why say something clearly when you can use a jaw-breaking euphemism?)这与简明英语(plain English)运动背道而驰。(详见《导读》四章六节)

Lesson Twenty-seven

课文导读

曾经的殖民地，如今的希望之洲，非洲正行进在崛起的路途上。历史、自然环境等因素导致非洲各国长期处于普遍的贫困状态，但依傍丰富的自然资源，国际上的友助，自身的拼搏，非洲在经历数十年的缓慢发展后，真正获得了发展的机会。非洲若想真正崛起，前方还有哪些困难？需要解决哪些问题？本文对此进行了多层面的剖析。

Pre-reading Questions

1. Do you have any friends or relatives, who have been to African countries?
2. What is their impression?

Text

The Hopeful Continent: Africa Rising
After decades of slow growth, Africa has a real chance to follow in the footsteps of Asia

1   THE shops are stacked six feet high with goods, the streets outside are jammed with customers and salespeople are sweating profusely under the onslaught[1]. But this is not a high street[2] during the Christmas-shopping season in the rich world. It is the Onitsha market in southern Nigeria, every day of the year. Many call it the world's biggest. Up to 3m people go there daily to buy rice and soap, computers and construction equipment. It is a hub for traders from the Gulf of Guinea, a region

blighted by corruption, piracy, poverty and disease but also home to millions of highly motivated entrepreneurs and increasingly prosperous consumers.

2   Over the past decade, six of the world's ten fastest-growing countries were African. In eight of the past ten years, Africa has grown faster than East Asia, including Japan. Even allowing for the knock-on effect of the northern hemisphere's slowdown, the IMF[3] expects Africa to grow by 6% this year and nearly 6% in 2012, about the same as Asia.

3   The commodities boom is partly responsible. In 2000—08 around a quarter of Africa's growth came from higher revenues from natural resources. Favourable demography is another cause. With fertility rates crashing in Asia and Latin America[4], half of the increase in population over the next 40 years will be in Africa. But the growth also has a lot to do with the manufacturing and service economies that African countries are beginning to develop. The big question is whether Africa can keep that up if demand for commodities drops.

Copper, gold, oil—and a pinch of salt[5]

4   Optimism about Africa needs to be taken in fairly small doses, for things are still exceedingly bleak in much of the continent. Most Africans live on less than two dollars a day. Food production per person has slumped since independence in the 1960s. The average lifespan in some countries is under 50. Drought and famine persist. The climate is worsening, with deforestation and desertification still on the march.

5   Some countries praised for their breakneck economic growth, such as Angola and Equatorial Guinea, are oil-sodden kleptocracies[6]. Some that have begun to get economic development right, such as Rwanda and Ethiopia, have become politically noxious. Congo, now undergoing a shoddy election, still looks barely governable and hideously corrupt. Zimbabwe is a scar on the conscience of the rest of southern Africa[7]. South Africa, which used to be a model for the continent, is tainted with corruption; and within the ruling African National Congress[8] there is talk of nationalising land and mines.

6   Yet against that depressingly familiar backdrop, some fundamental numbers are moving in the right direction. Africa now has a fast-growing

middle class: according to Standard Bank[9], around 60m Africans have an income of $3,000 a year, and 100m will in 2015. The rate of foreign investment has soared around tenfold in the past decade.

7   China's arrival has improved Africa's infrastructure and boosted its manufacturing sector. Other non-Western countries, from Brazil and Turkey to Malaysia and India, are following its lead. Africa could break into the global market for light manufacturing and services such as call centres. Cross-border commerce, long suppressed by political rivalry, is growing, as tariffs fall and barriers to trade are dismantled.

8   Africa's enthusiasm for technology is boosting growth. It has more than 600m mobile-phone users—more than America or Europe. Since roads are generally dreadful, advances in communications, with mobile banking and telephonic agro-info[10], have been a huge boon. Around a tenth of Africa's land mass is covered by mobile-internet services—a higher proportion than in India. The health of many millions of Africans has also improved, thanks in part to the wider distribution of mosquito nets and the gradual easing of the ravages of HIV/AIDS. Skills are improving: productivity is growing by nearly 3% a year, compared with 2.3% in America.

9   All this is happening partly because Africa is at last getting a taste of peace and decent government. For three decades after African countries threw off their colonial shackles, not a single one (bar the Indian Ocean island of Mauritius[11]) peacefully ousted a government or president at the ballot box. But since Benin set the mainland trend in 1991, it has happened more than 30 times—far more often than in the Arab world.

10   Population trends could enhance these promising developments. A bulge of better-educated young people of working age is entering the job market and birth rates are beginning to decline. As the proportion of working-age people to dependents rises, growth should get a boost. Asia enjoyed such a "demographic dividend"[12], which began three decades ago and is now tailing off. In Africa it is just starting.

11   Having a lot of young adults is good for any country if its economy is thriving, but if jobs are in short supply it can lead to frustration and violence. Whether Africa's demography brings a dividend or disaster is largely up to its governments.

More trade than aid

12   Africa still needs deep reform. Governments should make it easier to start businesses and cut some taxes and collect honestly the ones they impose. Land needs to be taken out of communal ownership[13] and title handed over to individual farmers so that they can get credit and expand. And, most of all, politicians need to keep their noses out of the trough[14] and to leave power when their voters tell them to.

13   Western governments should open up to trade rather than just dish out aid. America's African Growth and Opportunity Act[15], which lowered tariff barriers for many goods, is a good start, but it needs to be widened and copied by other nations. Foreign investors should sign the Extractive Industries Transparency Initiative[16], which would let Africans see what foreign companies pay for licences to exploit natural resources. African governments should insist on total openness in the deals they strike with foreign companies and governments.

14   Autocracy, corruption and strife will not disappear overnight. But at a dark time for the world economy, Africa's progress is a reminder of the transformative promise of growth. (From *The Economist*, December 3, 2011)

New Words

Angola /æŋˈgəʊlə/ *n.* a country in southwest Africa 安哥拉

autocracy /ɔːˈtɒkrəsɪ/ *n.* government by one person with unlimited power 专制, 独裁政治

ballot /ˈbælət/ *n.* a system of voting, usually in secret, or an occasion when you vote in this way 选票

bar /bɑː/ *prep.* except

Benin /beˈniːn/ *n.* a country in West Africa 贝宁

bleak /bliːk/ *adj.* (fig.) not hopeful or encouraging; dismal; gloomy 无望的; 阴郁的; 黯淡的

blight /blaɪt/ *v.* to ruin or destroy 损毁

boon /buːn/ *n.* sth very helpful and useful

bulge /bʌldʒ/ *n.* a sudden, usually temporary increase in number or quantity

communal /ˈkɒmjʊnəl/ *adj.* shared by a group of people or animals, esp. a group who live together 群体的

Congo /ˈkɒŋɡəʊ/ n. a country on the Equator in the western part of central Africa 刚果

deforestation /diːˌfɒrɪˈsteɪʃən/ n. the cutting or burning down of all the trees in an area 大量砍伐

demography /dɪˈmɒɡrəfɪ/ n. the statistical study of human population 人口统计学

desertification /dɪˌzɜːtɪfɪˈkeɪʃn/ n. the process by which useful land, esp. farm land, changes into desert 土地的沙化

dismantle /dɪsˈmæntl/ v. to bring to an end (a system, arrangement, etc.), esp. by gradual stages

dividend /ˈdɪvɪdənd/ n. share of profits paid to share-holders in a company, or to winners in a football pool 股息、红利、回报

Equatorial Guinea /ˌekwəˈtɔːrɪəl ˈɡɪnɪ/ n. a small country in west central Africa 赤道几内亚

Ethiopia /ˌiːθɪˈəʊpɪə/ n. a country in northeast Africa on the Red Sea 埃塞俄比亚

fertility /fəˈtɪlɪtɪ/ n. the ability to produce offspring; power of reproduction 生育能力；繁殖能力

hideous /ˈhɪdɪəs/ adj. extremely ugly or shocking to the senses; repugnant 极丑的,骇人听闻的 hideously adv.

infrastructure /ˈɪnfrəˌstrʌktʃə/ n. the basic systems and structures that a country or organization needs in order to work properly, for example roads, railways, banks, etc. 基础设施

kleptocracy /klepˈtɒkrəsɪ/ n. a government where officials are politically corrupt and financially self-interested 腐朽政府

oust /aʊst/ v. to force someone out and perhaps take their place

profusely /prəˈfjuːslɪ/ adv. produced or existing in large quantities 大量生存地

ravage /ˈrævɪdʒ/ v. to ruin and destroy; devastate 破坏,毁坏

Rwanda /ruˈændə/ n. a country in east central Africa 卢旺达

shackles /ˈʃæklz/ n. sth that prevents you from doing what you want to do 镣铐,禁锢

shoddy /ˈʃɒdɪ/ adj. unfair and dishonest 不公平,不诚实

slump /slʌmp/ v. to go down suddenly or severely in number or strength 暴跌,剧降

stack /stæk/ v. to put piles of things on or in a place 堆满,把……堆放在某处

strife /straɪf/ *n.* state of conflict; angry or violent disagreement; quarrelling 冲突；争斗；争吵

taint /teɪnt/ *v.* if sth bad taints a situation or person, it makes the person or situation seem bad 丑陋；腐败

tariff /ˈtærɪf/ *n.* a tax on goods coming into a country or going out of a country 关税

trough /trɒf/ *n.* a long narrow open container that holds water or food for animals 水槽，饲料槽

Notes

1. salespeople are sweating profusely under the onslaught—They are sweating a lot because they are very busy with customers. 此处的"onslaught"不能死抠"a fierce attack"的意思，是指买卖人招揽顾客拼命推销商品，所以汗流浃背。词义要视上下文而定。
2. high street—the main street of a town where most of the shops and businesses are or shops and the money people spend in them 商业街
3. IMF—The International Monetary Fund 国际货币基金组织
4. With fertility rates crashing in Asia and Latin America—As the birth rate drops in Asia and Latin America
   fertility rate—the birthrate of a population 生育率
   crash—to fail; become unsuccessful 跌，失败
5. a pinch of salt—used to describe a small amount of something. Here, it implies that although Africa is abundant in natural resources, it should be used in an economical way for, someday, it will be exhausted. 节俭方式，一点点
6. oil-sodden kleptocracies—Although some countries, such as Angola and Equatorial Guinea, are rich in oil resources, their government officials are politically corrupt and financially self-interested. 石油资源丰富，但是政府腐败。
7. oil-sodden—covered with oil or full of oil 吸饱石油的
   Zimbabwe is a scar on the conscience of the rest of southern Africa.—In Zimbabwe(津巴布韦), the Matabele unrest(玛塔贝利人的动乱) led to what has become known as the Matabeleland Massacres(大屠杀), which lasted from 1982 until 1985. Mugabe(津巴布韦总统穆加贝) ordered his North Korean-trained Fifth Brigade（第五旅）to occupy Matabeleland, crushing any resistance to his rule. It has been

estimated that at least 20,000 Matabele were murdered and tens of thousands of others were tortured in military internment camps(俘虏收容所). The slaughter only ended after Nkomo and Mugabe reached a unity agreement in 1988 that merged their respective parties, creating the Zimbabwe African Union-Patriotic Front(津巴布韦非洲爱国阵线). In 1980s, such slaughter is indeed a scar on the conscience in such a civilized world. 此句该刊第5段及根据英文资料的释义充分说明西方对非洲国家反对殖民统治、种族歧视和隔离政策及独立自主充满不满和仇恨。(见本课"读报知识")

  a scar on the conscience—great sadness, guilt, etc. after the unpleasant experience left in the heart which is difficult to get rid of 心灵上的创伤

8. African National Congress—South Africa's governing political party, supported by its Tripartite Alliance（三方联盟）with the Congress of South African Trade Unions (COSATU)（南非工会大会）and the South African Communist Party (SACP)（南非共产党）, since the establishment of non-racial democracy in April 1994. 南非非洲国民大会

9. Standard Bank—The Standard Bank of South Africa Limited is one of South Africa's largest financial services groups. It operates in 30 countries around the world, including 17 in Africa. 南非标准银行

10. telephonic agro-info—information related to agriculture given or obtained through telephoning 电话农业信息
  agro-info—由"agricultural information"拼缀而成。

11. the Indian Ocean island of Mauritius—an island nation in the Indian Ocean about 2,000 kilometres (1,200 mi) off the south east coast of the African continent. 印度洋毛里求斯岛

12. demographic dividend—a lot of advantages obtained from the population 人口红利，指一个国家的年轻劳动人口占总人口比重较大，抚养率比较低，为经济发展创造了有利条件。

13. communal ownership—an ownership of a territorial commune and its bodies of self administration. It is similar to municipal or public ownership, which is not part of state or private property. 群体所有

14. politicians need to keep their noses out of the trough—politicians should not interfere with government policies and practices. (This expression is a variant of the idiom "have one's nose in the

trough," which means "to be involved in sth which you hope will get you a lot of money or political power.") 不干预政治与实施
15. America's African Growth and Opportunity Act—a legislation that has been approved by the U. S. Congress in May 2000. The purpose is to assist the economies of sub-Saharan Africa and to improve economic relations between the United States and the region. 美国非洲增长和机遇法
16. Extractive Industries Transparency Initiative—an act to increase transparency over payments by companies from the oil and mining industries to governments and to government-linked entities, as well as transparency over revenues by those host country governments. 采掘业透明度行动计划

Questions

1. How is today's economic development in Africa compared with East Asia and the whole world?
2. When optimism is shown about Africa, what other obstacles is Africa facing now?
3. What is favorable to Africa's economic growth?
4. What measures should Africa take in order to achieve further development?
5. What are the main reasons leading to Africa's rising?

读报知识

报刊的政治倾向性

美英等国报刊均非公办,不代表政府,一贯标榜"客观"、"公正"、"独立"于政府和政党,"不受约束"、完全"自由办报",置身"意识形态之外"。是政府的监督员(watch dog),可批评政府各项政策,有乌鸦嘴之称,记者更戴上了无冕之王(uncrowned King)的桂冠。然而,通过美国前情报机构雇员 Edward Snowden 的揭秘,事实正好与此相反,他们一切都在政府的监控之下,违者遭殃。下面我们不妨来看看《经济学家》对本文第5段的评述:

非洲国家不是政治上不祥,就是贪污腐败,还批评南非国大党传

说要搞国有化，尤其对津巴布韦总统穆加贝不满甚至带有仇恨，说该国是其他南部非洲（注意 southern Africa 别与 South Africa 混淆）心灵上的创伤。为什么要这样攻击穆加贝领导的津巴布韦呢？

津巴布韦曾是英殖民地，1980年获得独立后，穆加贝一直掌权。2000年前后该国发生旱灾，要求国内外援助未能解决饥荒，于是穆采取了"土地改革"，没收白人占领的农场，分配给穷人，从而得罪了英国等大资本家和政客，对津进行制裁，并将它开除出英联邦（the Commonwealth [of Nations]）。根据注6和注7站在西方立场上的英文释义及本文的分析报道，"腐败"等负面消息不离题，尤其称是穆加贝屠杀了几万国人。《经济学家》是英国刊物，它的立场、观点都为英国政府帮腔，为白人农场主鸣不平。

非洲原来都是英法等西方列强殖民地，它们都是二战觉醒后通过反殖民统治获得独立的，所以西方当然是不高兴。现在非洲在崛起，西方也是不愿意看到的。阅历不深的年轻人读报刊时一定要擦亮眼睛，别让他们牵着鼻子走。《导读》在一章四节里对美英报刊的"立场"、"党派属性"、"惯用套路"、"用词"等做了详解。

Unit Nine
Society

Lesson Twenty-eight

课文导读

　　互联网的发展催生了以交流为目的的亿万网民,进而催化了婚恋交友网站的发展和繁荣。自1995年美国人创建婚恋交友网站 Match.com 至今,网上婚恋市场以欣欣向荣、势不可挡的态势蔓延至全球,婚恋网站已经发展成为利润丰厚的产业。在现实生活中,人们的社交圈狭窄,多元化的社交方式不足,而生活的压力又让人们少有空闲去体验传统的交友方式。网络的快捷和多元化恰恰提供了一个不错的交友平台,去交友网站寻求意中人逐渐成为一种选择方式,人们的婚恋观念也从传统的相亲模式向网络交友转变,因此也就有了对网络结识和传统结交的比较,哪一种方式更容易找到意中人呢？网络世界使你有机会结识更多的人,是否就意味着你的意中候选人就更多了？是否也意味着在道德问题上出轨更多？值得探讨。其实,要找到匹配的另一半,网上约会与传统约会方式一样各有利弊,不可一概而论。《时代》周刊的《网站约会让找意中人变得更难吗？》一文,从其独特的角度探讨了这一社会热点问题。

Pre-reading Questions

1. Do you know something about online dating?
2. Are there any of your friends or relatives who have met their spouse online?

Text

Does Online Dating Make It Harder to Find 'the One'?

By Alice Park

1　　Everyone knows someone who met their spouse online. A friend of mine whom I hadn't seen in years told me recently that she, too, met her husband on an Internet dating site. They're happily married, just moved into a new house, and are now talking about starting a family[1].

2   When I asked her if she thought online matchmaking was a better way than offline dating to find guys who were more compatible with her—and, therefore, better husband material—she laughed. "No, because I couldn't stand him when I first met him," she says of her husband. She thought he was full of himself and rude during their first encounter. It definitely wasn't love at first sight, she said—that took a while.

3   In other words, according to my friend, Internet dating is just as unpredictable as the non-digital version[2]. You never know how things are going to evolve until they do. But the benefit, she says, is that dating online gives you access to a lot more people than you'd ordinarily ever get to meet—and that's how she connected with her future husband.

4   These observations have been borne out[3] in a new study by social psychologists collaborating across the country. The extensive new study published in the journal Psychological Science in the Public Interest[4] sought to answer some critical questions about online dating, an increasingly popular trend that may now account for[5] 1 out of every 5 new relationships formed: fundamentally, how does online dating differ from traditional, face-to-face encounters? And, importantly, does it lead to more successful romantic relationships?

5　　　For their 64-page report, the authors reviewed more than 400 studies and surveys on the subject, delving into[6] questions such as whether scientific algorithms—including those used by sites like eHarmony, Perfect Match and Chemistry[7] to match people according to similarities—can really lead to better and more lasting relationships (no); whether the benefits of endless mate choices online have limits (yes); and whether communicating online by trading photos and emails before meeting in person can promote stronger connections (yes, to a certain extent).

6　　　Overall, the study found, Internet dating is a good thing, especially for singles who don't otherwise have many opportunities to meet people. The industry has been successful, of course—and popular: while only 3% of Americans reported meeting their partners online in 2005, that figure had risen to 22% for heterosexual couples and 6% for same-sex couples by 2007−09. Digital dating is now the second most common way that couples get together, after meeting through friends. But there are certain properties of online dating that actually work against love-seekers[8], the researchers found, making it no more effective than traditional dating for finding a happy relationship.

7　　　"There is no reason to believe that online dating improves romantic outcomes," says Harry Reis, a professor of psychology at University of Rochester[9] and one of the study's co-authors. "It may yet, and someday some service might provide good data to show it can, but there is certainly no evidence to that right now."

8　　　One downside to Internet dating has to do with one of its defining characteristics: the profile. In the real world, it takes days or even weeks for the mating dance to unfold, as people learn each other's likes and dislikes and stumble through the awkward but often rewarding process of finding common ground. Online, that process is telescoped and front-loaded, packaged into a neat little digital profile, usually with an equally artificial video attached.

9　　　That leaves less mystery and surprise when singles meet face to face. That's not necessarily a bad thing, as profiles can help quickly weed out[10] the obviously inappropriate or incompatible partners (who hasn't wished for such a skip button on those disastrous real-life blind dates[11]?), but it also means that some of the pleasure of dating, and building a relationship by learning to like a person, is also diluted.

10   It also means that people may unknowingly skip over potential mates for the wrong reasons. The person you see on paper doesn't translate neatly to a real, live human being, and there's no predicting or accounting for the chemistry[12] you might feel with a person whose online profile was the opposite of what you thought you wanted. Offline, that kind of attraction would spark organically.

11   The authors of the study note that people are notoriously fickle about what's important to them about potential dates. Most people cite attractiveness as key to a potential romantic connection when surveying profiles online, but once people meet face to face, it turns out that physical appeal doesn't lead to more love connections for those who say it is an important factor than for those who say it isn't. Once potential partners meet, in other words, other characteristics take precedence over the ones they thought were important.

12   "You can't look at a piece of paper and know what it's like to interact with someone," says Reis. "Picking a partner is not the same as buying a pair of pants."

13   Making things harder, many sites now depend on—and heavily market—their supposedly scientific formulas for matching you with your soul mate based on similar characteristics or personality types. It may seem intuitively logical that people who share the same tastes or attitudes would be compatible, but love, in many cases, doesn't work that way.

14   Some online dating sites, for example, attempt to predict attraction based on qualities like whether people prefer scuba diving to shopping, or reading to running, or whether they tend to be shy or more outgoing. But social science studies have found that such a priori predictors[13] aren't very accurate at all, and that the best prognosticators of how people will get along come from the encounters between them. In other words, it's hard to tell whether Jim and Sue will be happy together simply by comparing a list of their preferences, perspectives and personality traits before they meet. Stronger predictors of possible romance include the tenor of their conversations, the subject of their discussions, or what they choose to do together.

15   "Interaction is a rich and complex process," says Reis. "A partner

is another human being, who has his or her own needs, wishes and priorities, and interacting with them can be a very, very complex process for which going through a list of characteristics isn't useful."

16　　The authors also found that the sheer number of candidates that some sites provide their love-seeking singles—which can range from dozens to hundreds—can actually undermine the process of finding a suitable mate. The fact that candidates are screened via their profiles already sets up a judgmental, "shopping" mentality that can lead people to objectify their potential partners.[14] Physical appearance and other intangible characteristics may certainly be part of the spark that brings two people together, but having to sift through[15] hundreds of profiles may become overwhelming, forcing the looker to start making relationship decisions based on increasingly superficial and ultimately irrelevant criteria.

17　　And remember, says Reis, "Online dating sites have a vested interest[16] in your failure. If you succeed, the site loses two paying customers."

18　　Communicating online before meeting can help counter some of this mate-shopping effect, but it depends on how long people correspond electronically before taking things offline. A few weeks of email and photo exchanging serves to enhance people's attraction when they finally meet, researchers found, but when the correspondence goes on too long—for six weeks—it skews people's expectations and ends up lowering their attraction upon meeting. Over time[17], people start to form inflated or overly particular views about the other person, which leaves them at risk for being disappointed in the end.

19　　Considering the many pitfalls, what accounts for the enduring popularity—and success—of online dating sites? Part of it may be the fact that singles who use online dating sites are a particularly motivated lot. Their desire to find a spouse and get married may make them more likely to actually find a life partner on the site, or believe that they have. And they're also probably more likely to believe that the matchmaking algorithms that power so many sites really can find them that person who's "meant to be."

20　　It also offers an attractive solution for an age-old problem for singles—where to meet potential mates. As more people delay marriage, either for financial or professional reasons, and with more people constantly moving around to find better jobs, disrupting their social networks, the easily accessed digital community of like-minded singles becomes a tantalizing draw.

21   Still, those who go online looking for love are left navigating a minefield of odds—not unlike dating in the non-digital realm. But at least there's solace in matches like my friend's[18]. If there's one thing online dating does better than any matchmaker or network of friends who are eager to set you up with that "someone who's perfect for you," it's finding you lots and lots of candidates. "Like anything on the Internet, if you use online dating wisely, it can be a great advantage," says Reis. You just have to accept that not all of your matches will be your Mr. or Ms. Right. (From *Time*, February 7, 2012)

New Words

algorithm /ˈælgərɪðəm/ *n.* a set of rules that must be followed when solving a particular problem. 算法；计算程序

chemistry /ˈkemɪstrɪ/ *n.* kind of attraction sparked organically between two people(常指两性之间强烈的)吸引力

collaborate /kəˈlæbəreɪt/ *v.* to work together with sb in order to produce or achieve sth 合作

compatible /kəmˈpætəbl/ *adj.* having a good relationship with sb because of similar opinions and interests 情投意合的；般配的

criteria /kraɪˈtɪərɪə/ *n.* a standard or principle by which sth is judged or with the help of which a decision is made 标准

date /deɪt/ *n.* a romantic meeting *v.* to have a romantic relationship with sb

delve /delv/ *v.* to try to discover new information about sth 探究；钻研

dilute /daɪˈluːt/ *v.* to make a liquid weaker by adding water or another liquid to it 稀释

disastrous /dɪˈzɑːstrəs/ *adj.* extremely bad；terrible 糟糕的

disrupt /dɪsˈrʌpt/ *v.* to make it difficult for sth to continue in the normal way

downside /ˈdaʊnsaɪd/ *n.* the negative part or disadvantage of sth

draw /drɔː/ *v.* a performer, place, event etc that a lot of people come to see

fickle /ˈfɪkl/ *adj.* changing often and suddenly 变幻无常的；善变的

front-load /ˈfrʌntləud; ˈfrɔntˈləud/ v. to assign costs or benefits to the early stages of(装载)置前;(喻)提前

heterosexual /ˌhetərəˈsekʃuəl/ adj. sexually attracted to people of the opposite sex 异性恋的

inappropriate /ˌɪnəˈprəupriət/ adj. not suitable; cf. appropriate

incompatible /ˌɪnkəmˈpætəbl/ adj. different in important ways, and do not suit each other or agree with each other; cf. **compatible**

inflated /ɪnˈfleɪtɪd/ adj. ideas, opinions etc about sth make it seem more important than it really is 夸张的;过高的

intangible /ɪnˈtændʒəbl/ adj. difficult to describe, define or measure 不易捉摸的;难以确定的

intuitive /ɪnˈtjuːɪtɪv/ adj. showing or formed by the power of understanding or knowing sth without reasoning or learned skill 直觉的;直观的

match /mætʃ/ n. a marriage union or two people who are married

mentality /menˈtæləti/ n. attitudes and way of thinking 心态;思维方式

objectify /əbˈdʒektɪfaɪ/ v. to present sth or sb as an object 使客观化,使具体化

overwhelming /ˌəuvəˈwelmɪŋ/ adj. having such a great effect on you that you feel confused and do not know how to react 令人困惑的;不知所措的

pitfall /ˈpɪtfɔːl/ n. a danger or difficulty, esp. one that is hidden or not obvious at first

a priori [拉] 先验性的

profile /ˈprəufaɪl/ n. a short description that gives important details about a person 人物简介

prognosticator /prɒgˈnɒstɪkeɪtə/ n. one who foretells sth will happen in the future 预言者

property /ˈprɒpəti/ n. a stated quality, power, or effect that belonging naturally to sth 特性

scuba /ˈskjuːbə/ n. a portable apparatus containing compressed air and used for breathing under water 便携式水下呼吸器

skew /skjuː/ v. to change or influence sth with the result that it is not accurate, fair, normal, etc. 歪曲;曲解

sift /sɪft/ n. to examine and sort carefully

solace /ˈsɒləs/ n. a feeling of emotional comfort when sb is sad or disappointed. 安慰

stand /stænd/ v. to endure the presence or personality; endure or

undergo successfully; bear
stumble /ˈstʌmbl/ *v.* to put one's foot down awkwardly while walking or running and nearly fall over 跌跌撞撞地走
tantalizing /ˈtæntəlaɪzɪŋ/ *adj.* making you feel a strong desire to have sth that you cannot have 逗引人的,撩拨心弦的
telescope /ˈtelɪskəʊp/ *v.* to make a process seem to happen in a shorter time
tenor /ˈtenə(r)/ *n.* the general meaning or mood of sth spoken 大意;要领
vested /ˈvestɪd/ *adj.* settled, fixed
weed /wiːd/ *v.* to remove unwanted plants from a garden

Notes

1. start a family—to have a baby
2. non-digital version—traditional, face-to-face dating
3. These observations have been borne out. —These observations have been proved right.
    bear out—to show that sb is right or sth is true 证实;证明
4. Psychological Science in the Public Interest—PSPI, an academic journal of the Association for Psychological Science（美国心理学协会）that is published three times a year by SAGE Publications（塞奇出版社）《公众利益心理学》杂志
5. account for—If a particular thing accounts for a part or proportion of sth, that part or proportion consists of that thing; amount to（数量或比例上）占
6. delve into—to search thoroughly 钻研;深入研究
7. eHarmony, Perfect Match and Chemistry—the names of three well-known international online dating websites
8. there are certain... against love-seekers... —online dating weakens one's social or traditional morality because it usu. with the objective of developing a personal, romantic, or sexual relationship, that prevents love-seekers from finding their true love...
9. University of Rochester—private, founded in 1929, located in Rochester, New York 罗切斯特大学
10. weed out—to remove or get rid of people or things from a group because they are not wanted

11. blind date—a date between persons who have not previously met
12. account for the chemistry—to explain mutual attraction（此处 account for 意为 to explain or give the necessary information about，有别于第四段中的 account for）
13. a priori predictor—预设的预示因素
14. The fact that candidates are screened ... objectify their potential partners. 一个人简历在网上展示，看后便使人作出了判断，要像购物似的东看西比，将其潜在伴侣当做物品一样挑选（因为可供选择的对象太多了）。
15. sift through—to make a close and thorough examination of (things in a mass or group) 筛选
16. vested interest—if you have a vested interest in sth happening, you have a strong reason for wanting it to happen because you will get an advantage from it 既得利益
17. over time—If sth happens over time, it happens gradually during a long period of time.
18. in matches like my friend's—like my friend who has found her life partner or got married

Questions

1. Is online matching a better way than traditional dating according to the writer's friend who met her husband online?
2. What benefits does online dating create?
3. Does online dating lead to more successful romantic relationships?
4. How to understand that one of the disadvantages of online dating is the profile?
5. Although there are many pitfalls occurring in the online dating websites, why does its popularity keep rising?
6. Why does online dating appeal so much to people delaying their marriage?

> 新闻写作

句法上的简约

为适应信息化社会快节奏的需要，报道文章常使用简单句尤其是扩

展简单句(expanded simple sentence),其方法有:

(1) 多用介词引导的名词短语(noun phrase),少用从句(subordinate clause)。如:

No longer are the swarming peoples of Asia and Africa sunken, as for centuries past, **in a passive acceptance of their lot.** (*The New York Times*)

例句中用"(in a passive)acceptance of their lot"而不用从句"who accepted their lot"。

(2) 句法结构前移:如以简洁方法表现人物的性格特点,不用关系从句,而只是将职业、头衔或人名前加用的某些形容词或起修饰作用的同位语前置,使修饰语变长,类似中文。如:

A quiet, tubercular physicist named Robert Goddard appeared before a board of military-weapons experts. (*Newsweek*)

通常写法为 A quiet physicist named Goddard who was tubercular 或 a physicist, a quiet and tubercular man named Goddard,此例将 named 省去报刊中也常见,那就成了起修饰作用的同位语。

(3) 用一个主谓结构或句子直接置于被修饰语前作定语。如:

Changes in social mores, especially in the counterculture years of the 1960s, resulted in an **"anything goes" philosophy** that contributed directly to the rise in violence, drug abuse, divorce and out-of-wedlock births. (1996/8/5 *Financial Times*)。

通常的语序应该是: philosophy that anything goes(= anything is alright)。

(4) 用引号省去"that"作同位语结构。如:

The attitude "time is money" has more influence on business communication in US than it does anywhere else.

通常是: The attitude that time is money...

(5) 时间状语从句省掉连词、主语和助动词等成分,而将形容词和过去分词等用作起句。见下面一段文字:

(a) So consider these scenes from March 2004, described by two former top Justice officials who, like other ex-officials interviewed by *Newsweek*, did not wish to be identified discussing sensitive internal matters. (b) Attorney General John Ashcroft is really sick. (c) **About to give a press conference in Virginia**, he is stricken with pain so severe he has to lie down on the floor. (d) **Taken to the hospital for an emergency gallbladder operation**, he hallucinates under medication as he lies, near death, in intensive care. (2007/6/4 *Newsweek*)

在这段文字里,共有四个句子。a. 正常句;b. 简单句。关键在 c. d. 句,没有分别用时间状语从句"When he is about..."和"When he is taken...",而只是将形容词和过去分词引起的状语前置而省略了"When he is"。据王宗炎老先生在《向张道真同志进一言》文章"三、英语习惯和修辞问题"里认为,"**about to return** to the hall"不能放在主语前头,只能说"When he was about to return..."。可现在这种用法在报刊上较多,可能是一个省略的新趋势或与报刊文体有关。薄冰的《英语语法》说,像这样的结构可省去主语和助动词。

(6) 常用连字符号(hyphen)"-"而组成形容词性的自由连缀词组,带有一定的感情色彩,具有临时性和诙谐性特点。这也是一种定语前置,而且有增多趋势。如:

His only "non-political" gesture was to delete some pointedly wry reference to "total victory" and a "**pick-up-our-marble-and-go-home philosophy.**"(*Newsweek*)

不过,前置定词太多,相互关系反而不清,弄巧成拙,近年又有回摆趋势。这跟中文里,一些前置修饰语改为后置,相映成趣。

Lesson Twenty-nine

课文导读

　　社会在思想意识激烈的碰撞中不断前进。年轻人总是站在思潮的前列，推陈出新，在各方面对社会作出贡献。20世纪六七十年代的嬉皮士与主流文化和传统观念背道而驰，而80年代的雅皮士却热衷于追求财富、事业成功与物质享受，这一趋势在 X 一代和 Y 一代身上达到顶点。

　　Yawns 与他们前辈的思想和言行大相径庭。他们年轻、富裕、事业有成，但并不追求物质享受，相反却具有强烈的社会责任感和环保意识，提倡救困济贫，过着简朴、节俭的生活。学了这一课我们会得到很多启示，是向往奢华的生活方式，还是以俭朴为荣？

Pre-reading Questions

1. What is the most valuable thing in your life?
2. What is your ideal way of life?

Text

Yawns[1]: A generation of the young, rich and frugal
By Evelyn Nieves

1　　SAN FRANCISCO—They drive hybrid cars, if they drive at all, shop at local stores, if they shop at all, and pay off their credit cards every month, if they use them at all.[2]

2　　They may have disposable income, but whatever they make, they live below their means in a conscious effort to tread lightly on the earth[3].

3　　They are a new breed of Gen X'ers and Y's[4], Young and Wealthy but Normal, or Yawns.

4　　The acronym comes from *The Sunday Telegraph* of London, which noted that an increasing number of rich young Britons are socially aware, concerned about the environment and given less to consuming than to giving money to charity.[5]

5 Yawns sound dull, but they are the new movers and shakers[6], their dreams big and bold. They are men and women in their 20s, 30s and 40s who want nothing less than to change the world and save the planet.

6 Take Sean Blagsvedt, who moved from Seattle to India in 2004 to help build the local office of Microsoft Research. Moved by young children begging on the streets, Blagsvedt quit Microsoft and launched two networking sites, babajob.com and babalife.com, to link India's vast pool of potential workers with the people who need labor. The larger goal—to reduce poverty.

7 Far from the techie cafe life[7], Blagsvedt, 32, lives at babajob's headquarters in Bangalore, a 3,000-square-foot apartment where his mother and stepfather also live and 15 workers come and go every day.

8 "I'm a happy person," he said. "It's great to do something that you believe in doing."

9 The high-tech world has spawned its share of Yawns, but they can sprout anywhere.[8] In fact, Yawns are a subset of a growing global movement of the eco-socially aware. The state of the economy and the state of the planet have inspired people to consider what they buy and how they spend in ways not seen since the "Small is Beautiful"[9] and ecology movements of the 1970s[10].

10 The movement makes perfect sense, said David Grusky, a sociologist at Stanford University[11], since society tends to follow cycles—with anti-materialist periods like the hippie movement[12] generating a pro-materialist reaction—the yuppie period[13], and so on. Not to mention, he adds, that the evidence of major climate change and a concern with terrorism gives rise to more interest in spiritual as opposed to material objectives.

11 The upshot, he said, is that "a cultural and demographic perfect storm[14] may well push us decisively toward an extreme form of post-materialism in the coming period."

12 That helps explain why Earth Day[15] has become so big again, why products are all going "green" and why freecycle.org[16], an Internet community bulletin board where members offer items for free, has grown in five years from a dozen members in Tucson, Ariz., to a

network of more than 3,000 cities in 80 countries.

13   Deron Beal, the site's founder, counts 4 million members, and growing by 20,000 to 50,000 members each week.

14   "People have many reasons for freecycling," said Beal. "But the biggest reason is environmental-reusing and recycling instead of helping create more waste."

15   Could it also be that we are sick to death of buying stuff?

16   Pam Danziger, a consumer trends expert, thinks so. "The green thing is just a small part of it," said Danziger, whose firm, Unity Marketing, has new research showing luxury spending is way down. "Americans have been on a buying binge for the last 10 years," she said. "Our closets are full. Our attics are full. Our garages are full. Enough already!"

17   Yawns live small, but they already own whatever they want.

18   Rik Wehbring, a 37-year-old dot-com millionaire—he worked for multiple startups—limits himself to living on $50,000 a year. That's no chump change but well below what he could spend in San Francisco, where his rent eats up 40 percent of his allotted spending.

19   Wehbring doesn't own a television, his mp3 player cost $20 ("and it works just fine") and he drives (when he drives) a Toyota Prius[17].

20   He buys most of his food from local farmers' markets, is leaving the bulk of his estate to various environmental organizations and donates money to what he considers worthy causes. Everyday, he grapples with "how to live a low-carbon life."

21   But Wehbring doesn't buy clothes, or much of anything.

22   "I don't need a lot of material possessions," he said. "I haven't had to buy anything in a while."

23   Such frugality seems to run in his circle.[18]

24   Brad Marshland, 44, the husband of Wehbring's cousin, is a successful filmmaker living near Berkeley. He and his wife and two sons, ages 10 and 12, dry their clothes on a line, grow their own vegetables and buy what they need at garage sales and secondhand stores. (Secondhand stores are to Yawns what The Gap was to Yuppies.[19])

25   "We're pretty low on the stuff scale[20]," Marshland said.

26   Marshland offsets his family's "carbon footprint"—how much

energy it uses—by donating money to environmental groups online.

27   Yawns hate ostentation.

28   When Ray Sidney, a software engineer at Google, cashed in his stock options[21] in 2003, they yielded him more money than he could ever burn through[22] in his lifetime. (Billions? He won't say.) But instead of building himself a 10,000-square-foot mansion in the Googledom of Silicon Valley[23], he retired to a four-bedroom house in Stateline, Nev., and started giving money away.

Ray Sidney poses for a photograph at his home in Stateline, Nev. Sidney, a software engineer at Google, cashed in his stock options in 2003 and shares the money with local organizations where he lives and to a variety of charities. By Jim Grant, AP

29   He has given $400,000 to a local arts council to help build a new arts center, $1 million to a bus company to help launch a route so that casino workers wouldn't have to rely on private transportation to get to and from work, and $1.7 million for a new football field and track at a local high school, for example.

30   Sidney also donates millions to charities that try to cure diseases or save the world.

31   His one rich-guy, carbon hogging guilt trip[24]: a single engine plane he flies about once a week to see his girlfriend in San Francisco.

32   But his pet project these days is pure Yawn. He is building what he calls "an environmentally friendly affordable housing development" on 100 acres near his home in Stateline.

33   "This world and our society and the people in it are good and worthwhile," he said, "and I think it's worth spending money to keep it around and try to improve it." (From The Associated Press[25], May 4, 2008)

New Words

acronym /ˈækrənɪm/ *n.* a word made up from the first letters of the name of sth such as an organization 首字母缩略词

affordable /əˈfɔːdəbl/ *adj.* that can be afforded; able to spend, give, do etc, without serious loss or damage

allot /əˈlɒt/ *v.* to decide officially to give sth to sb or use sth for a particular purpose 分配；拨出

Ariz. *abbrev.* Arizona, a state in the SW of the US, north of Mexico, known for containing a large area of desert 亚利桑那州（美国）

attic /ˈætɪk/ *n.* the room in a building just below the roof 阁楼

Bangalore /ˌbæŋɡəˈlɔː/ *n.* a city of south-central India. It is a major industrial center and transportation hub in India. 班加罗尔（印度）

Berkeley /ˈbɜːklɪ/ *n.* a city on the eastern side of the San Francisco Bay area in California 伯克利（美国西部加利福尼亚州）

binge /bɪndʒ/ *n. infml* a short period when you do too much of sth, esp. drinking alcohol [非正式]（短期的）狂欢作乐；大吃大喝

Briton /ˈbrɪtən/ *n. fml* someone from Britain [正式]英国人

bulk /bʌlk/ *n.* the main or largest part of sth（某物的）主要部分；大半

bulletin board /ˈbʊlɪtɪn bɔːd/ notice board; a board on a wall which notices may be fixed to 布告牌

carbon footprint a measure of the amount of carbon dioxide produced by a person, organization, or location at a given time. It describes the environmental impact of carbon emissions. 二氧化碳排放量（的测量单位）

casino /kəˈsiːnəʊ/ *n.* a place where people try to win money by playing card games or roulette 赌场

chump change /tʃʌmp tʃeɪndʒ/ *slang* a small amount of money 一小笔钱

council /ˈkaʊnsɪl/ *n.* a group of people appointed or elected to make laws, rules, or decisions, or to give advice 委员会

cycle /ˈsaɪkl/ *n.* a number of related events happening in a regularly repeated order 循环，周而复始

demographic /ˌdiːməˈɡræfɪk/ *adj.* of or related to the study of human populations and the ways in which they change 人口学的，人口统计学的

disposable income /dɪˈspəʊzəbl ˈɪnˌkʌm/ the amount of money you have left to spend after you have paid your taxes, bills etc 可支配收入；税后收入

donate /'dəʊneɪt/ v. to give sth, esp. money, to a person or an organization in order to help them 捐赠，捐献

dot-com /dɒt-kʌm/ n. a company that does all or most of its business on the Internet 网络公司

estate /ɪs'teɪt/ n. all of someone's property and money, esp. everything that is left after they die 个人全部财产（尤指遗产）

frugal /'fruːgəl/ adj. careful to only buy what is necessary 节俭的 **frugality** /fruː'gælɪtɪ/ n.

garage sale a sale of used household belongings, typically held outdoors or in a garage at the home of the seller（在住宅车库里进行的）旧物出售

grapple (with) /'græpl/ v. to try hard to deal with (a difficult problem); to search mentally, with uncertainty and difficulty 尽力解决（难题等）；费力思考

guilt trip a feeling of guilt about sth（对某事的）负疚感

hybrid /'haɪbrɪd/ adj. consisting of or coming from a mixture of two or more other things; of mixed origin（两种或两种以上东西）混合的 **hybrid car** 混合动力车

mansion /'mænʃən/ n. a large house, usu. belonging to a wealthy person

multiple /'mʌltɪpl/ adj. including many different parts, types etc 多样的，多重的

Nev. abbrev. Nevada, a state in the western US

offset /'ɒfˌset/ v. to make up for; to balance 补偿，抵消

ostentation /ˌɒsten'teɪʃən/ n. unnecessary show of wealth, knowledge etc（财富、知识等的）卖弄，炫耀

pet /pet/ adj. of sth (usu. a theory, project, subject, etc) that you have particularly strong feelings about or particularly like or support 宠爱的；最喜欢的，最珍视的

pool /puːl/ n. a quantity or number of money, things, people etc that are collected together to be used or shared by several people or organizations 合伙使用的钱（或物资、人力等）

recycling /ˌriː'saɪklɪŋ/ n. the activity of reusing things that have already been used 回收利用

San Francisco /ˌsæn frən'sɪskəʊ/ a city and port in California, US

Seattle /sɪ'ætl/ a city and port in Washington State 西雅图

sociologist /ˌsəʊsɪ'ɒlədʒɪst/ n. a social scientist who studies the institutions and development of human society 社会学家

sprout /spraʊt/ v. to grow, appear, or develop 生长；发芽；发展

startup /'stɑːtəp/ *n.* a small business or company that has recently been started by someone 新兴公司
subset /'sʌbset/ *n.* a set that is part of a larger set 分支,(一)小部分
techie /'tekiː/ *n.* a person who knows a lot about computers and electronic equipment
tread (on) /tred/ *v.* to put one's foot when walking; to step 踩,踏
upshot /'ʌpʃɒt/ *n.* the result in the end; outcome 结果,结局
way /weɪ/ *adv.* far 远远地,大大地

Notes

1. Yawns——在本文中,这是"the Young and Wealthy but Normal"的首字母缩略词(acronym),指"年青、富裕,但是生活节俭的一代人"。
2. They drive hybrid cars ... if they use them at all. ——他们如果开车,就开混合动力车;如果购物,就去本地商店;如果使用信用卡,就每个月还清其欠款。此句中的三个条件从句都使用了 at all,强调所陈述条件可能性较小,即他们很少开车,很少购物,也很少使用信用卡。
3. tread lightly on the earth——move on the earth in a gentle way so that the earth is not disturbed
4. Gen X'ers and Y's——Generation X (Gen X) is a term used to describe the generation following the post-World War II baby boom (生育高峰期), especially people born from the early 1960s to the late 1970s. Generation X is generally marked by its lack of optimism for the future, nihilism(虚无主义), cynicism(犬儒主义), skepticism(怀疑论), alienation(疏远) and mistrust in traditional values and institutions. Gen Y is the generation following Gen X. They are primarily children of the Baby boomers, especially people born from the early 1980s to the late 1990. Generation Y are labeled for seeking instant gratification. X一代人和Y一代人。X一代可称为"后雅皮士时代",他们收入较高,花钱比较随意。在心理上,这一代人由于面临种种社会问题而有明显的悲观主义色彩,大多数没有明确的生活目标。Y一代人的父母是生育高峰期出生的人,因此他们处于又一个生育高峰,面临着吸毒、肥胖、教育费用增加以及不善于交流等问题。
5. The acronym comes from ... giving money to charity. ——这个首字母缩略词来自于伦敦出版的《星期日电讯报》,其中指出越来越多的年轻富裕的英国人具有社会责任感,他们关心环境,喜欢把钱捐给慈善事业而不是自己消费。

(be) given to—to be in the habit of or have a tendency to（习惯于；有……癖好；倾向于）

6. movers and shakers—opinion leaders; people who have power and influence, esp. those who are political or economic activists
7. techie café life—此处指把全部时间都花在工作上的一种生活方式。

    techie—a term derived from the word *technology*, for a person who displays a great, sometimes even obsessive, interest in technology, as well as high-tech devices, particularly computers 高科技（或计算机）迷
8. The high-tech world ... sprout anywhere.—Although the high-tech industry has produced a large number of yawns, more and more are appearing in every walk of life.
9. "Small is Beautiful"—*Small Is Beautiful*: *Economics As If People Mattered* is a collection of essays by British economist E. F. Schumacher. First published in 1973, *Small Is Beautiful* brought Schumacher's ideas to a wider audience. It was released during the 1973 energy crisis and emergence of globalization and dealt with the crisis and various emerging trends (like globalization) in an unusual fashion. *The Times Literary Supplement*（《泰晤士文学副刊》）ranked *Small Is Beautiful* among the 100 most influential books published after World War II.
10. ecology movements of the 1970s—Ecology became a central part of the World's politics as early as 1971, when UNESCO（联合国教科文组织）launched a research program called *Man and Biosphere*（人类与生物圈）, with the objective of increasing knowledge about the mutual relationship between humans and nature. A few years later it defined the concept of Biosphere Reserve（生物圈保护区）. In 1972, the United Nations held the first international Conference on the Human Environment in Stockholm（斯德哥尔摩）. This conference was the origin of the phrase "Think Globally, Act Locally."
11. Stanford University—private, founded in 1885 in California
12. the hippie movement—It was a peace movement during the Vietnam war, when people began to hate the war. On 5 September 1965, in an article in the *San Francisco Examiner*, Michael Fallon labeled the new "Bohemians（不受传统束缚者）" or "hippies." The label stuck and was thereafter applied to any young person who

experimented with drugs, exhibited an unconventional appearance, enjoyed new forms of music and art, expressed disdain(轻蔑)for mainstream values and institutions, investigated exotic religions, or espoused(信奉)a philosophy that combined the beats' existentialism(垮掉的一代的存在主义哲学)with a colorful, expressive joie de vivre(人生的乐趣)all their own. Now a hippy generally refers to a person who opposes and rejects many of the conventional standards and customs of society, especially one who advocates extreme liberalism in sociopolitical attitudes and lifestyles, often having long hair, wearing brightly-coloured clothes, taking illegal drugs, and rejecting middle-class materialism. 嬉皮士运动。流行于20世纪六七十年代。嬉皮士对社会现实不满，厌弃传统生活方式，实行群居，自由性爱，反对越南战争，主张和平。留长发，穿奇装异服，吸毒。

13. the yuppie period—The yuppies came into vogue in the 1980s. The term "yuppie" was derived from "young, urban professional person(城市少壮职业人士)". The yuppie population consists of that group of people in their thirties who are advancing rapidly in economic and social standing, having well-paid professional jobs and affluent lifestyles, and who represent a target audience for some advertisers, such as BMW automobiles or Fila sportswear. The term has come to have a somewhat pejorative connotation(贬义), particularly when applied to a specific individual. 雅皮士时期。雅皮士具有较强的职业意识，追求高待遇工作，注重物质享受，住在环境优美的市郊。

14. a cultural and demographic perfect storm—a combination of violent changes in cultural and demographic trends

15. Earth Day—Apr. 22, a day to celebrate the environment. The first Earth Day was organized in 1970 to promote the ideas of ecology, encourage respect for life on earth, and highlight growing concern over pollution of the soil, air, and water. Earth Day is now observed in 140 nations with outdoor performances, exhibits, street fairs, and television programs that focus on environmental issues. 世界地球日

16. freecycle.org—始于2003年的全球性环保网站。人们可以通过网站将自己不用的物品送与他人，也可免费得到自己想要的物品。

17. Toyota Prius—丰田公司生产的世界首款油电混合动力量产车,是环保理念与高科技结合的产品。
18. Such frugality seems to run in his circle.—It seems that all the people connected with him are as frugal as he is. 他圈内的人都如此节俭。
19. Secondhand stores are to Yawns what The Gap was to Yuppies.—Yawns like secondhand stores as much as Yuppies like The Gap.

    The Gap—嘉普(财富500强公司之一,总部所在地在美国,主要经营服装零售)
20. We're pretty low on the stuff scale—We have little demand for material possessions.
21. stock option an option giving the holder, usually an officer or employee, the right to buy stock of the issuing corporation at a specific price within a stated period 优先认股权,股票期权。一般是指企业在与经理人签订合同时,授予经理人将来以签订合同时约定的价格购买一定数量公司普通股的选择权,经理人有权在一定时期后出售这些股票,获得股票市价和行权价之间的差价,但在合同期内,期权不可转让,也不能得到股息。
22. burn through—consume freely
23. The Googledom of Silicon Valley—Googledom 一般指 google.com 通过网站链接和各项服务所提供的包罗万象的信息资源(the all-encompassing informational domain created by google.com's many websites and services),这里指 Google Inc. 位于硅谷的总部。
24. carbon hogging guilt trip—带着因尽情消耗能源而产生的负疚感的旅行

    hog—keep or use all of sth in a selfish or impolite way 贪心地攫取,把某物占为己有
25. Associated Press(*abbrev.* AP)—美联社,成立于1848年,总部设在纽约市。1976年就已有1,181家美国日报和约3,462家广播电台和电视台接受该社提供的新闻服务,现在已成为世界最大的通讯社。

Questions

1. What are the main characteristics of Yawns?
2. What is their dream?
3. What social-economic background has given rise to the consumer trends of Yawns?

4. How do you understand "post-materialism"?
5. What does "freecycling" mean? What's the most important reason for freecycling?
6. What do you think of the Yawns' life style?

语言解说

Generation 何其多？

　　Generation 虽不再时髦仍见诸报端，并造出新词。如 Generation O 即奥巴马（Obama）一代，虽然以前吸过毒，孩提时代不爱学习犹如 Generation Jones(1954 年至 1965 年出生)，但从 2009 年起一些人却在奥政府内领导着美国。有篇文章"The N.B.A. and China Hope They've Found the Next Yao"居然还有 Generation Yi(易建联一代)。肥胖的人多了，也称之为一代。社会学家在总结和描写历史时，往往将有共性、出生同时代的某一特定群体称为"代"（generation）。如美国根据时间先后顺序就可从南北战争到现在分为诸如 Missionary/Lost/G.I./Silent/Babyboom/Beat/Thirteenth/Millennial Generation 等这几代人。这里的所谓"代"是特指某一群体，并非一代。因此有的学者认为是用词不当。2001 年《美国新闻与世界报道》发表的一篇题为"'XX 一代'的说法恰当吗？"的文章指出，"代"常把某个小群体的经历和人生态度强加给同时期出生的整整一代人而无视其地区、种族、阶层等重大差异。马萨诸塞大学的一位教授主张摒弃这种不科学的提法。再则，即使这样划分，有的也含糊不清。由于社会学家这么用，记者用不着动脑子，也纷纷效仿，出现了诸如 Generation XXL 等滥用的现象。

Lesson Thirty

> 课文导读
>
> 科技的发展促进了社会生活的多样性,物质的丰富使人的需求日益增加。社会分工越来越细,许多新的职业也相应出现。如何在纷繁复杂、瞬息万变的职场立于不败之地?说难也不难。把握住时代的脉搏,看清楚社会需求变化的大趋势才是制胜的法宝。本文列出了美国当代最时尚最前沿的六大需求职业:医疗保健、数字化世界、全球化、临床基因图谱学的发展、保护环境以及反恐。虽然这些是美国最有吸引力的前卫职业,但对我国学生而言,也有重要参考价值。

Pre-reading Questions

1. What's your idea of a career?
2. Do you have any career plans for the future?

Text

Ahead-of-the-Curve Careers

By Marty Nemko

1   Cutting-edge careers are often exciting, and they offer a strong job market. Alas, the cutting edge too often turns out to be the bleeding edge[1], so here are some careers that, while relatively new, are already viable and promise further growth. They emerge from six megatrends:

2   **Growing healthcare demand.** The already overtaxed U.S. healthcare system will be forced to take on more patients because of the many aging baby boomers[2], the influx of immigrants, and the millions of now uninsured Americans who would be covered under a national healthcare plan likely to be enacted in the next president's administration. Jobs should become more available in nearly all specialties, from nursing to coding[3], imaging to hospice. These healthcare careers are likely to be

particularly rewarding. Health informatics specialists will, for example, develop expert systems to help doctors and nurses make evidence-based diagnoses and treatments. Hospitals, insurers, and patient families will hire patient advocates[4] to navigate the labyrinthine and ever more parsimonious healthcare system. On the preventive side, people will move beyond personal trainers to wellness coaches, realizing that doing another 100 pushups won't help if they're smoking, boozing, and enduring more stress than a rat in an experiment.

3　　**The increasingly digitized world.** Americans are doing more of their shopping on the Net. We obtain more of our entertainment digitally: Computer games are no longer just for teenage boys; billions are spent by people of all ages and both sexes. Increasingly, we get our information from online publications, increasingly viewed on iPhones[5] and BlackBerrys[6]. An under-the-radar career that is core to the digital enterprise is data miner[7]. Online customers provide enterprises with high-quality data on what to sell and for individualized marketing. Another star of the digitized world is simulation developer. The growing ubiquity of broadband connectivity is helping entertainment, education, and training to incorporate simulations of exciting, often dangerous experiences. For example, virtual patients allow medical students to diagnose and  treat without risking a real patient's life. A new computer game, Spore, allows you to simulate creating a new planet, starting with the first microorganism.

4　　**Globalization, especially Asia's ascendancy.** This should create great demand for business development specialists, helping U. S. companies create joint ventures with Chinese firms. Once those deals are made, offshoring managers are needed to oversee those collaborations as well as the growing number of offshored jobs[8]. Quietly, companies are offshoring even work previously deemed too dependent on American culture to send elsewhere: innovation and market research, for example. Conversely, large numbers of people from impoverished countries are immigrating to the United States. So, immigration specialists of all types, from marketing to education to criminal justice[9], will be needed to attempt to accommodate the unprecedented in-migration[10].

5   **The dawn of clinical genomics.** Decades of basic research are finally starting to yield clinical implications. Just months ago, it cost $1 million to fully decode a person's genome. Now it's $300,000 and just $1,000 for a partial decoding, which, in itself, indicates whether a person is at increased risk of diabetes, cancer, heart disease, Alzheimer's, and 15 other conditions. Within a decade, we will probably understand which genes predispose humans to everything from depression to violence, early death to centenarian longevity, retardation to genius. Such discoveries will most likely give rise to ways to prevent or cure our dreaded predispositions and encourage those in which we'd delight. That, in turn, will bring about the reinvention of psychology, education, and, of course, medicine. In the meantime, the unsung heroes who will bring this true revolution to pass will include computational biologists and behavioral geneticists[11].

6   **Environmentalism.** Growing alarm about global warming is making environmentalism this generation's dominant initiative. The most influential panel on the topic, the Intergovernmental Panel on Climate Change, and the most visible advocate of curbing carbon emissions, former Vice President Al Gore, shared the 2007 Nobel Peace Prize for insisting that vigorous action is needed.[12] The environmental wave is creating jobs in everything from sales to accounting in companies making green products, regulatory positions[13] in government, and grant writing, fundraising, and litigation work in nonprofits. Among the more interesting green careers[14], thousands of engineers are working on such projects as hydrogen-powered cars, more efficient solar cells, and coal pollution sequestration systems. But those jobs require very high-level training and skills and are at risk of being offshored. In contrast, so-called green-collar consulting is offshore resistant and often requires less demanding training (for example, learning how to do green-building audits).[15] It is a worthy option for people who love novelty and don't want to be stuck in the same office every day, for years. Many environmental consultants are peripatetic, solving new and different problems at constantly changing worksites—often blending office work with time in the great outdoors.

7   **Terrorism.** The expert consensus is that the United States will again fall victim to a major terrorist attack. Jobs in the antiterrorism field have already mushroomed since 9/11, but if another attack were to occur, even more jobs would surely be generated. Demand should particularly grow in such areas as computer security and Islamic-country intelligence, but their required skill sets[16] are difficult to acquire. More accessible yet also likely to be in demand is emergency planning. (From *U.S. News & World Report*, December 19, 2007)

New Words

accommodate /əˈkɒmədeɪt/ *v.* 1. to have or provide enough space for a particular number of people or things 容纳 2. to accept someone's opinions and try to do what they want, esp. when their opinions or needs are different from yours 迎合，迁就

ahead-of-the-curve /əˈhed-ɒv-ðə-kɜːvz/ *adj.* at the forefront of recent developments, trends, etc. 前沿的

Alzheimer's /ˈɑːltsˌhaɪməz/ *n.* Alzheimer's disease 阿耳茨海默氏病，早老性痴呆病（根据德国医生 Alois Alzheimer 命名）

ascendancy /əˈsendənsɪ/ *n.* a position of power, influence or control 优势；支配地位

bleeding edge the most advanced stage of a technology, art, etc, usu. experimental and risky（某一技术、艺术等的）最先进的阶段；最先进的技术（但通常要经实验而且具有一定的风险）

booze /buːz/ *v. infml* to drink alcohol, esp. a lot of it [非正式]饮酒；狂欢

centenarian /ˌsentɪˈnɛərɪən/ *n.* someone who is 100 years old or older 百岁（以上）老人

coding /ˈkəʊdɪŋ/ *n.* 指定（或确定）遗传密码

collaboration /kəˌlæbəˈreɪʃən/ *n.* the act of working together with another person or group to achieve sth 合作；协作

consensus /kənˈsensəs/ *n.* an opinion that everyone in a group will agree with or accept 共同意见，一致看法，共识

conversely /kənˈvɜːslɪ/ *adv. fml* used when one situation is the opposite of another [正式]相反地；另一方面

curb /kɜːb/ *v.* to control or limit sth in order to prevent it from having a harmful effect 控制，约束

cutting edge /ˈkʌtɪŋ edʒ/ the position of greatest importance or advancement; the leading position in any movement or field 刀锋；最前沿　**cutting-edge** *adj.* the most advanced; the newest 处于先锋地位的；最新的

diabetes /ˌdaɪəˈbiːtiːz/ *n.* a serious disease in which there is too much sugar in your blood 糖尿病

enact /ɪˈnækt/ *v.* to make a proposal into law 将……制定成法律

gene /dʒiːn/ *n.* a small part of the material inside the nucleus of a cell, that controls the development of the qualities that have been passed on to a living thing from its parents 基因

geneticist /dʒɪˈnetɪsɪst/ *n.* a person who studies or specializes in genetics 遗传学家

genome /ˈdʒiːnəʊm/ *n.* the total of all the genes that are found in one type of living thing 基因图谱：the human genome 人类基因图谱

genomics /dʒəˈnɒmɪks/ *n.* the study of genomes

grant /ɡrɑːnt/ *n.* a contract granting the right to operate a subsidiary business; a transfer of property（授予经营权等的）合同；财产转让契据

hospice /ˈhɒspɪs/ *n.* a special hospital where people who are dying are looked after 临终关怀医院

imaging /ˈɪmɪdʒɪŋ/ *n.* the creation of visual representations of objects, such as body parts or celestial bodies, for the purpose of medical diagnosis or data collection, using any of a variety of usually computerized techniques 造像；拍片

impoverished /ɪmˈpɒvərɪʃt/ *adj.* very poor

incorporate /ɪnˈkɔːpəreɪt/ *v.* to include sth as part of a group, system, plan etc 包含；吸收

influx /ˈɪnflʌks/ *n.* the arrival of large numbers of people or large amounts of money, goods, etc., esp. suddenly（突然）大量涌入

informatics /ˌɪnfəˈmætɪks/ *n.* information science; the sciences concerned with gathering, manipulating, storing, retrieving, and classifying recorded information 信息科学，信息处理

initiative /ɪˈnɪʃətɪv/ *n.* an important new plan or process that has been started in order to achieve a particular aim or to solve a particular problem 计划，措施

Islamic /ɪzˈlæmɪk/ *adj.* belonging or relating to Islam 伊斯兰教的；伊斯兰教国家的

labyrinthine /ˌlæbəˈrɪnθaɪn/ *adj.* of or like a labyrinth; very complicated（像）迷宫的；繁琐的

litigation /ˌlɪtɪˈgeɪʃən/ n. *law* the process of taking claims to a court of law, in a non-criminal case [法律](非刑事案件)诉讼

megatrend /ˈmegəˌtrend/ n. important trend 大趋势(mega-常置于名词和形容词前,表示"异常巨大的、非常重要的")

microorganism /ˌmaɪkrəʊˈɔːgənɪzəm/ n. a living thing which is so small that it cannot be seen without a microscope 微生物

novelty /ˈnɒvəltɪ/ n. sth new and unusual which attracts people's attention and interest 新奇的事物

overtax /ˌəʊvəˈtæks/ v. to make sb do more than they are really able to do, so that they become very tired 使(某人)负担过重(或过度疲劳),这里指使政府开支过大

parsimonious /ˌpɑːsɪˈməʊnɪəs/ adj. *fml* extremely unwilling to spend money; mean 过分节俭的;吝啬的

peripatetic /ˌperɪpəˈtetɪk/ adj. *fml* traveling from place to place, esp. in order to do your job (尤指为工作而)巡游的

predispose /ˌpriːdɪsˈpəʊz/ v. to make sb more likely to behave or think in a particular way or suffer from a health problem 使预先倾向于;使易感染

predisposition /ˌpriːˌdɪspəˈzɪʃən/ n. a tendency to behave in a particular way or suffer from a particular illness (以某种方式行事的)倾向;易患某种疾病的倾向

pushup /ˈpʊʃˌʌp/ n. *AmE* an exercise in which you lie on the floor on your front and push yourself up with your arms [美]俯卧撑

regulatory /ˈregjulətərɪ/ adj. *fml* having the purpose of controlling an activity or process, esp. by rules [正式]调整的;管理的,控制的

retardation /ˌriːtɑːˈdeɪʃən/ n. *fml* the process of making sth happen or develop more slowly 迟缓;阻滞

sequestration /ˌsɪkwesˈtreɪʃən/ n. the act of taking property away from the person it belongs to because they have not paid their debts 扣押(债务人的财产)

simulate /ˈsɪmjʊleɪt/ v. *fml* to give the effect or appearance of; to imitate 模仿,模拟

simulation /ˌsɪmjʊˈleɪʃən/ n. a model or representation of a course of events in business, science etc, esp. by computer calculation to study the effects of possible future changes or decisions 模拟研究;模拟试验;模拟操作

ubiquity /juːˈbɪkwɪtɪ/ n. the quality of being everywhere at the same time 无所不在;普遍存在

under-the-radar /ˌʌndə-ðə-ˈreɪdɑː/ *adj.* not noticeable; not popular

unprecedented /ʌnˈpresɪdəntɪd/ *adj.* never having happened before 前所未有的,无前例的

unsung /ˈʌnˈsʌŋ/ *adj.* not praised or famous although deserving to be 应该而未受到赞扬的:unsung hero 无名英雄

viable /ˈvaɪəbl/ *adj.* able to succeed in operation; feasible 可望成功的;切实可行的

wellness /ˈwelnɪs/ *n.* 1. the condition of good physical and mental health, esp. when maintained by proper diet, exercise, and habits 健康 2. an approach to healthcare that emphasizes preventing illness and prolonging life, as opposed to emphasizing treating diseases 保健

Notes

1. Alas, the cutting edge too often turns out to be the bleeding edge—唉！先锋往往是要冒风险的。"cutting edge"和"bleeding edge"都有"前沿"、"在某一领域最先进之事"的意思,后者仿前者和 leading edge 而造。用 bleeding 意含"要经实验而冒险的"、"带来不利影响、后果的"。

2. baby boomers—people born during a period when a lot of babies were born, esp. between 1946 and 1964 生育高峰潮代。第二次世界大战后,美国的出生率陡然激增。自 1946 年至 1964 年的 18 年间,美国出生人口高达 7,600 万,占 60 年代美国人口的将近三分之一。由此造成的人口年龄分布不均衡带来许多社会问题,如对教育、医疗、职业市场、城市和郊区经济等均有影响。

3. from nursing to coding—from taking care of patients to entering data into computer

4. patient advocates—people who help patients understand and navigate the healthcare system. They help ensure that the patient gets to see the desired specialist. They do Internet research so the patient is more informed when talking to the doctor.

5. iPhone—an Internet-enabled multimedia smartphone (智能电话) designed and marketed by Apple Inc (苹果公司)

6. BlackBerry—a wireless handheld device introduced in 1997 as a two-way pager (传呼机). The more commonly known smartphone Blackberry, which supports push e-mail, mobile telephone, text

messaging, internet faxing, web browsing and other wireless information services, was released in 2002.
7. data miner—a person who uses powerful softwares statistics to predict or explain customer behavior
8. Once those deals are made ... offshored jobs. ——一旦买卖成功,就需要外包经理去监管这些合作项目和越来越多的外包工作。

　　offshore—(1) *adj.* & *adv.* in a foreign country (2) *v.* move business processes or services to another country, esp. overseas, to reduce costs（生意或业务）向海外转移；外包（常用 offshoring 或 outsourcing 指外包。在美国，外包是一个有很大争议的问题。民主党说这是白领失业的一个主要原因,而共和党却支持这种做法,因为这是大公司节省成本的重要途径。本文也讨论了哪些工作可外包和哪些不能。）
9. criminal justice—the system of law enforcement（执法）, involving police, lawyers, courts, and corrections, used for all stages of criminal proceedings and punishment（刑事司法）
10. in-migration—入境移民。（该词的标准拼写应为 immigration,本文作者在 migration 前直接加前缀 in-,起到了强调的效果。）
11. the unsung heroes ... behavioral geneticists—那些即将带来这场真正的革命的无名英雄们包括计算生物学家和行为遗传学家。

　　bring ... to pass—make ... happen
12. The most influential panel... vigorous action is needed. ——这方面最有影响的专门委员会,即政府间气候变化专门委员会和最引人注目的控制碳排放的倡导者、(美国)前副总统阿尔·戈尔,因为坚持主张需要在这方面采取积极行动而共享 2007 年诺贝尔和平奖。

　　panel—此处 panel 来代替 a special committee,还可代替 committee 或 subcommittee。
13. regulatory positions—监管机构职务
14. green careers—careers in environmental protection or improvement（随着环境保护主义浪潮的高涨,green 的词义得到了扩展,可用来指所有与环境保护有关的人或事,如 a Green 指环保组织或绿党成员。）
15. In contrast ... less demanding training (for example, learning how to do green-building audits).——相比而言,所谓的绿领顾问行业不大可能转向国外,需要接受的训练也比较容易(例如,学习如何检验环保建筑)。

　　audit—the inspection or examination of a building or other

facility to evaluate or improve its appropriateness, safety, efficiency, or the like 对建筑物设施、安全性等的检验
16. skill sets—all the skills needed for doing a work or completing a task 一套技能

Questions

1. What are the causes of the growth in healthcare demand?
2. Why do patient families hire patient advocates?
3. What are the characteristics of a digitized world?
4. What effects will globalization have on the U.S. job market?
5. What clinical implications will genomics start to yield?
6. What are the main elements that contribute to the creation of cutting-edge careers?

语言解说

Administration 和 Government

本课中的"the next president's administration"指下一任总统组成的政府。因为本文发表于2007年,当时的美国总统是小布什,所以指布什以后的总统领导下的政府。"the Bush Administration"有人译为"布什政府",有人译为"布什行政当局",还有人在报上著文说,Administration 译为"政府"错了。那么到底哪个译法是正确的呢?词语对错应以英英词典的释义为准,先看 Longman Dictionary of English Language & Culture 中 "administration" 条下的第4义:[the]AmE (often cap.) (编者按:虽说 administration 在美语中作"政府"讲时常用大写,但报刊中却常用小写。) the (period of) government, esp. of a particular president or ruling party(〈美〉尤指一位总统或执政党领导的"政府",政府任期)。再看另一本政治权威词典,Safire's New Political Dictionary 的定义:"regime; the government of a specific leader"「政权;某一位(政党)魁首或领袖领导的政府」。这两本词典都定义 Administration 为"政府",且含有"临时"之意。如欲贬之,也可译为"布什政权"。另外,从"政府"的组成来看,the Bush Administration 与 the U.S. government 不同:前者指总统领导的内阁和阁员及他们为首的政府各部加上总统府办事机构和人员;后者则由行政、立法和司法三个部门组成。

综上所述,"the Bush Administration"译为"布什政府"或"布什行政

当局"似乎都有理。若我们判断的标准以词义为准,那么,译为"布什政府"才是正确的。倘若文章谈的是国会与行政当局的斗争,用的词是 Congress 和 the Bush Administration,那么译为"布什行政当局或机关"也是可以的。从美国报刊报道行政与立法当局斗争的用词来看,媒体往往用 the White House, the President 等词来指代行政当局。如报上出现 the administration,往往指文本前已提及过的 the Bush 或 Obama administration 之省略。所以在一般情况下,还是根据词义,译为"布什政府"合适。

至于见诸美国报端的"the Blair Administration"和英国报端的"the Bush government",显然是用法不当,因为英国是单一权力政体(unitary government),行政与立法机构的议会是一体,所以一般不用"administration"。若用"the Blair government"则常指布莱尔内阁或首相和内阁。由此也可说明新闻语言较随意。(见《导读》五章三节"英美政治比较")

Unit Ten
Business

Lesson Thirty-one

课文导读

模特在许多人眼中是美丽的代名词。美女模特在T型台上吸引众人的眼球。她们是世界时尚的弄潮儿,给人一种神秘高雅的感觉。然而个中滋味只有她们自知。

面对全球化的发展,这一行业正在慢慢发生变化。一批有才华的模特和全球化的模特圈正在改变T型台,受过良好教育的年轻女性纷纷入行。以往模特的职业生涯通常很短,薪水也低,现在却涌现出许多高收入的超模群体。以前的模特追求的是0号身材,瘦骨嶙峋;鉴于全球化的影响,现在的模特公司在世界范围内寻求体态强壮、高大健美的模特。然而,骨模仍有市场。现在该行业竞争激烈,要立于不败之地并非易事,时尚大牌和艺术总监不总是定海神针,模特自身的智慧才是不可或缺的。

通过学习此课,同学们不但可以了解西方模特现状和学习若干专有名词,如一般文章上很少出现的名模名字、时尚品牌和公司等。我们阅读各种题材的文章,能扩大视野,获得更广泛的知识。

Pre-reading Questions

1. Do you think modelling is attractive?
2. What kind of life do you think models live?

Text

Model economics: The beauty business

Brainy models and a global talent pool are changing the catwalk

On February 17th London's spring fashion week[1] begins. Across the capital, young women in vertiginous shoes and skimpy dresses will be teetering along catwalks. And thousands of young doughnut-dodgers[2] will be inspired to queue outside agents' offices for the slim chance of becoming the next Kate Moss[3].

2   Careers in modeling are typically short-lived, badly paid and less glamorous than pretty young dreamers imagine. Yet the business is changing. For one thing, educated models are in. This may sound improbable. In the film *Zoolander*[4], male models are portrayed as so dumb that they play-fight with petrol and then start smoking. But such stereotypes are so last year.[5]

3   Lily Cole, a redheaded model favoured by Chanel[6] and Hermès[7], recently left Cambridge University with a first-class degree in history of art. Edie Campbell, a new British star, is studying for the same degree at the Courtauld Institute[8] in London. And Jacquetta Wheeler, one of Britain's established catwalkers, has taken time out from promoting Burberry[9] and Vivienne Westwood[10] to work for Reprieve, a charity which campaigns for prisoners' rights.

4   Natalie Hand of London's Viva model agency, who represents Ms Campbell, says there has been a shift away from the "very young, impressionable models," who were popular in the past ten years, to "more aspirational young women.""There is an appetite now for models to be intelligent, well-mannered and educated," says Catherine Ostler, a former editor of *Tatler*, a fashion and society magazine.

5   This is new. The best-known models of yesteryear often led rags-to-riches lives, courtesy of the rag trade.[11] Twiggy, a star of the 1960s, was a factory worker's daughter. Ms Moss's mother was a barmaid.

6   But the big fashion houses and leading photographers are tiring of

the drama that comes with plucking girls as young as 15 from obscurity and propelling them to sudden stardom. Too often, models were showing up to photo-shoots hours late or drug-addled. This wasted a huge amount of time and money. Fashion houses are now keen to avoid trouble. Many find that educated models show up to work on time and don't go doolally as often.

7   Trends in the modelling business also follow those in the global economy. From the 1960s to the 1990s, America reigned supreme. The hottest "supermodels" were Americans such as Cindy Crawford and Christy Turlington. They were figures whose glossy confidence mirrored America's[12]. They never woke up for less than $10,000. They were cultural icons, too, celebrated in songs such as Billy Joel's "Uptown girl," the video of which starred Christie Brinkley, who became his wife[13].

Fat cheques
The world's best-paid models

Name	2011 earnings, $m	Comments
Gisele Bündchen	45	Giraffe-legged Brazilian; owns global underwear franchise. Has promoted Dior, Versace and Procter & Gamble's Pantene shampoo
Heidi Klum	20	Small-town German; has conquered America. Hosts "Project Runway" TV series
Kate Moss	14	Chirpy Brit from Croydon. Launched "heroin chic" look in 1993. Honoured with gold statue in British Museum
Adriana Lima	8	Brazilian newcomer; her GQ cover was the biggest-selling ever; Super Bowl ad hinted that flowers buy sex
Doutzen Kroes	6	Dutch ex-skater, known as "Helen of Troy" for launching so many products. Less well-known for promoting Friesian language

8   As in so many fields, the rewards for a handful of stars have shot up. Contracts are wrapped in secrecy, but sources say that a one-off deal for a shoot with a top model can begin at $75,000, rising to $1.5m for a global advertising campaign. For advertisers, the right face is lucrative. Procter & Gamble's campaign featuring Gisele Bündchen is said to have raised sales of its Pantene shampoo in Brazil by 40%.[14]

9   The stars pull in more from sidelines such as franchising goods in their own name (Elle Macpherson's underwear, Kate Moss's lipstick). Heidi Klum, a German model, serves as a judge on "Project Runway," a televised fashion-talent contest.[15]

10   Pay for lesser models has fallen sharply, however. This is partly because the labour pool has globalised and therefore grown much

bigger. International agencies now scout for talent in emerging economies[16]. In the 1990s they hired hordes of high-cheeked Slav teenagers. Now the hottest hunting-ground is Brazil, which produces Amazonian height and athletic looks.

11 Ashley Mears, an American sociologist and author of "Pricing Beauty", a study of the economics of modelling[17], says that although the industry has grown in the past decade, individual contracts have shrunk. Too many faces are chasing too few lenses.

12 Television fees have fallen, not least because technologies like TiVo[18] allow audiences to skip commercials. One British model told your correspondent that rates for the major fashion shows have roughly halved in recent years, and that many careers are now over in two seasons (a calendar year) rather than around six. The Model Alliance[19], an outfit that agitates for higher wages, estimates that the average regularly-employed model makes $27,000 a year. Part-timers and men make less.

13 The juiciest prize is to become the face of a luxury brand such as Dior or Burberry[20]. To have any chance, a model must first have magazine shoots under her designer belt. This fact allows fashion magazines to pay peanuts, even for a cover-shoot.[21]

14 There remains an iron divide between "editorial" models, who appeal to the expensive designers, and "catalogue" models, who are often slightly larger and more conventionally pretty. The catalogue models pose in normal clothes, which is less glamorous. But they earn a steadier income, and are less likely to be dropped by the time they reach their late 20s.

15 Agents take around 20% of a model's fee, plus another 20% from the client. Despite these high levies, agencies struggle. Since the financial crash, clients have been scrimping. And agencies must find models whose faces somehow capture the Zeitgeist, as defined by the big brands and their capricious artistic directors.

16 Large agencies are competing with a crowd of smaller upstarts, such as Viva London[22] and DNA[23] in New York. The giant Elite Model Management agency lost an American antitrust case on price-fixing in 2004[24] and drowned in a sea of recriminations. It has since been refounded under new ownership, though its Dutch branch faces a fresh

lawsuit, brought by the winner of a contest who claims the agency sacked her for putting on weight.

17   The sheer randomness of fashion makes it a tough business. Change is more predictable in other industries. IT firms, for example, can safely assume that computers will keep getting faster. But foreseeing next year's hot look is impossible. No one could have anticipated Kate Moss's early "grunge" look, which set a fashion for tangled long hair, boyish hips and pale complexions. Now the fashion is for models who look a little healthier, such as Doutzen Kroes[25], a former speedskater.

The exquisitely sensitive Karl Lagerfeld[26]

18   Despite angry campaigns against the cult of "Size 0"[27], skinny models are still in demand. This is partly because designers think clothes look better when there is no distracting flesh beneath them. Ms Mears adds that the industry keeps models thin to "signify elite luxury distinctiveness." Rough translation: if normal women have curves, then the elite want something different. This infuriates those who blame fashion for fostering eating disorders among the young. But the attitude shows little sign of shifting. Karl Lagerfeld, a designer, made headlines this week by describing Adele[28], a pop singer, as "fat."

19   Power in the fashion business depends on fame. "Super-brands" such as Gucci[29] and Burberry don't hesitate to throw their weight around[30]. Gucci flustered London's fashion week last autumn by ordering a clutch of the "mega-girls" to leave London early and fly to Milan for a more commercially important show.

20   Marc Jacobs[31], a prominent New York designer, caused a further shortage of models for British shows by detaining some prospective bookings in New York. Agents complained, but Mr Jacobs is bigger than any of them. "Where's the camaraderie?" asked Carole White of Premier Model Management[32], a London agency. On the catwalk, you walk alone. (From *The Economist*, February 11, 2012)

New Words

aspirational /ˌæspəˈreɪʃənl/ *adj.* having strong desire to do sth or have

sth important or great 有志向的，有抱负的
addled /'ædld/ *adj. infml* (of sb's brain) having become confused
agitate /'ædʒɪteɪt/ *v.* to argue strongly in public for or against some political or social change 鼓动，煽动，宣传
Amazonian /ˌæməˈzəʊnjən/ *adj.* strong and aggressive(used of women) 常作 amazonian(指妇女)男子气概的，强壮且咄咄逼人的
antitrust /ˌæntɪˈtrʌst/ *adj.* against trust or business monopolies 反托拉斯的，反垄断的
barmaid /'bɑːmeɪd/ *n.* a woman who serves drinks in a bar
brainy /'breɪnɪ/ *adj.* intelligent; smart
capricious /kəˈprɪʃəs/ *adj.* changing often, esp. suddenly and without good reason 反复无常
catwalk /'kætwɔːk/ *n.* a narrow raised footway sticking out into a room for models to walk on in a fashion show(时装表演时模特走的)T型台
camaraderie /ˌkɑːməˈrɑːdərɪː/ *n.* the friendliness and goodwill shown to each other by friends, esp. people who spend time together at work, in the army, etc.
complexion /kəmˈplekʃn/ *n.* the natural color and appearance of the skin, esp. of the face 面色，气色
cult /kʌlt/ *n.* a system of worship, esp. one that is different from the usu. and established forms of religion in a particular society 狂热的崇拜，迷信
detain /dɪˈteɪn/ *v.* to keep from proceeding; delay or retard 阻止；拖延
doolally /duːˈlælɪ/ *adj. infml* crazy
established /ɪˈstæblɪʃt/ *adj.* well-known and recognized by the public
exquisitely /ekˈskwɪzɪtlɪ/ *adv.* intensely, greatly (感觉)强烈的，剧烈的
feature /'fiːtʃə(r)/ *v.* to have or include as a prominent part or characteristic 由……主演；包含……作为主要部分或特点的
franchise /'fræntʃaɪz/ *v.* authorize someone to sell or distribute a company's goods or services in a certain area(授予出售或发行的)特许经营或销售权
fluster /'flʌstə(r)/ *v.* to cause to be nervous and confused
glamorous /'glæmərəs/ *adj.* full of or characterized by glamour 充满魅力的
glossy /'glɒsɪ/ *adj.* having a smooth, shiny, lustrous surface 表面光滑的，有光泽的；表面上时髦动人的
grunge /grʌndʒ/ *n.* a style of fashion, popular with young people in

the early 1990s, of wearing clothes that look dirty and untidy 邋遢装时尚

horde /hɔːd, həʊrd/ *n.* a large moving crowd, esp. one that is noisy or disorderly

icon /ˈaɪkɒn/ *n.* one who is the object of great attention and devotion; an idol

impressionable /ɪmˈpreʃənəbl/ *adj.* capable of receiving an impression; plastic 可塑的；有可塑性的

infuriate /ɪnˈfjʊərieɪt/ *v.* to make someone extremely angry

juicy /ˈdʒuːsɪ/ *adj.* yielding profit; rewarding or gratifying

levy /ˈlevɪ/ *n.* an official demand and collection, esp. of a tax 征税

maga-girl *n.* a super model

Milan /mɪˈlæn, miˈlɑːn/ *n.* a city in Italy 米兰

obscurity /əbˈskjʊərətɪ/ *n.* one that is unknown 不知名的人

one-off /ˈwʌnˌɒf, -ˌɔːf/ *adj.* sth that is not repeated or reproduced

outfit /ˈaʊtfɪt/ *n. infml* a group of people working together

pluck /plʌk/ *v.* to pull (esp. sth unwanted) out sharply 猛拉，猛扯

pool /puːl/ *n.* a group of people who are available to work or do an activity when they are needed（一批）备用或可用人员

recrimination /rɪˌkrɪmɪˈneɪʃn/ *n.* (*usu. pl.*) an act of quarrelling and blaming one another 吵架

runway /ˈrʌnweɪ/ *n.* a narrow walkway extending from a stage into an auditorium 延伸台道：从舞台通向观众席中的窄的走道

sack /sæk/ *v. infml* to dismiss from a job

scout /skaʊt/ *v.* to go looking for sth

scrimp /skrɪmp/ *v.* to save money slowly and with difficulty, esp. by living less well than usual

sideline /ˈsaɪdlaɪn/ *n.* an activity pursued in addition to one's regular occupation 副业

skimpy /ˈskɪmpɪ/ *adj.* a skimpy dress is very short and does not cover very much of a woman's body 太短太小或暴露的服装

skinny /ˈskɪnɪ/ *adj. infml* very thin, esp. in a way that is unattractive 消瘦的，皮包骨的

Slav /slɑːv/ *adj.* 斯拉夫人的

star /stɑː(r)/ *v.* to have as a main performer 以……为主角，主演

stardom /ˈstɑːdəm/ *n.* the status of a performer or an entertainer acknowledged as a star

stereotype /ˈsterɪətaɪp/ *n.* a fixed general image or set of characteristics that a lot of people believe represent a particular type of person or thing 模式化的陈规老套

tangle /ˈtæŋgl/ *v.* to (cause to) become a confused mass of disordered and twisted threads

teeter /ˈtiːtə(r)/ *v.* to stand or move unsteadily, as if about to fall 站立不稳，踉踉跄跄地走；本文中指模特走猫步

upstart /ˈʌpstɑːt/ *n. derog* someone who has risen suddenly or unexpectedly to a high position and takes advantage of the power they have gained 暴发户，新贵

vertiginous /vɜːˈtɪdʒɪnəs/ *adj. fml* causing or suffering from vertigo (a feeling of great unsteadiness), esp. by being at great height above the ground (尤指因处于高处令人)眩晕的，感到眩晕的

wrap /ræp/ *v.* to cover sth in a material folded around 包；裹

yesteryear /ˈjestəjɪə/ *n.* the year before the present year 去年；当年之前的一年

Zeitgeist /ˈzaɪtgaɪst/ *n. Ger.* the general spirit of a period in history, as shown in people's ideas and beliefs 时代精神，时代思潮

Notes

1. London's spring fashion week—London's fashion week is one of the big four fashion weeks in the world, held in the four fashion capitals of the world: New York City, London, Milan, and Paris. It is an apparel trade show held in London twice each year, in February and September.

2. doughnut-dodgers—people who avoid eating sweet food like doughnut, here refers to those young girls who go on diet to become slim.

3. Kate Moss—1974— , an English model who rose to fame in the early 1990s as part of the Heroin chic（海洛因时尚）model movement, best known for her waifish（瘦骨嶙峋的）figure, and her role in size zero fashion.

4. *Zoolander*—a 2001 American comedy film directed by and starring Ben Stiller. The film features a dimwitted（愚蠢的）male model named Derek Zoolander (a play on the names of Dutch model Mark Vanderloo and American model Johnny Zander), played by Stiller. 电影《超级名模》

5. But such stereotypes are **so last year.**—so outdated, outmoded, or out

of fashion(不如此理解,"are"就该是"were")

6. Chanel—a Parisian fashion house created by Coco Chanel, specializing in luxury goods 香奈儿

7. Hermès—a French manufacturer of quality goods established in 1837 爱马仕

8. Courtauld Institute—commonly referred to as The Courtauld, a self-governing college of the University of London specialising in the study of the history of art 英国考陶德艺术学院

9. Burberry—a British luxury fashion house, distributing clothing and fashion accessories and licensing fragrances 巴宝莉

10. Vivienne Westwood—1941— , an English fashion designer and businesswoman, largely responsible for bringing modern punk (朋克) and new wave fashions into the mainstream 维维安·韦斯特伍德

11. The best-known models of yesteryear often led rags-to-riches lives, courtesy of the rag trade.—The most famous models in the past years often led from-poverty-to-wealth lives, owing to the garment industry.

  a. rags-to-riches—usu. from rags to riches: becoming very rich after starting your life very poor

  b. rag trade-the garment industry

  c. courtesy of sb or sth—by the permission or generosity of 由于……的恩惠,承蒙……的允许

12. They were figures whose glossy confidence mirrored America's.—They were people whose attractive confidence reflected the confidence of America.

13. They were cultural icons... who became his wife.—他们还是文化偶像,在歌词中受到赞美,如比利·乔尔的《上城女孩》。这首歌的 MV 由克里斯蒂·布林克利主演,后来她嫁给了乔尔。

  a. Billy Joel—1949— , an American pianist, singer-songwriter, and composer. Since releasing his first hit song, "Piano Man," in 1973, Joel has become the sixth-best-selling recording artist and the fourth-best-selling solo artist in the United States, according to the RIAA(美国唱片业协会). He is also a six-time Grammy Award (格莱美奖) winner, a 23-time Grammy nominee and has sold over 150 million records worldwide.

  b. Christie Brinkley—1954— , an American supermodel and

actress.
14. Procter & Gamble's campaign featuring Gisele Bündchen is said to have raised sales of its Pantene shampoo in Brazil by 40%. 据说，吉赛尔·邦辰的代言广告令宝洁公司的潘婷洗发水在巴西的销售量增长了40%。

  a. Procter & Gamble—The Procter & Gamble Company（宝洁公司）, also known as P&G, is an American multinational consumer goods company headquartered in downtown Cincinnati, Ohio, USA.

  b. Gisele Bündchen—1980— , a Brazilian fashion model and occasional film actress and producer. She is the goodwill ambassador for the United Nations Environment Programme（联合国环境规划署亲善大使）. In the late 1990s, Bündchen became the first in a wave of Brazilian models to find international success.

15. Heidi Klum, a German model... a televised fashion-talent contest. 德国模特海蒂·克鲁姆在时尚达人电视比赛《超级名模时尚大比拼》中担任评委，该赛为电视淘汰赛。

  Project Runway—an American reality television series on Lifetime Television, previously on the Bravo network, created by Eli Holzman which focuses on fashion design and is hosted by model Heidi Klum. The contestants compete with each other to create the best clothes and are restricted in time, materials and theme. Their designs are judged, and one or more designers are eliminated each week.

16. emerging economies—surging economies are nations with social or business activity in the process of rapid growth and industrialization. The economies of China and India are considered to be the largest.

17. the economics of modelling—the way in which wealth is produced and used in the field of modelling

18. Tivo—a digital video recorder (DVR) developed and marketed by TiVo, Inc. and introduced in 1999

19. Model Alliance—(MA), a growing network of models and industry leaders dedicated to improving working conditions in the American fashion industry. Models have an industry voice through the MA. It seeks to improve the American modeling industry by empowering the models themselves.

20. The juiciest prize is to become the face of a luxury brand such as Dior or Burberry. ——If a model become a spokesman for a luxury brand such as Dior or Burberry, she can get the biggest reward.
    Dior——(Christian Dior S. A.), a French luxury goods company controlled and chaired by businessman Bernard Arnault who also heads LVMH Moët Hennessy-Louis Vuitton(酩悦·轩尼诗-路易·威登集团)——the world's largest luxury group. 克里斯汀·迪奥,简称迪奥

21. To have any chance ... even for a cover-shoot. ——要想获得这种机会,模特首先要有为设计师拍摄杂志照片的经历。这让时尚杂志花很少的钱就能请模特拍照,甚至是拍封面照。
    a. have/get sth under one's belt——to have achieved or experienced sth useful or important 获得某经历或某事
    b. peanut——a very small amount of money; a trifling sum
    c. cover-shoot——封面照片

22. Viva London——the sister agency to the well established VIVA Paris and shares the majority of its board

23. DNA——a modeling agency in New York City, established in 1996 by Jerome and David Bonnouvrier, and one of the top-three agencies in the world

24. The giant Elite Model Management agency lost an American antitrust case on price-fixing in 2004——行业巨头名模管理公司2004年在美国的一场操纵定价的反垄断诉讼中输掉了官司

25. Doutzen Kroes——1985— , a Dutch model and actress 杜晨·科洛斯

26. Karl Lagerfeld——1933— , a German fashion designer, artist and photographer based in Paris 卡尔·拉斐格

27. Size 0——A women's clothing size in the US catalog sizes system. Size 0 and 00 were invented due to the changing of clothing sizes over time, referred to as vanity sizing (虚荣尺码) or size inflation (尺码膨胀), which has caused the adoption of lower numbers. Modern size 0 clothing, depending on brand and style, fits measurements of chest-stomach-hips from 30—22—32 inches (76—56—81 cm) to 33—25—35 inches (84—64—89 cm). Size 00 can be anywhere from 0.5 to 2 inches (1 to 5 cm) smaller than size 0. "Size zero" often refers to extremely thin individuals (esp.

women), or trends associated with them.
28. Adele—1988— , an English singer-songwriter, musician and multi-instrumentalist
29. Gucci—the House of Gucci, better known simply as Gucci, an Italian fashion and leather goods brand, part of the Gucci Group, which is owned by French company PPR 古驰
30. throw one's weight around/about—to use one's position of authority to tell people what to do in an unpleasant and unreasonable way; to give orders to others, because one thinks one is important 指手画脚,作威作福,耀武扬威
31. Marc Jacobs—1963— , an American fashion designer. He is the head designer for Marc Jacobs, as well as Marc by Marc Jacobs, a diffusion line, with more than 200 retail stores in 80 countries 马克·雅各布斯
32. Premier Model Management—one of the world's leading model agencies, based in London, founded in 1981 by former model Carole White and her brother Chris Owen

Questions

1. What are the changes in the modeling business?
2. What kind of models is preferred now by fashion houses?
3. Why do models make less money?
4. What are the reasons for skinny models to be preferred by designers?
5. Who have more say in fashion business, supermodels or super-brands?

新闻写作

报刊常用套语

为了表明"客观公正",美英报刊记者以不肯定的第三者口气论述,如用"有人"、"人们"等;有的用"据称"、"据闻"、"据估计"等不确定的字眼及"事实不可容否认"、"可以认为","根据"等较确定的套语。有的为省时,常用固定写法用语(set expressions);还有以不确定的口气或审慎的态度报道,是怕事主找上门来纠缠。例如2003年美国女特工身份泄露案Valerie Plame Leak case 就涉及退休记者 Robert Novok,《纽约时报》记

者 Judith Miller 和《时代》周刊记者 Matt cooper,特别检察官以国家安全及保密法为由逼迫他们出庭作证。有的用"事实不容否认"、"可以认为"等,以证明所言非虚假新闻,有事实依据或目击证人等。这也是报刊常用被动语态的一个重要原因。我们不如读读安徽大学马祖毅先生写的《英译汉技巧浅谈》一书中关于这类常见写法。如:

It affords no small surprise to find that... 对于……令人惊讶不已
It can be safely said that... 我们有把握讲……
It cannot be denied that... 无可否认……
It has been calculated that... 据估计……
It has recently been brought home to us that... 我们最近痛切感到……
It is alleged that... 据称……
It is arranged that... 已经商定……,……已做准备
It is asserted that... 有人主张……
It is claimed that... 据称……,有人宣称……
It is demonstrated that... 据证实……,已经证明……
It is enumerated that.... 列举出……
It is established that... 可以认定……
It is generally recognized that... 一般认为……,普遍认为……
It is hypothesized that... 假设……
It is incontestable that... 无可置辩的是……
It is preferred that... 有人建议……
It is reputed that... 人们认为……,可以认为……
It is striking to note that... 特别令人注意的是……
It is taken that... 人们认为……,有人以为……
It is undeniable that... 事实不容否认……
It is universally accepted that... 普遍认为……,……是普遍接受的
It may be argued that... 也许有人主张……
It was described that... 据介绍……,有人介绍说……
It was first intended that... 最初就有这样的想法……
It was noted above that... 前面已经指出……,等等。

不过,据本人纵览近几年报道性文章,上述这类套语用得越来越少。(欲知更多套语,见《导读》四章七节)

Lesson Thirty-two

> 课文导读

通过这篇题为"不拘一格的谈判，立竿见影的成效"的文章，作者 Sergey Frank 向读者介绍了美国商人的谈判风格：看似自由、随便、不拘礼节，让人感觉轻松、愉快，但同时美国人的谈判又是目的明确、讲求实效的。作者明确指出，若想与美国人谈判成功，对方切不可被这种貌似轻松的谈判形式所误导，而应牢记美国人的谈判规则：遵守已经商定的议事日程或协议；大胆积极地展示自己的产品、服务等；要富有幽默感，但又要时刻小心该谈什么或不该谈什么，并遵守美国公司内部极其微妙的等级体系。

由此可见，在世界各国间交往日趋频繁的今天和明天，单单学会一门外语是远远不够的，一个出色的商务活动家或一场成功的商务谈判在很大程度上取决于对对象国文化的透彻了解。要真正做到这一点恐怕比单纯学会语言更需要花费时间和精力。顺畅的国际交流必须克服文化差异和由此产生的文化障碍。从中我们也不难得出另一个结论，一名优秀的语言翻译者更应是一位优秀的文化使者。

Pre-reading Questions

1. Do you like to go into bussiness after graduation?
2. Do you think that psychology is of high importance for business negotiations?

Text

Free talking and fast results

In the third of a fortnightly series on overcoming cultural barriers, **Sergey Frank** examines the US's casual but ruthlessly focused style of negotiating

How to negotiate

1   The US is an attractive market. Its business culture, which has

brought the world "shareholder value"[1] and "IPOs"[2], has been leading commercial thinking in recent years and will continue to do so. But whoever wants to succeed in the US needs to remember the rules of the game.

2　　US business is described by the lyrics of the song *New York, New York*: "If you can make it here, you can make it anywhere!"[3] Yet a euphoric approach to business is by no means enough.[4] Although business communication in the US is pleasant and easygoing, it is at the same time ruthlessly focused.[5]

3　　Communicating is a natural talent of Americans. When negotiating partners meet, the emphasis is on small talk and smiling. There is liberal use of a sense of humour that is more direct than it is in the UK. If you give a talk in America, you should speak in a relaxed way and with plenty of jokes to capture your audience's attention.

4　　Informality is the rule.[6] Business partners renounce their academic titles on their business cards. Sandwiches and drinks in plastic or boxes are served during conferences.[7] Your business partners tend to act casually in the office and chat about their family.

5　　This pleasant attitude persists in the negotiation itself. US negotiators usually attach little importance to status, title, formalities and protocol. They communicate in an informal and direct manner on a first-name basis. They are relaxed and casual with their gestures and body language, removing their jackets and adopting the most comfortable seating position.

6　　But the focus soon intrudes. The attitude "time is money" has more influence on business communication in US than it does anywhere else. After the neutral warm-up[8], US negotiating partners quickly come to the point. Even social get-togethers are often used to discuss business matters with the partner.

7　　Although Americans do business in a very pragmatic way, they want to win. Developing a personal relationship with the business partner is not as important as getting results.

8　　And US negotiators tend to want those results fast. As financial results are reported every quarter, it is essential to secure profitability on a short-term basis. Hence, many US contracts contain the provision "time is of the essence" within their preamble. Hence, too, US impatience in negotiations, which should not be perceived as impoliteness, but as the corollary of "time is money".

9   This attitude has a strong influence on negotiations, since strategic alliances and other long-term projects are evaluated in terms of their potential to achieve a quick return on investment.

10 Because the Asian negotiating approach tends to be long-term in nature, it is also one of the main reasons why so many joint ventures[9] and alliances between US and Asian companies have failed to meet expectations.

11 US negotiating partners are usually aware of this difference in negotiating style, thanks to the huge supply of literature and videos on Asian business. The trouble is that this material concerns itself mostly with the "what" behind the business and not on the more subtle questions of "how" and "why" business and communication patterns differ.[10] US executives preparing for projects abroad tend to make themselves familiar with most of the specific negotiating patterns of the other country. Yet once the negotiating situation changes, mistakes are common.[11]

12 When doing business in the US, you should take the following considerations into account.

13 ● Conducting negotiations on a highly professional level and making presentations with the help of state-of-the-art[12] technology is appreciated in the US. You should observe a negotiated agenda, or even a draft agreement. The negotiation will proceed in a well-prepared, calm, matter-of-fact and pragmatic manner, all laced with a substantial dose of humour.

14 ● Present and market your case in a positive way. You should not be too modest about your own company's products, services, and market position. Instead, take a "can-do" attitude.

15 ● Moreover, do not be misled by your negotiating partner's relaxed style of communication. Subjects such as religion, politics or ethnic background should only be touched on cautiously, even in private conversation.

16 ● The casual attitude in the US does not mean there is no hierarchy in US companies. On the contrary, status is expressed in a very subtle way, and it may take some time to gain a detailed

understanding of the ranking system.

17 The author is partner of Kienbaum Executive Consultants and managing director of the London office. www.kienbaum.co.uk (From *Financial Times*, August 2, 2000)

New Words

agenda /ə'dʒendə/ *n.* a list of the subjects to be discussed at a meeting（见《导读》"常见的多义词"）

alliance /ə'laɪəns/ *n.* an agreement in which two or more countries, groups etc. agree to work together in order to try to change or achieve sth 联盟，联合

communication /kə,mjuːnɪ'keɪʃən/ *n.* here talk

corollary /kə'rɒləri/ *n.* sth that is the direct result of sth else 自然的结果

euphoric /juː'fɒrɪk/ *adj.* feeling very happy and excited

fortnightly /'fɔːtnaɪtli/ *adj.* (happening) once two weeks

hierarchy /'haɪərɑːki/ *n.* a system within an organization in which people have authority and control over the people in the rank below them, who then have authority over the people below them 等级制度

lyrics /'lɪrɪks/ *n.* (*pl.*) the words of a song, especially a modern popular song

pragmatic /præg'mætɪk/ *adj.* dealing with problems in a sensible, practical way instead of strictly following a set of ideas

preamble /prɪ'æmbl/ *n.* a statement at the beginning of a book, document, or talk, explaining what it is about

protocol /'prəʊtəkɒl/ *n.* the system of rules on the correct and acceptable way to behave on official occasions 礼仪

renounce /rɪ'naʊns/ *v.* to publicly say that you will no longer keep something, or agree to give up ownership or possession of sth, esp. formally

return /rɪ'tɜːn/ *n.* the amount of profit that you get from sth

shareholder /'ʃɛəhəʊldə/ *n.* sb who owns shares in a business

subtle /'sʌtl/ *adj.* not easy to notice or understand unless you pay careful attention

Notes

1. "shareholder value" —the benefit that shareholders get from their shares 股东利益
2. "IPO"—(*abbrev.* Initial Public Offer) (股票的)首次公开发行
3. "If you can make it here, you can make it anywhere!"—If you can be successful here in New York (or in America), you can be successful in any other places! (这是一首名为 *New York, New York* 的流行歌曲中的一句歌词,意为:如果你能在这儿获得成功,你就能在其他任何地方获得成功!)

    make it—(*informal*) to be successful in a particular activity or profession

4. Yet a euphoric approach to business is by no means enough. —Adopting a pleasant method is not at all enough in dealing with business. 光凭一种轻松愉快或令人兴奋的手段来处理商务事务是远远不够的。

    euphoric approach—happy, pleasant or exciting way (in dealing with sb or sth)

5. Although business communication ... ruthlessly focused. —意为:在美国,尽管商务谈判看起来轻松愉快,但是这种谈判往往迫使参与者始终专心致志,紧紧围绕谈判主题。

    ruthless /'ru:θlis/—never stopping; unremitting 持久的,决不松懈的

6. Informality is the rule. — 不拘形式是常事。

    be the rule—used to say that sth is the usual situation

7. Sandwiches and drinks in plastic or boxes are served during conferences. —This is a typical example cited to indicate informality of the American. 意为:在会议或谈判其间,美国人通常上些用塑料或纸盒子装的三明治和饮料。
8. neutral warm-up—a period of talking about something without distinct characteristics of business in order to prepare for the activity coming after; time spent talking about something not business-related so as to prepare for the action coming after

    neutral /'nju:trəl/—having no distinct or positive qualities 无明显特性的

9. joint venture—合资企业;联营体
10. The trouble is that ... patterns differ. —The problem is that this

material is mostly about some particular aspects of the product or service of the business, but not the more subtle questions of the different histories and cultures between the East and the West. 问题是这些材料主要关注生意的目的,而不是更微妙的问题——商务活动和交际模式怎么不一样,又为什么不一样。

  a. this material——指前一句中的"the huge supply of literature and videos on Asian business"。

  b. concern itself mostly with——to be mainly about

  c. "what" behind the business——the specifics of the product being made or sold by the business

  d. "how" and "why" business and communication patterns differ——the different histories and cultures of the East and the West

11. US executives preparing for projects abroad ... are common.——To have a better understanding of these sentences, let us suppose an American is doing business with a Chinese. For example, a US executive might have studied beforehand and therefore understood how Chinese businesspersons negotiate a contract: first, establish personal relationships and trust with their foreign counterparts, agree in principle to general contract provisions, delay more specific negotiations until the last minute, and then take a hard line on contract terms that the other side thought would be treated more liberally. But when the negotiating situation changes——after the contract is signed——the American might misunderstand why the Chinese begins to re-negotiate certain contract terms that the American assumed are already decided by the signed contract. "Is the Chinese businessperson saying he won't honor the signed contract until I capitulate(投降;屈从) to certain changes in it?" thinks the American. "Am I being held up (as in a robbery)?" No. The explanation is that the Chinese continues to negotiate even after the contract is signed, whereas the American feels obligated to honor the original terms contained in the signed contract.

  这两句话恰好点明了前一句话的含义,即文化差异是个很微妙的问题,我们不能光看具体的生意目的有何不同,即文中的"what" behind the business,还要知道造成不同的原因,即文中的"how" and "why" business and communication patterns differ。这也是作者贯穿全文的中心思想:切不可被表象所误导,要知其实质。此外,作者在接下来的文章中就是按这种思路来给出建议的：表象是什么，实质是什么。

　　a. once the negotiating situation changes—after the contract is signed

　　b. mistakes are common—misunderstandings or misconceptions are found often.

12. state-of-the-art—using the most modern and recently developed methods, materials, or knowledge

Questions

1. In Sergey Frank's view, what is business communication like in the US?
2. How do you understand Sergey Frank's saying that "communicating is a natural talent of Americans"?
3. What has more influence on business communication in the US than anywhere else?
4. Make a brief account of a typical business communication or negotiation in the US. (Or: What is the US negotiating style? Cite examples to prove. Or: Summarize the major characteristics of business communication in the US and support each with an example.)
5. Why have so many joint ventures and alliances between US and Asian companies failed to meet expectations?
6. What suggestion will you give to people doing business in the US? (Or: What have you benefited from this text?)

学　习　方　法

勤上网和查词典

　　阅读时要做到彻底理解，不能只凭原来对某词的理解想当然，望文生义，也不能不懂装懂或不求甚解。而应该仔细阅读该词的全部词义，然后根据上下文确定其词义，不然易于误解。在翻译中，尤其是政治和科技文献的词语要求准确，差一点就会闹出大问题。

　　例如：本书主编在1987年编注《美英报刊文章选读》（上、下册）时选了《新闻周刊》关于两伊（伊朗和伊拉克）战争的一篇文章作课文，在文中遇到了"gunship"这个字时差一点犯了望文生义的错误。请见下面的原文：

The virtual absence of any opposing air cover turned the operation into a turkey shoot for the Iraqi warplanes, which were reportedly flying as many as 800 sorties a day. **Helicopter gunships** also joined the fray.

他乍一看 helicopter gunship 是"载直升机的炮舰或炮艇"的意思。可又一想，为了不犯"man-of-war"误解为"战士"的错误，就查一下 The *World Book Dictionary*，才知道应译为"武装或攻击直升机"（a helicopter carrying heavy machine guns and rockets for support of ground troops，为支援地面部队而携带着重机枪和火箭的直升机）。

再如：有人在翻译英国、爱尔兰和北爱尔兰各派就北爱问题达成的 Good Friday Agreement 时译为"美丽/美好星期五协议"。

The *New Oxford Dictionary of English* 对 Good Friday 的释义是：the Friday before Easter Sunday, on which the Crucifixion of Jesus is commemorated in the Christian Church. It is traditionally a day of fasting and penance. 复活节后星期日前的那个星期五，这天是基督教会纪念耶稣被钉死在十字架上和传统的斋日和苦修日。由此可见，应是"耶稣受难节"。那个协议应为"（耶稣）受难节协议"。

百度网站和英汉词典是从英文原文词典翻译编纂而成的。因译者文字水平和背景知识有限等因素，难免出错，因此，读者一定要在工作中多查英文网和英英工具书，不能贪图省事。需要勤上网和查词典的根本原因在于中西文化不尽相同，人们的思维和对事物的认识有差异。对于有些词语、语法，英美人不会产生误解，而对中国人来说，如不上网或查词典及通过学习，则极易理解有误。这里不举复杂的、会使我们误解的段落或句子，只列出若干初学者极易误解的词语。

cooker 非"厨师"，而是"炊事用具"；

fresh paint 非"新鲜漆"，而是"油漆未干"；

general doctor 非"多面手医生"，而是级别较低的"通科医生"；

industrial relations 不是含糊的"工业关系"，而是"劳资关系"；

man-of-war 非"战士"，而是"军舰"；

nonperson 非"不是人"，而是"无足轻重或无权利之人"，"被遗忘或被漠视的人"；

official's time-out 非"官方暂停"，而是"裁判员暂停"；

press book 非"新闻或报刊书"，而是剪刀加糨糊贴成的"剪报册"；

policy bank 非"政策银行"，而是一种"赌博彩票的庄家"；

sleeping policeman 非"在睡眠中的警察"，而是"减速杠"；

student-driven car 非"学生开的车",而是"教练车";
Sunday driver 非"星期天开车者",而是"不常开车的新手";
Whistle blower 非"吹哨子的人",而是"敢于揭露上司或政府机构的谎言或丑闻者";
yellow press 非"黄色报刊",而是"低级报刊",指故作耸人听闻报道、哗众取宠的报章杂志;
Yellow Pages 非"色情专页",而是电话号码本中厂商地址和广告。

像上述这类易引起中国读者误解的词语很多,如果有人能编出一本这样的词典来,定受国内广大英语学习者的欢迎。

Lesson Thirty-three

课 文 导 读

　　海洋航运,一直是货物运输的重要方式,但是美丽的大海并不平静,偶尔也会掀起怒涛,将往来的船只吞没。有史可查的海难事件数不胜数。生命融入海洋,和时间一起消逝了,而沉睡在海底的宝藏却让今天日益势利的人们日夜垂涎。一些人在经济利益的驱动之下,对海底文物进行破坏性打捞,给千百年来积淀下来的海底宝藏带来一场浩劫。因此,当奥德赛公司宣布他们找到了美国殖民时期沉入海底的重达17吨的50万枚银币和几百枚金币时,一场争论就在海下寻宝商和考古学家之间展开。不仅如此,现在连沉宝属于沉船国还是属打捞公司和沉船地的司法争斗已经展开。看来其争夺的范围比本文还要复杂和广泛。

　　值得注意的是,标题里的"find"貌似动词而实为意义不同的名词,指的是:"sth good or valuable that is found";再如 catch 作名词时与动词意思也有区别,可指"捕获量"、"捕获物"等意义。

Pre-reading Questions

1. Have you ever read any book or seen any film about treasure exploration?
2. Have you ever tried to explore treasure?

Text

A Bountiful Undersea Find, Sure to Invite Debate
By Terry Aguayo

1　　MIAMI, May 18—Explorers for a shipwreck exploration company based in Tampa said Friday that they had located a treasure estimated to be worth hundreds of millions of dollars in what may be the richest undersea treasure recovery to date.

Greg Stemm, left, co-founder of Odyssey Marine Exploration, examining coins recovered from a shipwreck in the Atlantic Ocean.

2   Deep-ocean explorers for the company, Odyssey Marine Exploration[1], located more than 500,000 silver coins weighing more than 17 tons, along with hundreds of gold coins and other artifacts, in a Colonial-era shipwreck[2] in an undisclosed location in the Atlantic Ocean, the company said in a statement.

3   The retail value of the silver coins ranges from a few hundred dollars to $4,000 each, with the gold coins having a higher value, the company said.

4   "All recovered items have been legally imported into the United States and placed in a secure, undisclosed location where they are undergoing conservation and documentation," according to the statement.

5   Citing security and legal concerns, Odyssey has not disclosed details about the discovery[3], including the origin of the coins and the identity or location of the site, dubbed Black Swan, but has said it is "beyond the territorial waters[4] or legal jurisdiction of any country." Phone calls seeking comment were not returned on Friday.

6   The 6,000 silver coins that have so far been conserved are in "remarkable condition," Greg Stemm, the company's co-founder, said

in the statement.

7 "We are excited by the wide range of dates, origins and varieties of the coins," Mr. Stemm said, "and we believe that the collecting community[5] will be thrilled when they see the quality and diversity of the collection."

8 The bountiful find is sure to reignite the long-running debate between undersea explorers and archaeologists, who view such treasure hunting as modern-day piracy.

9 Kevin Crisman, an associate professor in the nautical archaeology program at Texas A&M University[6], said salvage work on shipwrecks constituted "theft of public history and world history."

10 He said the allure of treasure hidden under the sea seemed to blind the public to the ethical implications. "If these guys went and planted a bunch of dynamite around the Sphinx[7], or tore up the floor of the Acropolis[8], they'd be in jail in a minute," Mr. Crisman said.

11 Anticipating such comments, John Morris, the chief executive of Odyssey, said in a statement: "We have treated this site with kid gloves[9], and the archaeological work done by our team out there is unsurpassed. We are thoroughly documenting and recording the site, which we believe will have immense historical significance."

12 Robert W. Hoge, a curator at the American Numismatic Society[10] in New York, questioned the secrecy surrounding the discovery and said that while it might be perfectly legitimate, the findings would have been better preserved in the hands of archaeologists.

13 "Whenever these finds are made by treasure hunters, their first thought is to sell instead of preserving," Mr. Hoge said. "They need to make money because they're a corporation with enormous expenses. They're not there to preserve history."

14 The find, which was announced on the same day that the publicly traded Odyssey held its annual stockholder meeting, came four years after the company found thousands of coins worth $75 million after excavating the Republic[11], a steamship lost in 1865 off Savannah, Ga. The company, which had reported losses for 2005 and 2006, saw its stock rise almost 81 percent to $8.32 by the time the market closed on Friday.

15 This year, Odyssey received permission from the Spanish

government to resume a search that had been suspended on the wreck of the Sussex, a British warship that sank in the Mediterranean in 1694 with a cargo of coins that may be worth billions of dollars.

16 The company has not disclosed the methods or equipment it used in the Black Swan find.

17 The largest documented previous find occurred in 1985, when the treasure hunter Mel Fisher found the Nuestra Señora de Atocha, a Spanish galleon that sank off the Florida Keys in 1622. The treasure included thousands of silver coins worth more than $400 million.

18 *John Schwartz and William J. Broad contributed reporting from New York.* (From *The New York Times*, May 19, 2007)

New Words

archaeology /ˌɑːkɪˈɒlədʒɪ/ *n.* the study of the buried remains of ancient times, such as houses, pots, tools, and weapons 考古学
archaeologist /ˌɑːkɪˈɒlədʒɪst/ *n.* 考古学家 **archaeological** /ˌɑːkɪəˈlɒdʒɪkəl/ *adj.*

artifact /ˈɑːtɪfækt/ *n.* an object made by human work, esp. a tool, weapon, or decorative object that has special historical interest

bountiful /ˈbaʊntɪfəl/ *adj.* generous; in large quantities

conserve /kənˈsɜːv/ *v.* to keep from being wasted, damaged, lost, or destroyed; to preserve **conservation** /ˌkɒnsɜːˈveɪʃən/ *n.*

constitute /ˈkɒnstɪtjuːt/ *v.* to form or make up; be

curator /kjʊəˈreɪtə/ *n.* a person in charge of a museum, library etc.

document /ˈdɒkjʊmənt/ *v.* to prove or record with documents **documentation** /ˌdɒkjʊmenˈteɪʃən/ *n.*

dub /dʌb/ *v.* (esp. in newspapers) to name humorously or descriptively(把……戏称为)

dynamite /ˈdaɪnəmaɪt/ *n.* a powerful explosive 甘油炸药

ethical /ˈeθɪkəl/ *adj.* connected with ethics 伦理的, 道德的

excavate /ˈekskəveɪt/ *v.* to uncover (sth from an earlier time under the earth) by digging

Florida Keys a chain of small islands and reefs off the southern coast of Florida 佛罗里达群岛

galleon /ˈgælɪən/ *n.* a large sailing ship used in former times, esp. by the Spaniards

implication /ˌɪmplɪˈkeɪʃən/ *n.* a possible later effect of an action, decision etc.

jurisdiction /ˌdʒʊərɪsˈdɪkʃən/ *n.* the right to use the power of an official body, esp. to make decisions on questions of law 司法权；管辖权

legitimate /lɪˈdʒɪtɪmɪt/ *adj.* correct or allowable according to the law

Mediterranean /ˌmedɪtəˈreɪnjən/ *n.* a sea surrounded by the countries of S Europe, N Africa, and SW Asia 地中海

nautical /ˈnɔːtɪkəl/ *adj.* of sailors, ships, or sailing

numismatic /ˌnjuːmɪzˈmætɪk/ *adj.* of or relating to coins or currency; of or relating to numismatics 钱币的；钱币学的

piracy /ˈpaɪərəsɪ/ *n.* robbery by pirates; the action of pirating 海上抢劫；非法翻印

reignite /ˌriːɪgˈnaɪt/ *v.* to cause to start again

resume /rɪˈzjuːm/ *v.* to begin again after a pause

retail /ˈriːteɪl/ *n.* the sale of goods in shops to customers, for their own use and not for selling to anyone else 零售

salvage /ˈsælvɪdʒ/ *n.* the act or process of saving sth from destruction, esp. saving a wrecked ship or its goods from the sea

Savannah /səˈvænə/ *n.* a port city of southeast Georgia, US, near the mouth of the Savannah River 萨凡纳港市

suspend /səsˈpend/ *v.* to stop or cause to be inactive or ineffective for a period of time

Tampa /ˈtæmpə/ *n.* a city, port, and holiday resort in west-central Florida in the US

undisclosed /ˈʌndɪsˈkləʊzd/ *adj.* not made known publicly; kept secret

unsurpassed /ˌʌnsəˈpɑːst/ *adj.* excellent

wreck /rek/ *n.* a ship lost at sea or (partly) destroyed on rocks

Notes

1. Odyssey Marine Exploration—奥德赛海洋探险公司。Odyssey 这一名称来自于古希腊诗人荷马（Homer）的史诗《奥德赛》。《奥德赛》是关于特洛伊战争中的希腊首领、伊萨卡国王奥德修斯在战争结束后，经过十年的漫长艰难的旅程，终于回到家乡的故事。"Odyssey" 一词现常用来比喻漫长艰难的旅程。(*The Odyssey*, which recounts the adventures of Odysseus during his return from the war in Troy to his home in the Greek island of Ithaca. Odysseus was the king of Ithaca, a leader of the Greeks in the Trojan War, who reached home after ten years of wandering. Figuratively, an "odyssey" is any difficult,

Lesson Thirty-three   103

prolonged journey.)
2. a Colonial-era shipwreck—殖民地时期的沉船。(The Colonial era [1492－1776] of the US refers to the period from the start of European settlement to the time of independence from Europe, when the thirteen colonies of Britain declared themselves independent in 1776. 美国的殖民时期指自哥伦布发现美洲大陆到美利坚合众国独立,是美国早期发展时期。)
3. Citing security and legal concerns, Odyssey has not disclosed details about the discovery—Because they worry about the security of the coins and the lawfulness of their ownership, Odyssey has not given detailed information about the discovery.

    cite—to mention sth, esp. as an example or as proof of what one is saying
4. territorial waters—the parts of the sea close to a country's coast which it considers to be under its control, esp. with regard to fishing rights(领海)
5. the collecting community—the group of people in a society who have the same hobby of collecting sth. such as stamps, coins, paintings, etc.

    community—a group of people united by shared interests, religion, nationality etc. (团体;界。见本课的"语言解说"。)
6. Texas A&M University—a coeducational public research university located in College Station, Texas, also known as A&M or TAMU. It was established in 1876 as the Agricultural and Mechanical College of Texas, the first public institution of higher education in that state. Now the letters "A&M" no longer have any explicit meaning but are retained as a link to the university's past.
7. the Sphinx—A sphinx is an ancient Egyptian image of a lion, with a human head. This mythical beast symbolized the pharaoh(法老)as an incarnation(化身)of the sun god. Thousands of sphinxes were built in ancient Egypt; the (Great) Sphinx is the most famous sphinx which is close to the Pyramids of Giza in Egypt and is visited by many tourists. It is considered one of the Seven Wonders of the World. (古埃及的狮身人面像。最著名的狮身人面像位于埃及吉萨的金字塔附近,被认为是世界七大奇迹之一。)
8. the Acropolis—A Greek word meaning "high point of the city," the

Acropolis is the elevated, fortified section of various ancient Greek cities. The Acropolis of Athens, a hill with a flat oval top, was a ceremonial site beginning in the Neolithic Period(新石器时代) and was walled before the 6th cent. B.C.. Devoted to religious rather than defensive purposes, the area was adorned with some of the world's greatest architectural and sculptural monuments. The top was reached by a winding processional (游行的) path at the west end, where the impressive Propylaea (通廊) stood. From there, the Sacred Way led past a colossal bronze statue of Athena (雅典娜) and the site of the old temple of Athena to the Parthenon(帕台农神庙). To the north was the Erechtheum(厄瑞克修姆庙) and to the southwest the temple of Nike Apteros (Wingless Victory 胜利神庙). (雅典卫城,包含四个古希腊艺术最大的杰作——帕台农神庙、通廊、厄瑞克修姆庙和雅典娜胜利神庙,是希腊最杰出的古建筑群,集中展示了希腊的古代文明。)

9. with kid gloves—with great care; very carefully
    kid gloves—gentle methods of dealing with sb or sth (as if with gloves made of very soft leather)
10. the American Numismatic Society (ANS)—美国钱币协会。
11. the Republic—"共和国"号沉船。美国内战刚刚结束时,"共和国"号满载货物和钱币从纽约出发,准备前往新奥尔良,不幸遇上罕见的飓风,沉入了冰冷的海底。2003年,奥德赛公司寻找了整整12年之后,终于在距佐治亚州海岸100英里的洋面下找到"共和国"号。打捞上来的金银钱币卖了7,500万美元,而他们前期投入的成本只有200万美元。

Questions

1. Why has Odyssey kept secret the origin of the coins and the identity or location of the site?
2. Did the coins originate from the same time and place?
3. What is the long running debate between undersea explorers and archaeologists about?
4. What did archaeologists think about savage work on shipwrecks?
5. What are the archaeologists worried about? What have caused their worries?
6. Do you think treasure hunters can preserve the historical sites they

have discovered? Why or why not?

语言解说

Community

该词的基本意义可概括为"a group of people"或"a group of nations",但是,在不同的上下文或与不同的词搭配,意思也异。细究起来,此字比上述定义要广得多。见例句：

1. 社会；集团,共同体。如用于"the international community",一般意为"国际社会"；用于"the Atlantic Community"译为"大西洋集团"；"the European Community"译为"欧洲共同体"。还有的学者认为：一般而言,其大写译为"共同体",小写译为"大家庭"。但记者在写新闻报道时并不一定遵守大小写规则,在报刊上该大写的字却小写的现象相当普遍。

2. 界或某界人士。如：intelligence community（情报界）; the business community（商界）；本课中的"the collecting community"（收藏界）。再如：

The reports of a respected foreign correspondent were a different matter. Snow's stories in the foreign press (and the English-language *China Weekly Review*, published in the international Settlement in Shanghai) quickly filtered through the Chinese intellectual community（知识界）.(*The China Quarterly*)

3. 派。例如：Shiite community（指穆斯林的什叶派）。

4. 居民；侨民；移民。例如：the indigenous community（土著居民）; the Turkish community（土耳其裔居民）；a large foreign community; a large Mexico community。

5. 群落；民族；民众。例如：a gay community; a black community。

6. 地方；社区；地段；街道。例如：a community college, a community nurse

此外,据上述的例1所示,the world/international/global community 或 the community of nations 一般意为"国际社会",事实上根据不同上下文和不同历史时代背景可作"联合国、国际大家庭和世界各国人民"讲。(详见《导读》二章一节)

Unit Eleven
Science

Lesson Thirty-four

课文导读

在搜索引擎上输入关键词,搜寻自己想要知道的信息;在社交网络上发布文章和照片,分享自己的心情和生活……你可知道,这些在网络时代人们习以为常的活动,是由遍布全球的互联网公司及其数据中心所支撑的。而互联网公司及其数据中心要使用惊人的能耗,无论用户需求多寡,各大网站的数据中心均全天 24 小时不间断运作,这些数据中心的服务器机群是增长最快的二氧化碳排放源之一。尽管搜索引擎巨头谷歌也是此类污染制造者大户,但它似乎是互联网公司中"最有诚意"改变目前造成污染状况的公司。早在 2007 年,谷歌公司就开始进行实现碳中和的尝试,并决意打造全美第一家零碳排放公司。其努力和尝试,是否能真正实现它宣称的零碳排放的目标?是否能成为其他互联网公司仿效的对象?且看本文作者如何评说。

通过本课的阅读,读者可以学到一些环保词语和知识。

Pre-reading Questions

1. What do you know about zero carbon?
2. Do you think real zero carbon is possible?

Text

Google's zero-carbon quest

The search giant has an ambitious plan to achieve its goal: becoming the world's most energy-efficient company.

By Brian Dumaine

1   As the double-decker bus turns onto Charleston Road and starts winding through Google's Mountain View, Calif.[1], campus, I stretch

out in the business-class-size seat, admiring the smoothness of the black leather and the plush gray carpeting at my feet. A spacious table expands to hold a laptop, which can connect to the vehicle's Wi-Fi system[2]. This $800,000 luxury double-decker is one of 73 buses that Google owns and operates. (It leases 26 others.) Each day the fleet transports about 4,500 employees, or about a third of those working at the Googleplex[3], as the company's headquarters is known.

2   It turns out that Google (GOOG) isn't offering a free ride simply as an employee perk—the buses actually save the company money. Yes, there's the added productivity of 4,500 employees working an extra couple of hours each day while riding to and from work. But Google's bus service is about much more than that. Real estate in Mountain View is expensive. Underground parking spaces cost as much as $85,000 to construct. (Really!) If Google had to build a parking space for each of the bus riders, the price tag would run to almost $400 million. And that's not counting the lost opportunity cost[4] of not using that land for new office buildings.

3   Google has made other investments in transportation too. If, during the day, a Google-ite[5] needs to run an errand or pick up a sick kid at school, he or she can hop into one of 52 electric and hybrid cars parked on campus. The company also encourages employees to drive electrics. It has spent an estimated $3 million to $4 million to install

395 chargers—the largest corporate electric-vehicle infrastructure in the country.

4 Finding creative solutions to energy issues has become a major priority for Google co-founder and CEO Larry Page[6] in recent years. For the obvious reasons—a growing population, increasingly scarce resources, and climate change—he believes that the corporate world needs to operate more sustainably, and he is determined to build the nation's first zero-carbon company. This means a business that ultimately is so energy efficient and uses so much clean power that it emits no greenhouse gas—a very tall order indeed. Experts aren't sure whether it's even possible for a company to emit no carbon, but Google is trying to come as close to that goal as possible. "As we became a bigger user of energy, we wanted to make sure we were not just part of the problem, but part of the solution," says Urs Hölzle, Google's employee No. 8 and a senior vice president[7] who oversees the company's green initiatives.

5 To reach its audacious zero-carbon goal, Google is taking a three-pronged approach. First, it's making its server farms, office buildings, and commuting habits more energy efficient. (Apparently Page's Boeing 767, which he owns with co-founder Sergey Brin[8], doesn't get counted in the equation.) Then the company is investing heavily—$915 million to date—in solar and wind producers to make clean energy more available. And finally it is buying enough carbon offsets[9] to make the company carbon neutral[10]—at least on paper—until it can meet its overall goal.

6 If the plan works, Page will have created a blueprint that other companies can use to reduce their own energy use and—as important—save money at the same time. But Google has already learned some hard lessons.

7 In June 2007, Page and his top execs issued a staff memo declaring that the company would become carbon neutral. The catch? The existing power infrastructure is so dependent on fossil fuels that no major company in the world has yet achieved this goal without buying carbon credits[11]. Page began buying carbon credits from organizations that, say, capture methane from landfills to offset the greenhouse gas Google emits. Then he set the company on a long march to reduce the

amount of energy it consumes while increasing its use of carbon-free wind and solar power.

8   Later that year Page, to the amazement of many in the IT industry, also announced that Google was getting into the clean-energy business. In a Nov. 27, 2007, press release, the company introduced an additional initiative based on the formula RE < C, which translates as "renewable energy is cheaper than coal." Page believed Google could become carbon neutral faster by applying the formidable brainpower of its engineers to the problem. He wanted to help produce one gigawatt of renewable power—about the equivalent produced by a nuclear power plant—that was cheaper than coal within a few years. This goal, however, turned out to be more devilish than anyone thought.

9   Page asked his managers to focus on a basic question: How much carbon are we emitting? Google's executives started asking themselves how they could use less power in their data centers, how they could make their office buildings more efficient, and where they could buy clean energy for their operations.

10   Becoming a zero-carbon company is no easy task. In 2011—some four years after Page's memo—Google reported that it still had emitted 1.5 million tons of carbon in the previous year. It was the first time Google had publicly revealed its carbon footprint[12]. To put that in perspective, Google's 30,000 employees and its fleet of data centers last year emitted the same amount of CO_2 as a city the size of Fargo, N. D. (pop. 202,000)[13]. The good news: If the company hadn't embarked on

Page's quest to become carbon neutral, the numbers would have been much worse. That 1.5 million tons of carbon is more than Google emitted in 2007, but much less than would have been expected considering that the company's annual revenue since then has more than doubled, to $38 billion.

11   Google's largest source of greenhouse gas emissions is its data centers—those buildings stuffed with computers that handle each of the 3 billion searches its customers perform every day. According to Jonathan Koomey, a Stanford professor, server farms account for about 2% of America's total electricity use. (That's roughly the same greenhouse gas impact as the airline industry's.) However, they are one of the fastest-growing sources of CO_2 emissions.

12   Server farms also account for Google's biggest use of energy. One thing the company realized early on is that the managers in charge of building data centers were not the same people who operated them. "It's incredible how much people waste in a company," says Google executive Hölzle. "The facility department pays construction costs and utility bills, but the IT people buy the servers, so they don't care about how much electricity they use."

Server farms: not green but grey

To eliminate that conflict, Google made sure that the person paying the utility bills and the one buying the computers was the same.

13   Now the economic incentive exists to cut energy use. Typically a server farm consumes as much energy for lighting and cooling as for the computers themselves. By using customized hardware and applying innovative cooling techniques, the need for air conditioning is reduced. Joe Kava, Google's director of data center operations, cites as an example the search giant's new server farm in Finland—on the site of a former paper mill—that sits on the Gulf of Finland[14] and uses seawater in its cooling system.

14   No matter how efficient Google makes its server farms, it will still need clean power to meet its zero-carbon goals. Soon after Page launched the RE < C program in 2007, he set up a handful of green

skunkworks projects[15] and created a team to make venture investments in green energy. Google put money into promising companies like BrightSource Energy[16], which is building a cutting-edge, solar thermal plant in the Mojave Desert[17]. The search giant even had an internal engineering team working to improve a type of concentrating solar power technology called the solar power tower. It invested in AltaRock[18] to foster innovations in geothermal energy. It also sponsored research to develop the first geothermal map of the U. S. to better understand the potential for geothermal energy.

15   Driving the price of renewables below that of fossil fuels is an ambitious goal, especially for a company that has no background in power generation. The energy field, as Google eventually learned, is much more capital-intensive and has a far longer time horizon than is typical in Silicon Valley—where a new company with a garage full of software geeks can scale to billions in revenue seemingly overnight. After four years of effort, Google quietly dropped its RE < C program in late 2011.

16   Google execs explain that relatively speaking, not much money was invested—perhaps $50 million. (Google has kept its equity investments in BrightSource and AltaRock but has disbanded its green-tech engineering efforts.) It couldn't have helped that the company had been taking flak from a group of shareholders who didn't understand why Google was spending money on clean tech. In 2011, Justin Danhof, the general counsel of a conservative think tank, the National Center for Public Policy Research[19], filed a shareholder proposal criticizing Google's lack of transparency about its green investments. (It didn't pass.)

17   While Google has abandoned its quest to be an innovator in clean-energy technology, it hasn't stopped investing in green power. Today Google has signed contracts to buy about 12% of its total energy from wind and solar farms, up from 4% just two years ago. (Add in existing sources of clean energy on the grid, and that number rises to 27%.) "As a company we are looking at ways we can support the renewables industry," says Rick Needham, Google's director of energy and sustainability. "We have a long vision of being a company powered by renewable energy, but how do we get from here to there?" Google pays more for clean energy than it would for power off the grid. However, it

has locked into long-term pricing contracts for renewables and expects those contracts to eventually make money as conventional power becomes more expensive over time.

18 Google has also been investing directly in wind and solar projects to the tune of $915 million. It began in 2008 by financing a couple of wind farms—in North Dakota and Oregon—in need of funding after the financial meltdown had frozen the capital markets. A key to Google's strategy is that it wants the money it invests to expand utilities' solar and wind operations; otherwise it won't be adding capacity to the system. As the wind projects become operational and begin selling electricity to big utilities, Google gets a piece of the cash flow. This type of deal—a form of tax equity investment—gets sweetened by federal tax credits.

19 Google was one of the first companies—if not the first—outside the banking, energy, and utility sectors to start investing in these tax deals. Instead of keeping its cash in the corporate treasury and earning only 1% or 2% on it, it can earn as much as 15% to 20% through the tax credit investments, says Google.

20 The company may be increasingly cleaning up its act, but it is still a polluter. In the meantime, it continues to buy carbon offsets. Carbon offsets, however, are controversial. One common way is to, say, pay an organization to plant a tree to offset the carbon you emit when you fly cross-country. But how do you know if the tree ever gets planted or if someday a drought kills it? Some criticize offsets as just a guilt-free way to indulge in polluting habits.

21 Well aware of the problems posed by offsets, Google searched for ones that were verifiable and additional—meaning that the reduction in carbon is real and wouldn't have happened without Google's buying the offset. It decided the best way to create carbon offsets was to pay for reductions in methane emissions from landfills and swine farms. Says Jolanka Nickerman, Google's program manager for carbon offsets: "The gold standard for offsets is methane gas, which is 20 to 25 times more potent than carbon dioxide." These methane-capture projects can cost anywhere from $500,000 to $1 million. In Yadkinville, N.C.[20], Google, in partnership with Duke Energy[21] (DUK) and Duke University[22], helps the Loyd Ray Farms, home to 9,000 hogs, capture

methane from manure to power its operations.

22 So far the company has spent upwards of $15 million investing in or purchasing carbon credits for dozens of such projects. That will offset about 5 million tons of CO_2—more than enough to make Google a carbon-neutral company on paper.

23 When asked how long it will take to become a truly zero-carbon company, Google execs say they don't really know. What they do know is that the green program has made the company stand for something more than just making money. That's a message that Google's bus riders are reminded of each day. (From *Fortune*, July 12, 2012)

New Words

audacious /ɔːˈdeɪʃəs/ *adj.* showing great courage or confidence in a way that is impressive or slightly shocking 大胆的，雄心勃勃的

campus /ˈkæmpəs/ *n.* the land and buildings belonging to a large company（包括土地和建筑物在内的属于大公司的）园区

catch /kætʃ/ *n. usu. sing.*, *infml* a hidden problem or difficulty 诀窍，关键

cutting-edge /ˈkʌtɪŋˈedʒ/ *adj.* in accordance with the most fashionable ideas or leading in nature 尖端的，前沿的

devilish /ˈdevəlɪʃ/ *adj.* very bad, difficult, or unpleasant 阴暗，魔鬼般的

electrics /ɪˈlektrɪks/ *n.* electric cars 电动车

embark /ɪmˈbɑːk/ *v.* to start sth, esp. sth new, difficult, or exciting 启动新奇事物

equation /ɪˈkweɪʒn/ *n.* the set of different facts, ideas, or people that all affect a situation and must be considered together（涉及平衡的）影响因素，综合体

equivalent /ɪˈkwɪvələnt/ *n.* sth that has the same value, purpose, job etc as sth else 等同物；等价物；对应物

exec /ɪɡˈzekjətɪv/ *n.* an informal word for EXECUTIVE 行政长官

facility /fəˈsɪləti/ *n.* rooms, equipment, or services that are provided for a particular purpose（为某种目的而提供的）设施；设备

flak /flæk/ *n. infml* strong criticism 强烈的反对

fleet /fliːt/ *n.* a group of vehicles that are controlled by one company, motorcade（某家公司控制的）车队

formidable /ˈfɔːmɪdəbl/ *adj.* very powerful or impressive, and often frightening 令人敬畏的；可怕的

geothermal /ˌdʒi(ː)əʊˈθəməl/ *adj.* relating to or coming from the heat inside the earth 地热的

grid /grɪd/ *n.* the network of electricity supply wires that connects POWER STATIONS and provides electricity to buildings in an area 电力网，输电网

hog /hɒg/ *n. esp. AmE* a large pig that is kept for its meat 肉（肥）猪

hybrid /ˈhaɪbrɪd/ *n.* sth that consists of or comes from a mixture of two or more other things（两种或两种以上不同事物组成的）混合体，混合动力汽车

infrastructure /ˈɪnfrəstrʌktʃə(r)/ *n.* the basic systems and structures that a country or organization needs in order to work properly, for example roads, railways, banks etc 基础设施

initiative /ɪˈnɪʃətɪv/ *n.* the ability to make decisions and take action without waiting for sb to tell you what to do 主动，首先发起

lease /liːs/ *v.* to grant the temporary possession or use of (lands, tenements, etc.) to another, usu. for compensation at a fixed rate 出租，租用

manure /məˈnʊə, -ˈnjʊə/ *n.* waste matter from animals or human droppings that are mixed with soil to improve the soil and help plants grow 粪肥，有机肥

meltdown /ˈmeltdaʊn/ *n.* a situation in which prices fall by a very large amount or an industry or economic situation becomes much weaker（价格的）暴跌；（行业或经济的）崩溃

methane /ˈmiːθeɪn/ *n.* a gas that you cannot see or smell, which can be burned to give heat 甲烷，沼气

neutral /ˈnjuːtrəl/ *adj.* neither moral nor immoral; neither good nor evil, right nor wrong 中性的；中和的

North Dakota /ˌnɔːθdəˈkəʊtə/ a state in the Midwestern region of the U.S., along the Canadian border（美国）北达科他州

offset /ˈɒfset/ *n.* a compensating equivalent 抵消，补偿 *v.* compensate for or counterbalance 抵消，弥补

Oregon /ˈɒrɪɡən/ a state in the Pacific Northwest region of the U.S.（美国）俄勒冈州

perk /pɜːk/ *n.* sth that you get legally from your work in addition to your wages, such as goods, meals, or a car（工资以外的）额外收入，津贴

plush /plʌʃ/ *adj. infml* very comfortable, expensive, and of good

quality 高贵而舒适的
potent /ˈpəʊtnt/ *adj.* powerful and effective 强有力的，有能力的
prong /prɔːŋ, prɔŋ/ *n.* one of two or three ways of achieving sth which are used at the same time (**three-pronged** *adj.* 三方面的)
scale /skeɪl/ *v.* to climb to the top of sth that is high and difficult to climb 攀登
sustainable /səˈsteɪnəbl/ *adj.* able to continue without causing damage to the environment **sustainably** *adv.* **sustainability** *n.* 可持续
utility /juːˈtɪlətɪ/ *n. usu. pl.* a service such as gas or electricity provided for people to use 公用事业(如煤气、电力等)
verifiable /ˈverɪfaɪəbl/ *adj.* capable of being tested (verified or falsified) by experiment or observation 可考验的

Notes

1. Mountain View, Calif. —a city in Santa Clara County, California. It is named for its views of the Santa Cruz Mountains. Situated in Silicon Valley, Mountain View is home to many high technology companies. Today, many of the largest technology companies in the world are headquartered in the city, including Google, Symantec(赛门铁克,美国著名软件公司), and Intuit(直觉软件公司). 山景城
2. Wi-Fi system—Also spelled Wifi or WiFi, short for wireless fidelity(无线保真技术), and a trademark of the Wi-Fi Alliance 无线网络系统
3. Googleplex—the corporate headquarters complex(建筑群)of Google, Inc., located at 1600 Amphitheatre Parkway in Mountain View, Santa Clara County, California. "Googleplex" is a blend of "Google" and "complex", and a reference to "googolplex"(1 后跟着 10 的 100 次方个零,指巨大得无法想象的,天文数字), the name given to the large number 10 googol(10 的 100 次方). 谷歌公司总部
4. opportunity cost—a key concept in economics, which refers to benefit that could have been gained from an alternative use of the same resource. The notion of opportunity cost plays a crucial part in ensuring that scarce resources are used efficiently. Thus, opportunity costs are not restricted to monetary or financial costs: the real cost of output forgone, lost time, pleasure or any other benefit that provides utility should also be considered opportunity costs. 机会成本

5. Google -ite—谷歌人,谷歌员工

    -ite—*suf.* a follower, supporter
6. Google co-founder and CEO Larry Page—1973— , an American computer scientist and Internet entrepreneur. In 1998, Sergey Brin and Larry Page founded Google, Inc. Page ran Google as co-president along with Brin until 2001 when they hired Eric Schmidt as Chairman and CEO of Google. On April 4, 2011, Page took on the role of chief executive officer of Google, replacing Eric Schmidt. As of 2012, his personal wealth is estimated to be $20.3 billion, ranking him #13 on the Forbes 400 list of richest Americans. 劳伦斯·"拉里"·佩奇
7. Urs Hölzle, Google's employee No. 8 and a senior vice president—Hölzle(乌尔斯·霍泽尔) is Senior Vice President(高级副总裁) for Technical Infrastructure at Google. In this capacity Urs oversees the design, installation, and operation of the servers, networks, and data centers that power Google's services. As the No. 8 of Google's first ten employees and its first VP(副总裁) of Engineering, he has shaped much of Google's development processes and infrastructure.
8. Sergey Brin—1973— , is a Russian-born American computer scientist and Internet entrepreneur who, with Larry Page, co-founded Google. Together, Brin and Page own about 16 percent of the company. 谢尔盖·布林
9. carbon offsets—reduction in emissions of carbon dioxide or greenhouse gases made in order to compensate for or to offset(补偿) an emission made elsewhere 碳补偿
10. carbon neutral—the achieving of net zero carbon emissions by balancing a measured amount of carbon released with an equivalent amount of offset 碳中和
11. carbon credits—a highly regulated medium of exchange used to offset, or neutralize(中和) carbon dioxide emissions. A single carbon credit generally represents the right to emit one metric ton of carbon dioxide or the equivalent mass of another greenhouse gas. 碳信用
12. carbon footprint—the measure given to the amount of greenhouse gases produced by burning fossil fuels, measured in units of carbon dioxide (i.e. kg) 碳足迹

13. Fargo, N. D. (pop. 202,000)—Fargo is the largest city in the U.S. state of North Dakota, accounting for nearly 16% of the state population.
14. the Gulf of Finland—the easternmost arm of the Baltic Sea(波罗的海). It extends between Finland (to the north) and Estonia(爱沙尼亚) (to the south) all the way to Saint Petersburg(圣彼得堡) in Russia. 芬兰湾
15. green skunkworks projects—projects typically developed by a small and loosely structured group of people who research and develop projects primarily for the sake of radical innovation. 绿色臭鼬工厂项目
16. BrightSource Energy—an Oakland, California, corporation that designs, builds, finances, and operates utility-scale solar power plants(太阳能电厂). Greentech Media(绿色科技媒介公司)ranked BrightSource as one of the top 10 greentech startups(创业公司)in the world in 2008. 亮源能源公司
17. the Mojave Desert—an area that occupies a significant portion of southeastern California and smaller parts of central California, southern Nevada, southwestern Utah and northwestern Arizona in the United States. It is named after the Mohave tribe of Native Americans. 莫哈维沙漠
18. AltaRock—AltaRock Energy Inc., headquartered in Seattle, Washington and having a technology development office in Sausalito, California, is a privately held corporation that focuses on the development of geothermal energy resources and Enhanced Geothermal Systems (EGS). 艾塔洛克能源公司
19. a conservative think tank, the National Center for Public Policy Research—保守智库美国全国公共政策研究中心

    think tank—a group of people with experience of knowledge of a particular subject, who work to produce ideas and give advice reports on the implications.
20. Yadkinville, N. C.—a town in Yadkin County, North Carolina, U. S. It is the county seat and largest city of Yadkin County. 北卡罗来纳州亚德金维尔市
21. Duke Energy—the largest electric power holding company in the U. S. It is headquartered in Charlotte, North Carolina, with assets

also in Canada and Latin America. 杜克能源公司
22. Duke University—private, located in Durham, North Carolina. 杜克大学

Questions

1. Why does Google offer the free ride of luxury double-decker buses to its employees on Mountain View campus?
2. What makes Larry Page determined to build the nation's first zero-carbon company?
3. How is Google going to reach its audacious zero-carbon goal?
4. What green powers are mentioned in the passage? And what is the conventional power?
5. What has Google done to make it a carbon-neutral company? Do those measures really work?

语言解说

科技旧词引申出新义

尤为值得注意的是，科技用语转用后，不断扩展引申出新义。如：作为域名的"dotcom"引申为"因特网和其他信息技术"、"上网公司"、"网络公司"、"高科技公司"等，"dotcom crash"就指这类高科技公司的泡沫或神话的破灭。soft landing 指人造卫星、飞船等软着陆，后来引申到经济体制改变而未引起较大震荡或破坏。hardware 原指计算机硬件，扩展引申为"军事武器和装备"，泛指设施，现又喻"法"；software 指计算机软件，扩展引申为"武器研发、计划和使用说明"，泛指服务，战争中的人类的"思想"，作"thinking"是美军界行话，还喻"创新"，现又引申为与"法"相配合的"德"和"宗教"。chemistry 喻"(人际)关系，人缘"，"electricity"喻"热情"。"ground zero"原指核爆炸"损失最大的中心点"，现喻"9·11"事件后"原世界贸易中心大楼的遗址"。chad 喻手工重新计票，brain cell 喻"智力"，brain dead"极其愚蠢的"。rocket science 火箭科学，现喻"复杂、高深难懂之事"。countdown 本来指发射卫星飞船时的"倒计时"，现喻在竞选或其他重大事件中"最后的紧张令人生畏、激动人心的时刻"、"行将出现的摊牌局势"。firestorm 指核弹等爆炸引起的"大火暴"，现可喻"强烈的反响"或"不满"、"愤怒"或"竞选前最后几天"等。"hemorrhage"本义为"大出血"引申为"人才等流失"。创世大爆炸的"Big Bang"喻"影响深远

的举措"。"lightening rod"喻"替罪羊"。defuse 为去掉引爆信管,现可指"缓和"或"解除"易引危险或不利之事。fulcrum 是杠杆的"支点",喻"支柱"、"支持物"。The rubber meets the road. 指"汽车轮胎在高速公路面临安全性能的考验",引申为"紧要关头或真材实料的考验"。fault lines "断层线",现喻"党派"等分界线。political fault-line 政治断层带,指政治的关键地区、重要地方或国家等,如同地球上的大陆板块断层带。有时喻地方虽小,却极其重要,因为其变动(地震)会带来极大震荡。见下列两例句:

(1) Traditionally, American party politics has had **fault lines**—blacks vote differently from whites and southerners from northerners. (*The Atlantic*)

从传统上看,美国的党派政治一直界线分明:黑人与白人、南方人与北方人投票趋向不同。(即黑人和南方人往往将票投给自由派的民主党候选人,而白人和北方人则投给保守派的共和党人。)

(2) Palestine, a tiny place, straddles one of **the world's political fault-line**. The crack from the small point threatens the peace of larger nations, the economy of every oil importer. (*Time*)

巴勒斯坦地方虽小,却横跨一条世界政治地震断层带上。一丝风吹草动,就叫一些更大国家不得安宁,殃及每个石油出口国经济。

另一种语义是,专有名词转化成普通名词或动词,语义也引申扩展了。如本课中的"Google"作动词,意为用"谷歌搜索或传播信息"。"YouTube"(从视频传到网上)。一个网上的 527 group 名叫"Swift Boat Veterans for Truth"(寻求越战真相快艇老兵)。"swift boat spot"是 2004 年大选中用来攻击民主党总统候选人 John Kerry 越战经历的电视广告,作动名词 swift-boating(*v*. swift-boat),意为"声讨候选人弄虚作假","揭露(官员、候选人的谎言、欺骗、造假或扩大其军旅经历等)";从反对派或政敌来说也有"诽谤"之意思。

Lesson Thirty-five

> 课 文 导 读

　　人们谈癌色变,因为它夺去了太多人的亲朋好友。为战胜它,国内中医有以毒攻毒的,有用保守疗法的;国外普遍以外科手术为主。然而,手术后的化疗使患者痛苦不堪,可见这不是一个理想的疗法。哈佛大学医学院曾有一份调查报告称,70%的患者都是被此病吓死的。可见患者在治疗中的精神和心理因素也极为重要。

　　本文所谈治癌之法可说是另辟蹊径,纳米弹或粒子可以发光,光可产生热能,这样它不用CT等仪器就能发现癌的位置,又能将产生的热能射线将癌细胞杀死,而使未受癌症扩散的细胞毫发无损。不过,美国赖斯大学以West女士为首的实验团队仍处于实验阶段,从《新科学家》杂志的报道来看,其前景光明,但愿它能成功,为人类添福。

　　"纳米球使癌症无藏身之处"一文代词多,编者尽可能帮读者进行语法分析。有的词无论在网上或词典里都不可能找到适合其上下文中的意义,这是常有的事,那就只能根据语境和其他文外知识等来确定词义。还有的词如"control",或许我们只知道其广义,但在本文"control mice"中,不能理解为"控制的鼠"。此处词义变窄,成了"用作检查实验、调查等结果作比较标准的集群或个体"。简言之,即"对照实验或实验的对照物",即"被用来与实验鼠作对比之鼠",以检查结果。我们在读报时对理解不透的词语,应多在网上或工具书中查出合适的词义,切不可望文生义。

Pre-reading Questions

1. How much do you know about cancer? Is it curable or incurable?
2. Do you have any relatives or friends who have suffered or are suffering from the disease? How about them now?

Text

Nanospheres leave cancer no place to hide

By Celeste Biever

1   Gold-coated glass "nanoshells"[1] can reveal the location of tumours and then destroy them minutes later in a burst of heat.

2   Using these particles to detect and destroy tumours could speed up cancer treatment and reduce the use of potentially toxic drugs. It could also make treatment cheaper, says Andre Gobin of Rice University in Houston, Texas, who helped to create the particles.

Nanospectra developing AuroLase™ therapy, a medical device which incorporates a new class of particles to selectively destroy solid tumors.

3   In 2003 Gobin's supervisor Jennifer West showed that gold-coated silica nanospheres could destroy tumours in mice, while leaving normal tissue intact. The blood vessels surrounding tumours are leakier than those in healthy tissue, so spheres injected into the bloodstream tend to accumulate at tumour sites. Illuminating the tumour with a near-infrared laser then excites a "sea" of loose electrons around the gold atoms via a process called plasmon resonance. This creates heat, killing all the nearby cells.[2]

4   However, before this can happen doctors first have to make sure they find all the tumour sites, which requires an MRI or CT scan. This extra stage can mean multiple hospital visits and more drugs for the patient.

5   Now the team has shown how to tweak the size of the nanoshells so that they also scatter some of the radiation. That means any cancer sites will "light up" under low-intensity infrared, so they can then be zapped with the laser. "We can use one single particle to accomplish two tasks and neither feature is diminished greatly[3]," says Gobin.

6   To achieve this, the team had to carry out a delicate balancing act. Smaller spheres convert more radiation to heat, which makes them better at destroying tumours[4], but larger ones scatter more radiation,

which is vital for the imaging stage. Previously, the spheres were 120 nanometres in diameter, which meant they only scattered 15 per cent of the light shone on them, and converted the rest to heat.[5] West's team increased their size to 140 nanometres, causing them to convert 67 per cent of the light to heat, and to scatter the remaining 33 per cent.

"We are extremely encouraged by the results of these first animal tests. These results confirm that nanoshells are effective agents for the photothermal treatment in vivo tumors."
— *Jennifer West*

7   The team injected the new particles into mice with colon carcinoma tumours[6] and used a technique called optical coherence tomography[7] to test their ability to act as an imaging agent. This involves shining low-power near-infrared light onto the tissue and then measuring where the scattered light bounces back[8]. They found that the nanoparticles caused tumour tissue to light up 56 per cent more strongly than healthy tissue.

8   The team then applied a higher-power infrared laser to each tumour site for 3 minutes to heat the tissue. After a few weeks, they found the tumours had been almost completely destroyed. Eighty per cent of the mice treated survived for more than seven weeks, while all the control mice[9], who did not receive the nanoshells, died after three weeks.

9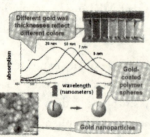

Montage. Gold-coated 120-nm-diameter silica nanospheres reflect different colors

Using one particle to detect and destroy tumours could cut treatment length. Since optical coherence tomography only penetrates up to 2 millimetres, the imaging step will only be useful for locating tumours near the surface, such as cervical, mouth and skin cancers, says Gobin. However, the team plans to modify the nanoshells so that they work with more deeply penetrating radiation, such as X-rays. Houston-based Nanospectra Biosciences[10], which West co-founded, will begin trials of the spheres in humans in the next two months. (From *New Scientist*[11], June 21, 2007)

New Words

accumulate /əˈkjuːmjʊleɪt/ v. to make or become greater in quantity or size 积留,积聚

blood stream /blʌd striːm/ n. the blood as it flows round the body 血流

blood vessel /blʌdˈvesl/ n. any of the tubes of various sizes through which blood flows in the body 血管

carcinoma /ˌkɑːsɪˈnəʊmə/ n. a cancer arising in the epithelial tissue of the skin or of lining of the internal organs 由皮肤上皮的细胞组织或内部器官的内壁引起的癌

cervical /ˈsɜːvɪkəl/ adj. of a neck or cervix 颈部的;子宫颈的

coherence /kəʊˈhɪərəns/ n. a fixed relationship between the phase(相)of waves in a beam of radiation of a single frequency. Two beams of light are coherent when the phase difference between their waves is constant. (光波、光等的)相干性,相参性

colon /ˈkəʊlən/ n. the lower part of the bowels in which food changes into solid waste matter and passes into the rectum 结肠

convert /kənˈvɜːt/ v. to cause to change into another form, substance, or state

CT (*abbrev.*)computerized tomography 计算机断层照相术

delicate /ˈdelɪkɪt/ adj. needing careful or sensitive treatment in order to avoid failure or trouble 小心对待的;微妙的

diameter /daɪˈæmɪtə/ n. a straight line passing from one side of a circle to the other side through the center of the circle 直径

diminish /dɪˈmɪnɪʃ/ v. to cause to become or seem smaller or less; to decrease

illuminate /ɪˈljuːmɪneɪt/ v. to give light to 照明,照亮

image /ˈɪmɪdʒ/ v. to make a visual representation of (sth) by scanning it with a detector or electromagnetic beam 造像;成像: an imaging stage/agent/step 成像阶段/媒介/步骤

infrared /ˌɪnfrəˈred/ adj. of or being rays or light of wavelength that cannot be seen or give heat 红外线的: near-infrared 近红外线的

intact /ɪnˈtækt/ adj. whole because no part has been touched, spoilt, or broken 完整无缺的;未受触动或损伤的

intensity /ɪnˈtensɪtɪ/ *n.* the quality of existing in a high degree 密度：low intensity 低密度
millimetre /ˈmɪlɪˌmiːtə/ *n.* 毫米（常作 mm）
modify /ˈmɒdɪfaɪ/ *v.* to change the form or quality of sth, esp. slightly
MRI (*abbvev.*) magnetic resonance imaging 磁共振成像
nanosphere /ˈnænəˌsfɪə/ *n.* 纳米球
optical /ˈɒptɪkəl/ *adj.* of or using light, esp. for the purpose of recording and storing information in a computer system 光学的；光的
particle /ˈpɑːtɪkl/ *n.* a very small piece 粒子
plasmon /ˈplɑːzmɒn/ *n.* 细胞基因组，胞质团
resonance /ˈrezənəns/ *n.* sound produced or increased in one object by sound waves from another 共鸣，共振
scan /skæn/ *n.* the act of examining closely
scatter /ˈskætə/ *v.* to throw in various random directions; to emit 散射；放射
silica /ˈsɪlɪkə/ *adj.* a chemical compound that is found naturally as sand, quartz, and flint and is used in making glass 二氧化硅
sphere /sfɪə/ *n.* a round shape in space; ball-shaped mass; (here refers to) nanosphere
supervisor /ˌsjuːpəˈvaɪzə/ *n.* a person who observes and directs the execution of (a task, project, or activity) 主管；指导者
tissue /ˈtɪʃʊ/ *n.* the substance that animal or plant cells are made of 动植物细胞的组织
tomography /təʊˈmɒɡrəfɪ/ *n.* technique for displaying a representation of cross section through a human body or other solid object using X-rays or ultrasound X 线体层照相术，X 线断层照相术
toxic /ˈtɒksɪk/ *adj.* poisonous 有毒的
tumour /ˈtjuːmə/ *n.* a mass of diseased cells in the body which have divided and increased too quickly, causing swelling and illness 肿块，肿瘤；赘生物
tweak /twiːk/ *v.* to make small changes to (sth) in order to improve its performance 对……做小的改变
zap /zæp/ *v.* to attack or destroy 杀死，除掉

Notes

1. Gold-coated glass "nanoshells"—从文字上讲并不难理解，但"nanoshells"与标题中"nanospheres"，第 2 段的"these particles"，第 3 段的"gold-coated silica nanospheres"和"spheres injected into the

bloodstream"以及第 7 段段首的"The team injected the new particles into mice..."等中,"nanosphere, nanoshell, sphere 和 particle"是否词异义同或有何区别? 本文第 2 段说明, nanosphere 和 nanoshell 都是 Rice University 的 Gobin 先生创造用来对付癌症的粒子或纳米粒子。从上下文看,这些词义也同,如 gold-coated glass nanoshells 和 gold-coated silica nanospheres 是一个意思,因为玻璃是以二氧化硅(silica)为原料做成的。以上这些不同的表达法与语言避免重复使用同一个词或词组有关。

2. The blood vessels.... nearby cells. —肿瘤周围的血管比健康组织的血管的通透性好,所以注射进血液中的纳米球就会聚集在肿瘤所在的位置。用近红外线激光照射肿块就会在金原子周围激起大量自由电子。通过这一称之为胞质团共振过程,它会产生热能,从而杀死所有的周围肿瘤细胞。

    a. spheres—here refers to the (gold-coated silica) nanopheres
    b. a sea of sth—a lot of it

3. We can use... diminished greatly—We can use only one nanoparticle to light up the cancer sites and at the same time destroy the cancer cells, and both tasks can be accomplished.

    feature—here refers to either one of the two tasks

4. Smaller spheres ... destroying tumours—In this clause, "them" stands for (nano) spheres.

5. Previously, the spheres ... to heat. —先前,纳米球体的直径是 120 纳米,这就是说,纳米球只能将 15% 照射到球体上的光散发出去,而将其余的射线转换成热能。

    In this sentence, "which" refers to the preceding clause, both "they" and "them" stand for the spheres.

6. colon carcinoma tumour—结肠内壁癌的肿块

7. optical coherence tomography—光学相干层析技术:一种用宽带光源的短程相干特性对活体组织内部结构断层成像的技术

8. bounce back—rebound 跳回,弹回;文中指反射回

9. control mice—a group of mice used as standard of comparison for checking the results of the experiment 用于对照实验的老鼠

    control—a group or individual used as a standard of comparison for checking the results of a survey or experiment

10. Houston-based Nanospectra Biosciences—总部设在(得州)休斯敦的纳米光谱生物科学公司

11. *New Scientist*—《新科学家》杂志创刊于 1956 年,由里德爱思唯尔集团 (Reed Elsevier) 的子公司里德商业信息有限公司 (Reed Business Information Ltd) 出版。这是一种面向大众的科学杂志,内容包括科学和技术的最新发展、科技新闻,以及关于未来科技发展的推测性文章。

虽然《新科学家》不是供同行阅读和评论的杂志,但它是科学家和大众了解他们自己的研究领域和兴趣之外的其他学科发展状况的途径。许多普通出版物上的科学文章都以其内容为根据。

1996 年,《新科学家》开辟了网络版,每天发布最新消息。其总部设在伦敦,还出版美国版和澳大利亚版。

Questions

1. In the author's view, can gold coated glass nanoshells be used to cure cancer? How can they?
2. Which of them are better for the treatment of cancer—nanoparticles or drugs? Why?
3. What does plasmon resonance produce, and can it serve the purpose of destroying cancer cells?
4. What purpose do MRI and CT serve in the treatment of some diseases before nanoshells can be used to cure cancer?
5. Do the different sizes of nanospheres work differently? Why?
6. What animal and technique did the West's team use for its experiment? Did its experiment succeed?

语言解说

Nano/Virtual/Cyber

由于各国都提倡创新,科技新语不断、造词能力出众和旧词不断引申出新义(见《导读》二章九节"科技用语")。下面只对与本课和本书有关的 nano、virtual 和 cyber 加以解说:

纳米技术,在英文里是 nanometer(nm) / nanoscale technology 或 nanotechnology,nano 常作为前者的缩略词。纳米是一米的 10 亿分之一,是一个计量单位的概念。自从扫描隧道显微镜发明后,世界上便诞生了一门以 0.1 至 100 纳米或毫微米(记为 nm)这样的尺度为研究对象的前沿学科,这就是"纳米科技"。

"nano-"作前缀派生出许多新词,如本文就有:nanosphere(纳米球),

nanoshell(纳米炮弹)、nanoparticle(纳米粒子)、nanometer(纳米,毫微米)、nanospectrum(*pl.* nanospectra)(纳米光谱;纳米射频或幅度)等词。对于这些词若不是从事这一行者似乎很陌生,但 nanocomputer(纳米电脑)、nanomaterial(纳米材料)、nanomachine(纳米机器)和 nanosurgery(纳米或毫微外科手术,其精密度比显微外科手术要高一万倍)等词语,或许我们听到过它的神秘功能。

本书在第三版第 6 课"Best Graduate School"一文中还出现过一度相当流行的科技用语:virtual。virtual 用于计算机,应被视为新词或熟词新义;英文词典对 virtual 一字的释义是 in computing: not physically existing but made to appear so from the point of view of users; involving the replication of a physical object by an electronic equivalent。用于计算机,virtual 指的是非物体的有形存在;用电子复制出相同实物的。由此概括地译为"虚拟的"。随着此字的出现而造出许多新词,如 virtual reality/environment/landscape/space/sex/shopping/therapy/world 等。virtual reality,可缩合为 virtuality,还可缩略为 VR,指的是"创造一种可以看到的模拟环境,通过接触或移动模拟实物,使人能产生一种身临其境的感觉"。也有人译为"虚拟/虚幻/灵境/仿真技术";virtual newsland 指交互网上的"新闻传真天地";virtual institution "虚拟教育机构或大学","网上教育机构或大学";virtual surgery "远程遥控手术";virtual doctor "远程诊断大夫"。由此看来,要真正理解和译对"virtual"这个字并非易事。

近年来,由于电脑和互联网的大量发展和使用,与此相关的词汇层出不穷,这里只谈 cyber。如 1995 年 5 月出版的一期《时代》周刊提到 cyber 时说,"Cyber has become the prefix of the day"。*The New Oxford Dictionary of English* 的释义是:"relating to electronic communication networks and virtual reality",即有关电子通讯网络(系统)和虚拟现实。构成的词如 cybernetics "控制论",cyberland "网络天地",cyberspace "网络天空/宇宙",cybercommunity "交互网络社会",cybercafe "装有联通网电脑的咖啡馆",cyberspeak "电脑用语或术语"。不仅如此,在本书 "Pentagon Digs in on Cyberwar Front"这课里 cyber 用作前缀构成 cyberattack、cyberweapon 等词外,还单独与其他词搭配。如 cyber capability/domain/power/program/security 等,说明它正从构词成分演化成词的发展过程。

Lesson Thirty-six

课文导读

学外语是一门苦差事，需要的是笨功夫。只要你足够勤奋使自己双语在握，就等于掌握了一把开启新世界大门的钥匙，自然会受益匪浅，好处多多。此外，学习外语还可以提高你的认知能力，让你更聪明。研究表明，学习一门新语言可以提高智力，降低认知偏差，改善你的注意力，降低注意力的分散，甚至能够延缓老年痴呆症的发病。2012 年 3 月 18 日，《纽约时报》刊载了《科学》杂志撰稿人 Yudhijit Bhattacharjee 的署名文章"Why Bilinguals Are Smarter"，对双语如何影响人们的认知能力和解决问题的能力，甚至会影响人们的情感做了介绍。作者通过列举一系列权威的实验和研究，形象直观地描述掌握双语带给人们的好处。

Pre-reading Questions

1. What practical benefits have you got when you take English as your second language?
2. If you married someone from a different culture, what language would you like to teach your baby in the future?

Text

Why Bilinguals Are Smarter
By Yudhijit Bhattacharjee

1   Speaking two languages rather than just one has obvious practical benefits in an increasingly globalized world. But in recent years, scientists have begun to show that the advantages of bilingualism are even more fundamental than being able to converse with a wider range of people. Being bilingual, it turns out, makes you smarter. It can have a profound effect on your brain, improving cognitive skills[1] not related to language and even shielding against dementia in old age.

Lesson Thirty-six 129

2   This view of bilingualism is remarkably different from the understanding of bilingualism through much of the 20th century. Researchers, educators and policy makers long considered a second language to be an interference, cognitively speaking, that hindered a child's academic and intellectual development.

3   They were not wrong about the interference: there is ample evidence that in a bilingual's brain both language systems are active even when he is using only one language, thus creating situations in which one system obstructs the other. But this interference, researchers are finding out, isn't so much a handicap as a blessing in disguise[2]. It forces the brain to resolve internal conflict, giving the mind a workout that strengthens its cognitive muscles[3].

4   Bilinguals, for instance, seem to be more adept than monolinguals at solving certain kinds of mental puzzles. In a 2004 study by the psychologists Ellen Bialystok and Michelle Martin-Rhee, bilingual and monolingual preschoolers were asked to sort blue circles and red squares presented on a computer screen into two digital bins—one marked with a blue square and the other marked with a red circle[4].

5   In the first task, the children had to sort the shapes by color, placing blue circles in the bin marked with the blue square and red squares in the bin marked with the red circle. Both groups did this with comparable ease. Next, the children were asked to sort by shape, which was more challenging because it required placing the images in a bin

marked with a conflicting color. The bilinguals were quicker at performing this task.

6   The collective evidence from a number of such studies suggests that the bilingual experience improves the brain's so-called executive function—a command system that directs the attention processes that we use for planning, solving problems and performing various other mentally demanding tasks. These processes include ignoring distractions to stay focused, switching attention willfully from one thing to another and holding information in mind—like remembering a sequence of directions while driving.

7   Why does the tussle between two simultaneously active language systems improve these aspects of cognition? Until recently, researchers thought the bilingual advantage stemmed primarily from the ability for inhibition that was honed by the exercise of suppressing one language system: this suppression, it was thought, would help train the bilingual mind to ignore distractions in other contexts. But that explanation increasingly appears to be inadequate, since studies have shown that bilinguals perform better than monolinguals even at tasks that do not require inhibition, like threading a line through an ascending series of numbers scattered randomly on a page.

8   The key difference between bilinguals and monolinguals may be more basic: a heightened ability to monitor the environment. "Bilinguals have to switch languages quite often—you may talk to your father in one language and to your mother in another language," says Albert Costa, a researcher at the University of Pompeu Fabra[5] in Spain. "It requires keeping track of changes around you in the same way that we monitor our surroundings when driving." In a study comparing German-Italian bilinguals with Italian monolinguals on monitoring tasks, Mr. Costa and his colleagues found that the bilingual subjects not only performed better, but they also did so with less activity in parts of the brain involved in monitoring, indicating that they were more efficient at it.

9   The bilingual experience appears to influence the brain from infancy to old age (and there is reason to believe that it may also apply to those who learn a second language later in life).

10   In a 2009 study led by Agnes Kovacs of the International School for Advanced Studies[6] in Trieste, Italy, 7-month-old babies exposed to two

languages from birth were compared with peers raised with one language. In an initial set of trials, the infants were presented with an audio cue and then shown a puppet on one side of a screen. Both infant groups learned to look at that side of the screen in anticipation of the puppet. But in a later set of trials, when the puppet began appearing on the opposite side of the screen, the babies exposed to a bilingual environment quickly learned to switch their anticipatory gaze in the new direction while the other babies did not.

11   Bilingualism's effects also extend into the twilight years. In a recent study of 44 elderly Spanish-English bilinguals, scientists led by the neuropsychologist Tamar Gollan of the University of California, San Diego[7], found that individuals with a higher degree of bilingualism—measured through a comparative evaluation of proficiency in each language—were more resistant than others to the onset of dementia and other symptoms of Alzheimer's disease[8]: the higher the degree of bilingualism, the later the age of onset.

12   Nobody ever doubted the power of language. But who would have imagined that the words we hear and the sentences we speak might be leaving such a deep imprint? (From *The New York Times*, Mar 18, 2012)

New Words

anticipate /æn'tɪsɪpeɪt/ v. to expect sth 预料；预期
adept /ə'dept/ adj. good at sth that needs care and skill 内行的；熟练的
ample /'æmpl/ adj. enough or more than enough 足够的；丰裕的
ascending /ə'sendɪŋ/ adj. (次序)渐进的；上升的
bilingual /ˌbaɪ'lɪŋgwəl/ adj. involving or using two languages 双语的；n. 会用两种语言的人
converse /kən'vɜːs/ v. to talk informally with another or others; exchange views, opinions, etc. by talking 交谈
cognitive /'kɒgnətɪv/ adj. relating to the mental process involved in knowing, learning, and understanding things 认知的；认识过程的
cue /kjuː/ n. a signal for sth else to happen 暗示，提示
dementia /dɪ'menʃə/ n. a state of mental disorder 痴呆
distraction /dɪ'strækʃn/ n. sth that stops you paying attention to what you are doing 使人分心的事
handicap /'hændɪkæp/ n. a permanent or mental condition that makes it difficult or impossible to use a particular part of your body or

mind 生理缺陷；弱智；残疾

hone /həʊn/ *v.* to develop and improve sth, esp. a skill, over a period of time 磨炼；训练

inhibition /ˌɪnhɪˈbɪʃn/ *n.* when sth is restricted or prevented from happening or developing 压制，抑制（作用）

interference /ˌɪntəˈfɪərəns/ *n.* an act of deliberately getting involved in a situation where you are wanted or needed 介入，干预，干涉

monolingual /ˌmɒnəˈlɪŋɡwəl/ *adj.* knowing or able to use only one language 单语的；*n.* 只用一种语言的人

neuropsychologist /ˌnjʊərəʊsaɪˈkɒlədʒɪst/ *n.* 精神心理学家

obstruct /əbˈstrʌkt/ *v.* to block a road, an entrance, a passage etc. so that sb or sth can't get through 阻碍

random /ˈrændəm/ *adj.* done or chosen, etc. without sb deciding in advance what is going to happen 随机的，随意的

scatter /ˈskætə(r)/ *v.* to move or to make people or animals move in every direction 散开，使分散

sequence /ˈsiːkwəns/ *n.* the following of one thing after another; succession 次序，顺序

shape /ʃeɪp/ *n.* the form that sth has 形状，外形

shield /ʃiːld/ *v.* to serve as a protection for 保护

simultaneous /ˌsɪmlˈteɪniəs/ *adj.* existing, occurring, or operating at the same time; concurrent 同时发生的

suppress /səˈpres/ *v.* to put an end, often by force, to a group or an activity that is believed to threaten authority 镇压，平定

tussle /ˈtʌsl/ *n.* a rough physical contest or struggle 扭打，争斗

twilight /ˈtwaɪlaɪt/ *n.* the period just before the end of the most active part of sb's life 暮年

willfully /ˈwɪlfəlɪ/ *adj.* deliberate, voluntary, or intentional 故意地

workout /ˈwɜːkaʊt/ *n.* a period of exercise

Notes

1. cognitive skill—also known as cognitive ability or cognitive functioning. It is a set of abilities, skills or processes that are part of nearly every human action. Cognitive abilities are the brain-based skills we need to carry out any task from the simplest to the most complex. 认知技能

2. a blessing in disguise—a common expression for a seeming misfortune that turns out to be for the best 因祸得福

3. cognitive muscles—cognitive abilities 认知能力
4. sort blue circles and red squares presented on a computer screen into two digital bins—one marked with a blue square and the other marked with a red circle. —将电脑屏幕上的蓝色圆圈和红色方块分别放进两个标记蓝色方块和红色圆圈的电子收纳箱中。The test by the psychologists is an application of Stroop Test（斯特鲁测验）, a popular psychological test that is widely used in clinical practice and investigation. It is a demonstration of interference in the reaction time of a task. When the name of a color (e. g., "blue," "green," or "red") is printed in a color not denoted by the name (e. g., the word "red" printed in blue ink instead of red ink), naming the color of the word takes longer and is more prone（倾向于）to errors than when the color of the ink matches the name of the color. 斯特鲁测验又称Stroop Color-Word Test,是公认的衡量行为控制系统能力最好办法之一。该测试向受测者展示不同颜色的单词,要求受测者说出字体颜色。难点在于,这些单词是一些颜色的名称。"蓝色"一词可能是用红色墨水书写的,而你必须说红色。但是,"蓝色"一词却非常突出地一直闪现在你的大脑中,你很想说蓝色。这时你就需要一种抑制该想法的系统,才能说出红色。

   sort sth into sth—to put things in a particular order or arrange them in groups according to size, type etc
5. the University of Pompeu Fabra—a university in Barcelona, Spain, founded in 1990（西班牙）庞培法布拉大学
6. the International School for Advanced Studies—(*abbrev.* SISSA) an international, state supported, post graduate teaching and research institute with a special statute, located in Trieste（迪里亚斯特）, Italy. Instituted in 1978, SISSA's aim is to promote science and knowledge, particularly in the areas of Mathematics, Physics and Neuroscience（神经系统科学）. 意大利国际高等研究院
7. the University of California, San Diego—UC San Diego or UCSD, public, located in California, established in 1960, one of the ten University of California campuses 加州大学圣地亚哥分校
8. Alzheimer's disease—also Alzheimer disease, the most common form of dementia. There is no cure for the disease, which worsens as it progresses, and eventually leads to death 阿尔茨海默病,又称老年痴呆症

Questions

1. What practical benefits can you get by being bilingual except conversing with various people?
2. Some researchers claim that bilingualism can be interference, but in what way does the interference influence our brain system?
3. According to a study in 2004, bilingual experience improves the brain's executive function that directs the attention processes we can use for arduous tasks, what do the processes refer to?
4. What is the major difference between bilinguals and monolinguals?
5. How bilingualism affect people in their old age?

广告与漫画

内容和语言特色

1. 广告(advertisement)在美英报刊尤其是报纸中,约占篇幅的一半以上。西方广告内容广泛,千奇百怪。除了新产品、新技术、求职、招聘、娱乐、旅行、烟酒、购车置业等外,甚至还有色情和出租丈夫的广告。有些广告有助于我们了解这些国家的社会生活,甚至政治、经济、科技等动态。广告使用的照片和文字必须要有针对性,能打动和招徕看客,激起欲望。因此文字必须简明、生动、形象,经常运用比喻、双关、夸张、对仗、拟人化等修辞手段。下面举一幅为例:

2004年大选时,小布什(George W. Bush)和切尼(Dick Cheney)针对民主党候选人John Kerry,用奔袭的狼群作比喻,作竞选广告:

狼群下面的说明文字:PAD FOR BY BUSH-CHENEY 04 AND THE REPUBLICAN NATIONAL COMMITTEE AND APPROVED BY PRESIDENT BUSH

主题是:Primal Fear: Bush said Kerry's weakness would draw predators.

首要恐惧:布什说克里的软弱会招来食肉动物,"软弱招人欺"。他鼓吹"弱肉强食"的森林法则,美国这么强大,谁敢侵犯?显然是玩弄竞选伎俩。

2. 漫画(cartoon)有别广告,画家从新闻取材,通过夸张、比喻、象征、寓意等手法,借幽默、诙谐的画面,针砭时弊。漫画犹如社论,立场鲜明,内行一看,就知奥妙。有些漫画十分含蓄,缺乏背景知识和想象力,一头雾水。有时一画或一言寓两事。语言简洁,常用时髦词、委婉语和名言。如:"The Bug Stop here.(我来拍板,责无旁贷。)"稍不注意,易欣赏或理解有误。下面举一幅为例:

次贷危机后,开放信贷又遭讽:代表美国者:Finally! Credit Markets Are Thawing! ("信贷市场终于解冻了!")救生圈上字:The Economy[经济(有救了)]

北极熊代表失业者:Yipee(哎呀!)(对 Thawing 表示惊恐)Thawing 是双关语,冰融化了,北极熊也像次贷危机(subprime mortgage crisis)时的房贷者一样要被淹死了。(2009/4/2 *Time*)

(详见《导读》三章一、二节)

Lesson Thirty-seven

> 课 文 导 读

  1859 年,达尔文在《物种起源》一书中探究了万物和人类自身的起源,提出"物竞天择,优胜劣汰"的进化论。作为一个基础的科学理论,进化论在美国大多数公立学校里一直被作为标准的科学教材。但围绕进化论的争论从 19 世纪持续至今。进化论从猿进化到人的理论从一开始就被认为是对宗教的侵犯,完全与《圣经》中描述的上帝创造万物,亚当和夏娃被赶出伊甸园的故事相违背。因此,有人在驳斥进化论时提出了这样的荒谬问题:"究竟你的祖父还是曾祖父是猴子?"1925 年,田纳西州甚至发生了因中学教师教授进化论而被迫接受审判的斯科普斯案(猴子案审判)。20 世纪 60 年代,美国几个州的法律规定,在学校教进化论被视为一种犯罪行为。尽管美国高等法院在 1968 年推翻了这条法律,但反对进化论的活动仍时隐时现,一直没有中断。这是对进化论第一回合的挑战。
  2005 年秋天,进化论又面临第二回合"智慧设计"论的挑战。一些基督徒宣扬,动植物复杂和精妙的结构,不可能是自然演进的结果,达尔文的进化论无法回答生命起源的问题,必定有外界智力起了引导作用,尽管他们解释不了这个智力从何而来。卷入这场争论的除了实力强大的宗教界人士外,还有保守派总统小布什。可至今人们也未发现外星人,智力在史前时期也不能创造出人,只不过是一种变相的上帝造人说罢了。后来最高法院做出裁决,宣布在课堂上教授"智慧设计论"违法,才算平息了这场争论。
  这场关于"进化论的论战"看似好笑,但并不奇怪。90% 以上的美国人信教,他们从小就受到与进化论相悖的上帝造人说的影响。美国宗教界右翼和政界的保守派是这派人的代表,他们不断向进化论发难。科学不进则退,如照他们的意志行事,到头来美国科技世界领先地位终有一天会处于岌岌可危的境地。

Pre-reading Questions

1. What do you know about Darwin and his theory of evolution?

2. Do you believe that God created man?

Text

The Evolution Wars

When Bush joined the fray last week, the question grew hotter: Is "intelligent design"[1] a real science? And should it be taught in schools?

By Claudia Wallis

1   Sometime in the late fall, unless a federal court intervenes, ninth-graders at the public high school in rural Dover, Pa., will witness an unusual scene in biology class. The superintendent of schools, Richard Nilsen, will enter the classroom to read a three-paragraph statement mandated by the local school board as a cautionary preamble to the study of evolution. It reads, in part:

2   *Because Darwin's theory[2] is a theory, it is still being tested as new evidence is discovered. The theory is not a fact. Gaps in the theory exist for which there is no evidence ... Intelligent design is an explanation of the origin of life that differs from Darwin's view. The reference book* Of Pandas and People[3] *is available for students to see if they would like to explore this view ... As is true with any theory, students are encouraged to keep an open mind.*

3   After that one-minute reading, the superintendent will probably depart without any discussion, and a lesson in evolutionary biology will begin.

4   That kind of scene, brief and benign though it might seem, strikes horror into the hearts of scientists and science teachers across the U.S., not to mention plenty of civil libertarians[4]. Darwin's venerable theory is widely regarded as one of the best-supported ideas in science, the only explanation for the diversity of life on Earth, grounded in decades of study and objective evidence. But Dover's disclaimer on Darwin would appear to get a passing grade from the man who considers himself America's education President[5]. In a question-and-answer session with Texas newspaper reporters at the White House last week, George W. Bush weighed in on the issue. He expressed support for the idea of combining lessons in evolution with a discussion of "intelligent design"

—the proposition that some aspects of living things are best explained by an intelligent cause or agent, as opposed to natural selection. It is a subtler way of finding God's fingerprints in nature than traditional creationism.[6] "Both sides ought to be properly taught," said the President, who appeared to choose his words with care, "so people can understand what the debate is about... I think that part of education is to expose people to different schools of thought."

5   On its surface, the President's position seems supremely fair-minded: What could possibly be wrong with presenting more than one point of view on a topic that divides so many Americans? But to biologists, it smacks of faith-based science. And that is provocative not only because it rekindles a turf battle that goes all the way back to the Middle Ages but also because it comes at a time when U.S. science is perceived as being under fresh assault politically and competitively.[7] Just last week, developments ranging from flaws in the space program to South Korea's rapid advances in the field of cloning were cited as examples that the U.S. is losing its edge. Bush's comments on intelligent design were the No. 1 topic for bloggers for days afterward. "It sends a signal to other countries because they're rushing to gain scientific and technological leadership while we're getting distracted with a pseudoscience issue," warned Gerry Wheeler, executive director of the 55,000-member National Science Teachers Association[8] in Arlington, Va. "If I were China, I'd be happy."[9]

A SUBTLER ASSAULT

6   Darwin's theory has been a hard sell to Americans ever since it was unveiled nearly 150 years ago in *The Origin of Species*. The intelligent-design movement is just the latest and most sophisticated attempt to discredit the famous theory, which many Americans believe leaves insufficient room for the influence of God.[10] Early efforts to thwart Darwin were pretty crude. Tennessee famously banned the teaching of evolution and convicted school-teacher John Scopes of violating that ban in the "monkey trial"[11] of 1925. At the time, two other states—Florida and Oklahoma—had laws that interfered with teaching evolution. When such laws were struck down by a Supreme Court decision in 1968, some states shifted gears and instead required that "creation science" be

taught alongside evolution.[12] Supreme Court rulings in 1982 and 1987 put an end to that. Offering creationism in public schools, even as a side dish to evolution, the high court held, violated the First Amendment's separation of church and state [13].

7   But some anti-Darwinists seized upon Justice Antonin Scalia's dissenting opinion in the 1987 case.[14] Christian fundamentalists, he wrote, "are quite entitled, as a secular matter, to have whatever scientific evidence there may be against evolution presented in their schools."[15] That line of argument—an emphasis on weaknesses and gaps in evolution—is at the heart of the intelligent-design movement, which has as its motto "Teach the controversy." "You have to hand it to the creationists. They have evolved,[16]" jokes Eugenie Scott, executive director of the National Center for Science Education[17] in Oakland, Calif., which monitors attacks on the teaching of evolution.

HOLES IN DARWIN?

8   Since the 1987 decision, a devoted band of mostly religious Christians, including hundreds of scientists, engineers, theologians and philosophers, has written papers and books, contributed to symposiums on the perceived problems with Darwin's theory. The headquarters for such thinking is the Center for Science and Culture at a nonpartisan but generally conservative think tank called the Discovery Institute, founded in Seattle in 1990.

9   What exactly is their critique of Darwin? Much of it revolves around the appealing idea that living things are simply too exquisitely complex to have evolved by a combination of chance mutations and natural selection.[18] The dean of that school of thought is Lehigh University[19] biologist and Discovery Institute senior fellow Michael Behe, author of the 1996 book *Darwin's Black Box*, a seminal work on intelligent design. Behe's main argument points to the fact that living organisms contain such ingenious structures as the eye and systems like the mechanism for clotting blood, which involves at least 20 interacting proteins. He calls such phenomena "irreducibly complex" because removing or altering any part invalidates the whole.[20]

10   Other arguments in this new brand of anti-Darwinism focus on missing pieces in the fossil record, particularly the Cambrian period[21],

when there was an explosion of novel species. Still other advocates, including mathematician, philosopher and theologian William Dembski, who is heading up a new center for intelligent design at Southern Baptist Theological Seminary[22], use the mathematics of probability to try to show that chance mutations and natural selection cannot account for nature's complexity. In contrast to earlier opponents to Darwin, many proponents of intelligent design accept some role for evolution—heresy to some creationists. They are also careful not to bring God into the discussion (another sore point for hard-line creationists), preferring to keep primarily to the language of science. This may also help them avoid the legal and political pitfalls of teaching creationism.

BIOLOGISTS ASK, WHAT HOLES?

11   Many scientists have been reluctant to engage in a debate with advocates of intelligent design because to do so would legitimize the claim that there's a meaningful debate about evolution, "I'm concerned about implying that there is some sort of scientific argument going on. There's not," says noted British biologist Richard Dawkins, professor of the public understanding of science at Oxford University, whose most recent book about evolution is *The Ancestor's Tale*. He and other scientists say advocates of intelligent design do not play by the rules of science. They do not publish papers in peer-reviewed journals, and their hypothesis cannot be tested by research and the study of evidence. Indeed, Behe concedes, "You can't prove intelligent design by an experiment." Dawkins compares the idea of teaching intelligent-design theory with teaching flat earthism[23]—perfectly fine in a history class but not in science. He says, "If you give the idea that there are two schools of thought within science—one that says the earth is round and one that says the earth is flat—you are misleading children."

12   Scientists say it is, in fact, easy to gainsay the intelligent-design folks. Take Behe's argument about complexity, for example. "Evolution by natural selection is a brilliant answer to the riddle of complexity because it is not a theory of chance," explains Dawkins. "It is a theory of gradual, incremental change over millions of years, which starts with something very simple and works up along slow, gradual gradients to greater complexity. Not only is it a brilliant solution to the

riddle of complexity; it is the only solution that has ever been proposed." To attribute nature's complexity to an intelligent designer merely removes the origin of complexity to the unseen designer. "Who designs the designer?" asks Dawkins.

13   As for gaps in the fossil record, Dawkins says, that is like detectives complaining that they can't account for every minute of a crime—a very ancient one—based on what they found at the scene. "You have to make inferences from footprints and other types of evidence." As it happens, he notes, there is a huge amount of evidence of evolution not only in the fossil record but also in the letters of the genetic code[24] shared in varying degrees by all species. "The pattern," says Dawkins, "is precisely what you would expect if evolution would happen."

14   Mathematical arguments against evolution are equally misguided, says Martin Nowak, a Harvard professor of mathematics and evolutionary biology. "You cannot calculate the probability that an eye came about," he says. "We don't have the information to make this calculation." Nowak, who describes himself as a person of faith, sees no contradiction between Darwin's theory and belief in God. "Science does not produce any evidence against God," he observes. "Science and religion ask different questions."

WHAT SHALL BE TAUGHT?

15   But for those who read *Genesis*[25] literally and believe that God created the world along with all creatures big and small in just six days, there's no reconciling faith with Darwinism. And polls indicate that approximately 45% of Americans believe that. It's no wonder that almost one-third of the 1,050 teachers who responded to a National Science Teachers Association online survey in March said they had felt pressured by parents and students to include lessons on intelligent design,

creationism or other nonscientific alternatives to evolution in their science classes; 30% noted that they felt pressured to omit evolution or evolution-related topics from their curriculum.

16 The new, presumably Constitution-proof way of providing coverage for communities that wish to teach ideas like intelligent design is to employ such earnest language as "critical inquiry" (in New Mexico), "strengths and weaknesses" of theories (Texas), and "critical analysis" (Ohio).[26] It's difficult to argue against such benign language, but hard-core defenders of Darwin are wary. "The intelligent design people are trying to mislead people into thinking that the reference to science as an ongoing critical inquiry permits them to teach I. D. crap in the schools," says David Thomas, president of New Mexicans for Science and Reason.

17 The new school year is certain to bring more battles over teaching evolution, not only in Kansas and Pennsylvania but also in the many states that are preparing new standards-based tests in science. By raising the profile of intelligent design, the President has doubtless emboldened those who differ with Darwin and furthered one goal of that movement: he has taught all of us the controversy. —With reporting by Melissa August/Washington, Jeremy Caplan/New York, Jeff Chu and Constance E. Richards/Greenville, Rita Healy/Denver, Christopher Maag /Cleveland, Bud Norman/Wichita, Adam Pitluk/ Dallas, Jeffrey Ressner/ Los Angeles and Sean Scully/Philadelphia (From *Time*, August 15, 2005)

New Words

Arlington /'ɑːlɪŋtən/ *n.* a town of E Massachusetts, a residential suburb of Boston
assault /ə'sɔːlt/ *n.* violent attack
benign /bɪ'naɪn/ *adj.* gentle and mild
blogger /'blɒgə/ *n.* a person who writes weblogs 博主,写博客的人
cloning /'kləʊnɪŋ/ *n.* 无性繁殖,克隆技术
clot /klɒt/ *v.* to form an almost solid lump
clout /klaʊt/ *n.* power or influence over other people or events
crap /kræp/ *n.* sth worthless or useless; nonsense
creationism /kriː'eɪʃənɪzəm/ *n.* 上帝造世说,神造论

disclaimer /dɪsˈkleɪmə/ *n.* a statement that you are not responsible for sth or you are not connected with it
discredit /dɪsˈkredɪt/ *v.* to cause people to stop respecting or believing an idea or person
dissent /dɪˈsent/ *v.* to disagree with other people about sth
Dover *n.* a borough located in York County, Pennsylvania
embolden /ɪmˈbəʊldən/ *v.* to make sb brave
fair-minded *adj.* treating everyone equally
fray /freɪ/ *n.* a quarrel, argument, or fight
gainsay /ɡeɪnˈseɪ/ *v.* to refuse to accept sth as truth
gradient /ˈɡreɪdɪənt/ *n.* a slope or the degree of steepness of a slope 坡度，倾斜度
heresy /ˈherəsɪ/ *n.* a belief that disagrees with the official principles of particular religion 异端，异教
incremental /ˌɪnkrɪˈmentəl/ *adj.* increasing in value by a regular amount（增加的）
irreducible /ˌɪrɪˈdjuːsəbl/ *adj.* that can't be made smaller or simpler
　irreducibly *adv.*
legitimize /lɪˈdʒɪtɪˌmaɪz/ *v.* to make acceptable and right
libertarian /ˌlɪbəˈtɛərɪən/ *n.* 自由论者，自由意志主义者
mandate /ˈmændeɪt/ *v.* to command or order
mutation /mjuːˈteɪʃən/ *n.* a change in genetic structure of an animal or plant（生物物种的）突变，变异
Pa. (*abbrev.*) Pennsylvania
pitfall /ˈpɪtfɔːl/ *n.* a likely mistake or problem in a situation 隐患，陷阱
preamble /priːˈæmbl/ *n.* an introduction to a speech or piece of writing 导言，开场白
provocative /prəˈvɒkətɪv/ *adj.* causing an angry reaction, usu. intentionally（煽动的）
pseudoscience /ˌsjuːdəʊˈsaɪəns/ *n.* a system of thought or a theory which is not formed in a scientific way 伪科学
rekindle /riːˈkɪndl/ *v.* to light a fire or flame again
secular /ˈsekjʊlə/ *adj.* not having any connection with religion
seminal /ˈsemɪnl/ *adj.* containing important new ideas and being very influential on later work
seminary /ˈsemɪnərɪ/ *n.* a college for training ministers or priests 神学院
smack /smæk/ *v.* to have a distinctive flavor or taste

superintendent /ˌsjuːpərɪnˈtendənt/ *n.* a person who is officially in charge of a place, job, activity
symposium /sɪmˈpəʊziəm/ *n.* a formal meeting in which people who know a lot about a particular subject have discussions about it
theologian /ˌθiːəˈləʊdʒən/ *n.* a person who studies religion and religious belief 神学家
thwart /θwɔːt/ *v.* to stop sth from happening or sb from doing sth
turf /tɜːf/ *n.* the area which a group considers its own 势力范围
turf battle a fight or an argument to decide who controls an area or an activity
unveil /ʌnˈveɪl/ *v.* to show or tell people sth that was previously kept secret
venerable /ˈvenərəbl/ *adj.* deserving respect because of age, high position or religious or historical importance

Notes

1. intelligent design—the assertion that some features of living things are best explained as the work of a designer rather than as the result of a random process like natural selection. This means that various forms of life began abruptly through an intelligent agency, with their distinctive features already intact—fish with fins(鳍) and scales (鳞), birds with feathers, beaks(喙)and wings, etc.
2. Darwin's theory (Darwinism)—the theory of biological evolution developed by Charles Darwin and others, stating that all species of organisms arise and develop through the natural selection of small, inherited variations that increase the individual's ability to compete, survive, and reproduce. Notice that Darwinism is not synonymous with evolution, but rather with evolution by natural selection. Modern biology suggests a number of other mechanisms involved in evolution which were unknown to Darwin, such as genetic drift (遗传漂变). The phrase "survival of the fittest(适者生存)" was taken to be emblematic(标志性的) of Darwinism.

   Charles Robert Darwin—1809－1882, a British naturalist who achieved lasting fame as the originator of the theory of evolution through natural selection. Of his 19 books, his 1859 book *On the Origin of Species* established evolution as the dominant scientific theory of diversification in nature. It is now recognized as a leading work in natural philosophy and in the history of mankind. Darwin continued his research and wrote a series of books on plants and animals until his death in 1882. His works were violently attacked and energetically defended, then; and, it seems, yet today. In a national recognition of Darwin's pre-eminence, he was buried in Westminster Abbey, only a few feet away from Sir Isaac Newton.

3. *Of Pandas and People—The Central Question of Biological Origins* is a controversial 1989 school textbook that espouses(支持)the idea of intelligent design. It presents various creationist arguments against the scientific theory of evolution.

4. That kind of scene ... plenty of civil libertarians. —Scientists and science teachers would be frightened at the idea of teaching intelligent design in biology class although this doesn't seem to produce any ill effect, not to mention civil libertarians. 这一幕,尽管短暂而且可能看似无害,但将令全美各地的科学家和自然科学教师惊骇不已,更不用说众多公民自由主义者了。

   civil libertarian—one who is actively concerned with the protection of individual civil liberties and civil rights. For civil libertarians, the introduction of intelligent design in public school will impose one religion upon all citizens, which means putting undue stress on people of diverse backgrounds and different religions. This strongly goes against their ideology of protecting freedom of religion.

5. But Dover's disclaimer on Darwin ... America's education President. —But the American President would nod in agreement with the idea of introducing intelligent design in school. 不过,自视为美国的教育总统的那个人看来会同意多佛否认达尔文理论的声明。

   a. disclaimer on Darwin—denial of Darwin's theory
   b. get a passing grade—get an approval

6. It is a subtler way... than traditional creationism. —The traditional creationism openly claims that it is God who created the universe, whereas intelligent design avoids mentioning god and explains the living things by an intelligent cause. But in fact, the two theories are similar in that they all acknowledge a common creator. 和传统的神创论相比,它是一种更隐晦的认为自然中有上帝印记的理论。

creationism—the belief that God created the universe, including the world and everything in it, in the way described in the Bible.

7. And that is provocative ... politically and competitively. —On the one hand, the accounts of creation have become controversial since the Middle Ages, and the intelligent design will again stir up a new controversy; on the other hand, the U.S. science is under political and competitive attack now. Therefore, the President's position at this moment will cause a lot of discussion. 此举引人争议,不仅因为它让一场一直追溯到中世纪的论战死灰复燃,而且因为它的出现正值美国科学界面临新的国内政治和国外竞争抨击之际。

8. National Science Teachers Association—(NSTA) the largest organization in the world committed to promoting excellence and innovation in science teaching and learning. It was founded in 1944 and headquartered in Arlington, Virginia.

9. "If I were China, I'd be happy"—Here Gerry Wheeler put China in the opposite of America, so if America fell behind in scientific research, China would be happy. This might be comprehensible as different countries are opponents in scientific and technological competitions, but what Gerry said here also showed a disapproval of communism.

10. The intelligent-design movement is just ... insufficient room for the influence of God—People who believe in God find it hard to accept Darwin's theory because it fully denies the role of God in the nature. Some movements simply made use of this situation to cause people to stop believing Darwin's theory, and the intelligent-design movement is the latest one and the most complicated one.

    the intelligent-design movement—an organized campaign that began in the late-1980s to promote the intelligent design arguments in the public sphere, primarily in the United States. The ID movement has attracted considerable press attention and pockets of public support, esp. among conservative Christians in the US. Principal ID proponents have stated a goal of greatly undermining or eliminating altogether the teaching of evolution in public school science and to also secure recognition of creationists claims of scientific legitimacy by opening the door to supernatural explanations.

11. the "monkey trial" —On May 25, 1925, John T. Scopes, a teacher

in Dayton, Tennessee was charged with violating the law passed on March 13, 1925, which forbade the teaching in any state-funded educational establishment in Tennessee of "any theory that denies the story of the Divine Creation of man as taught in the Bible, and to teach instead that man has descended from a lower order of animals." This is often interpreted as meaning that the law forbade the teaching of any aspect of the theory of evolution. It has often been called the "Scopes Monkey Trial." 猴子案审判,即斯科普斯案审判,是对因讲授达尔文进化论而触犯田纳西州法律的中学教师斯科普斯的审讯,该州禁止公立学校讲授任何否定《圣经》创世说或认为人类是由猴子等动物进化而来的理论。结果斯科普斯被判有罪。1927年田纳西州最高法院宣布撤销该判决。

12. When such laws were struck down ... be taught alongside evolution. —The US Supreme Court abrogated (废除) the law of forbidding teaching the theory of evolution in 1968. Some states had to change their previous practice of banning the teaching of evolution, but they still wanted creationism to be taught, so they required the teaching of both theories.

  a. strike down—render ineffective, cancel

  b. Supreme Court—the highest federal court in the United States. It has ultimate judicial authority within the United States to interpret and decide questions of federal law including the Constitution of the United States. It is head of the judicial branch of the United States Government. 美国最高法院

  c. shift gears—start sth in a different way, esp. in the amount of energy or effort you use

13. violated the First Amendment's separation of church and state—The First Amendment reads "Congress shall make no law respecting an establishment of religion ..." The law of teaching creationism in public school will obviously help an establishment of Christianity. 将教授神创论写进法律当然会强化人们对于基督教的信奉,这有悖于宪法第一条修正政教分离的条款。

  the First Amendment—an amendment to the Constitution of the United States guaranteeing the right of free expression; includes freedom of assembly and freedom of the press and freedom of religion and freedom of speech. It is a part of the United States

Bill of Rights. 宪法第一条修正,即人权法第一条,规定人民享有宗教信仰自由,言论自由,出版、集会和向政府请愿的自由。

14. But some anti-Darwinists seized upon Justice Antonin Scalia's dissenting opinion in the 1987 case. —In the 1987 case (mentioned in the last paragraph), Antonin Scalia disagreed with forbidding the offering of creationism in public schools, although the High Court finally ruled so. Some anti-Darwinists just made use of what he said to justify the teaching of creationism.

　　Antonin Scalia—a U. S. Supreme Court Associate Justice (最高法院法官) since 1986. He is the first Italian-American Justice of the Supreme Court of the United States.

15. Christian fundamentalists ... presented in their schools. —What Scalia wrote means people who believe in creationism have the right to teach their theory in schools. He used the words "scientific evidence there may be against evolution" to indicate "creationism".

　　Christian fundamentalists—Christians who believe that everything in the Bible is completely true. Fundamentalism refers to the movement which arose mainly within American Protestantism in the late 19th century by conservative evangelical (福音的) Christians who, in a reaction to modernism, actively affirmed a "fundamental" set of Christian beliefs: the inerrancy of the Bible, the virgin birth of Christ and the authenticity of his miracles. 基督教原教旨主义者,原教旨主义是由新教保守神学家针对现代主义和自由主义神学派提出的神学主张,他们强调《圣经》的绝对正确。原教旨主义者常作"极端保守派"讲。

16. You have to hand it to the creationists. They have evolved. —You have to admire the creationists. In order to stop believing evolutionism, they changed their way from interfering with teaching evolution to encouraging teaching both evolution and intelligent design (i. e. teach the controversy). What Scott says here implies that intelligent design is a variation of creationism and the only difference is the way of their movement. Notice here Scott uses the word "evolve" to joke that, although they are creationists, they have changed according to different situations, which means they have undergone the process of evolution.

　　hand it to sb—sb is so skillful and successful that you admire

him a lot.
17. National Center for Science Education—(NCSE) a nonprofit organization affiliated with the American Association for the Advancement of Science that defends the teaching of evolution and opposes the teaching of religious views in science classes in America's public schools.
18. Much of it revolves around ... and natural selection.—Their critique of Darwin focuses on the attractive idea that the making of living things is so delicate and complex that chance mutation and natural selection simply can not explain their existence.
  a. chance mutations—a random and sudden structural change within a gene or chromosome(染色体) of an organism resulting in the creation of a new character or trait not found in the parental type
  b. natural selection—the process which results in the continued existence of only the type of animals and plants which are best able to produce young or new plants in the conditions in which they live
19. Lehigh University—private, based in Bethlehem, Pennsylvania
20. He calls such phenomena ... invalidates the whole.—He said the living organism was so complex that no part in the mechanism could be reduced or removed because doing so would make the whole organism invalid or unacceptable. In fact, when proponents of intelligent design say something is "irreducibly complex", what they really mean is that they can't explain it.
21. the Cambrian period—the first period in the Paleozoic era (古生代). During the Cambrian (550 — 505 million years ago), there were wide-spread seas and several scattered landmasses. The average climate was probably warmer than today, with less variation between regions. There were no land plants or animals, but there were marine organisms with either shells or skeleton. Because the dominant animals were trilobites (三叶虫), the Cambrian is sometimes referred to as the Age of trilobites. 寒武纪
22. Southern Baptist Theological Seminary—南方浸信会神学院
23. flat earthism—the idea that the Earth is flat, as opposed to the view that the Earth is very nearly spherical (球形的). People from early antiquity generally believed the world was flat, but by 1st century, its spherical shape was generally acknowledged.
24. genetic code—the arrangement of genes which controls the development

of characteristics and qualities in a living thing 遗传密码
25. Genesis—the first book of the Bible, which describes how God made the world 《圣经·旧约》的首篇《创世记》
26. The new, presumably Constitution-proof way ... "critical inquiry"... "strengths and weaknesses" ... "critical analysis" (Ohio).—为了满足希望教授智慧设计等理论的群体的愿望,新出现的可能不违宪的办法是使用"批判性探索"(新墨西哥州)、理论的"优点和缺点"(得克萨斯州)以及"批判性的分析"(俄亥俄州)等严肃的字眼。

Constitution-proof way—way that avoids violation against the Constitution

Questions

1. What will happen in the public high school in rural Dover in the late fall? Why do scientists feel horrible about it?
2. What is President Bush's attitude towards "intelligent design"? What is the effect of his attitude?
3. Has evolutionism been well accepted in America since its birth? What was "monkey trial"?
4. What are the problems with Darwin's theory according to the advocates of "intelligent design"?
5. Do earlier anti-Darwinists and the proponents of "intelligent design" hold the same point of view? Why?
6. Why do many scientists resist engaging in the new evolution war?
7. Why will science teachers choose such expressions as "critical inquiry", "strengths and weaknesses" and "critical analysis" when they teach ideas like "intelligent design"?
8. What is your opinion on the war between Darwin's theory and "intelligent design"?

读报知识

宗 教

说到美国国情,人们首先想到自由民主的政治制度,强大的军事经济实力,发达的科技,先进的教育体系,等等,很少人会想到宗教,更不会有与上面提到的美国政治、经济、文化等联系起来,也想不到美国竟有一半以上的人认为,上帝是美国民主的道德支柱。美国人大约90%信教,它不仅是世界上世俗(secular)大国,也是宗教大国。法规制约行为,宗教控制内心。也就是说,宗教是他们的灵魂。

现在的中国,无神论者(atheist)占绝大多数,对西方国家的宗教及其语言相当陌生,可是对我们这些学习英语和新闻的学生而言,要理解词语、解读文章,离不开宗教知识。不懂圣经故事和希腊神话,就等于不了解我国的儒家文化一样。也就是说,只了解表面上的美国,而非真正的美国。要了解美国的宗教,必须知道现代基督教和犹太教。

基督教的三大教派

经历几次的分化和改革,现代基督教(Christianity)有三大派别。它们是天主教(Catholicism or Catholic Church)、新教(Protestantism or Protestant Church)和东正教(Eastern Orthodox /Orthodox Church,或无Eastern,译为正教)。犹如政党党中有党、派中有派一样,新教因政治和社会原因分化成不同的宗派(denominations),如公理宗(Congregationalism)、路德宗(Lutheranism)、英国圣公会(Anglicanism)、循道宗(Methodism)、长老会(Presbyterianism)和浸礼会(Baptism)等。

1. 天主教:天主教与罗马教廷关系紧密,所以有些人仍称Roman Catholic Church(罗马天主教),是世界上最大的统一基督教派别和宗教团体。天主教实行教皇至上论(Ultramontanism),教皇享有至高无上的权力。高级神职人员除教皇(Pope)外,依次为cardinal(红衣主教)、archbishop(大主教)、bishop(主教)和father(神父)。教皇对所在国的红衣主教等有任命权(这一点是我国与罗马教廷建交谈不拢的主要原因)。在美国,天主教徒占20%,仅次于新教,有神父约8万,连同其他神职人员共约20万人,美国天主教在海外十分活跃,有近万人从事传教活动。但在美国政界,天主教不如新教活跃,担任过总统的只有肯尼迪(John Kennedy)一人信奉天主教,所以有人认为其在1963年被刺有教派背景。因该教禁止教神职人员结婚,闹出许多性丑闻,令教廷震惊和蒙羞。现代主义的兴起也给传统的天主教教义带来了威胁。

2. 东正教:东正教也称正教,希腊、俄罗斯、塞尔维亚、阿尔巴尼亚、保加利亚和乌克兰是以东正教为主的国家,在美国信徒极少。

3. 新教:a. 美国新教:新教曾被译为"更正教"、"抗罗教"、"耶稣教"等,是美国最大的基督教教派,人们普遍把美国看做一个重要的基督教国家,教徒占50%,在美国社会,具有举足轻重地位。Protestant或Protestanism源出德文Protestanten(抗议者)。16世纪,新教诸侯和城市代表强烈抗议天主教会等级森严的僧侣制、僵硬的教条、腐败堕落的行为。其后 protestant 衍生为新教各宗派的共同称谓。新教主张教会制度多样化,不赞成强求一律,强调直接与上帝相通,无须神父(father)中介。主要教派有:the Bapist Church(浸礼会,最大,尤其在南方信徒众多)、the Anglican Church(英国圣公会)、the Methodist Church(卫理公会,也译为循道会、美以美会)、the Lutheran Church(路德会、信义会)、the Congregationalist Church(公理会)、the Presbyterian Church(长老会),等等。新教教士 minster/clergyman/pastor/ecclesiastic(牧师)等与天主教神职人员不同,可以结婚。

b. 英国国教:the Established Church 指 the Church of England 或 the Anglican Church(英国国教会或圣公会)。最高牧首(the Supreme Governor)和基督教的保护者(defender of the Faith)或世俗领袖(Secular head)是现任英国女王。宗教领袖是坎特伯雷大主教(the Archbishop of Canterbury 或 the Primate of All England 全英首主教),其他高级神职人员依次为大主教(Archbishops)、主教(Bishops)和教长(Deans),根据首相提名,由君主任命,均为贵族院议员。其他一般神职人员(ecclesiastic)有 rector/vicar(牧师)、curate(助理牧师)、deacon(执事)等。

犹太教

犹太教(Judaism)历史上最悠久,基督教和伊斯兰教(Islam)都发源于它。犹太教是美国第三大宗教,犹太教徒(Jewish)虽然仅占人口总数 1%,只有六百多万人,美国却是世界上犹太教徒最多、影响力很大的国家,有五千多所会堂(synagogue)。他们在外交上积极支持以色列,成立了 Israeli Lobby(以色列游说集团或以色列帮),政治能量可观,如 2000 年曾推出民主党内保守派人物(Demopublican)Joseph Lieberman 为该党副总统候选人,在新闻界和财界也颇具影响。

至于教会"势力无孔不入"和"政教貌离神合"等详见《导读》五章一节。

Unit Twelve
Sports and Entertainment

Lesson Thirty-eight

课文导读

　　2012年2月14日,在美国职业篮球联赛赛场上,纽约尼克斯队对阵多伦多猛龙队,美籍华裔球员林书豪(Jeremy Lin)在比赛结束前不足一秒的情况下投入一记三分制胜球,帮助尼克斯队击败对手。至此,尼克斯队已经取得六连胜,林书豪也成为NBA史上第一位在前五场首发比赛中场均获得20多分并送出7次助攻的球员。林从板凳球员一跃成为耀眼明星的传奇让人们津津乐道,但他的NBA成功之路并不平坦。本文即从这个角度展现了他坎坷曲折的篮球追梦之路。

　　这是一篇颇具特色的体育人物报道,写得生动活泼,作者开篇即以Lin-sane, Lin-fectious, Lin-destructible 和 Lin-derella 等一系列即兴杜撰的新词,将横空出世的NBA新星林书豪及其在NBA赛场内外激起的热潮表现得活灵活现,读起来恍如身临其境,一个活生生的林书豪跃然纸上。他现在仍在Houston Rockets打2013—2014年常规赛。应该说亚洲球员在体格上与欧美非球员相比还是吃亏的,动辄受伤或体力不支,唯有打前锋或控球后卫且具有几手百发百中的命中率,才能真正在NBA站稳脚跟。姚明和易建联的例子就证明了这一点。

　　通过此课,学生们不仅可以学到一些体育用语,还可体会到报刊语言的若干特点。

Pre-reading Questions

1. What do you know about NBA?
2. Which NBA superstar do you like best?

Text

Basketball: The incredible story of Jeremy Lin, the new superstar of the NBA

By Brendan Meyer

1 The NBA has gone Lin-sane.[1]

2 It's been stricken with Lin-fectious love from fans all over, and stunned by Lin-destructible play from an unlikely hero.[2] New York Knicks point guard Jeremy Lin has inspired the NBA world, overcoming all obstacles in becoming sports' newest Cinderella, or Lin-derella, story.[3]

3 The 23-year-old, who is the NBA's first American-born of Chinese or Taiwanese descent, has made NBA history the last two weeks, scoring 136 points in his first five career starts, surpassing Allen Iverson, Michael Jordan, and Shaquille O'Neal for the most ever in that span[4].

4 But just two weeks ago, Lin was not a household name. He did not have the fastest selling jersey in the NBA, and did not have fans all over the world belting and cheering his name. He was the last player on the Knicks bench[5], a third-string point guard on the verge of being cut for the third time this season. So what has changed in two weeks?

5 Nothing.

6 Lin is the same, versatile basketball player he has always been, and has finally gotten his first chance to show it to the world. After receiving no Division I collegiate basketball scholarship[6] offers out of high school, going undrafted in the NBA draft[7], and being cut by two NBA teams, Lin is now one of the most well known athletes in all of sports.

7 But in a sport where most NBA stars are African American or Caucasian, there is no question that racial stereotyping led to the delay of Lin's opportunity to show off his talent. Now, he's proving all of his critics wrong.

8 "I feel like Asians in general don't get the respect that we may deserve whether it comes to sports, basketball, or whatever it might be," Lin said in an online interview in mid-December. "Maybe I can help break the stereotype."

9   This stereotype has paved an obscure path for Lin, affecting him at each stage of his career, creating one of the most unique basketball journeys.

10   The recruiting process for collegiate athletes is similar to the recruiting process for football's next star[8]. Scouts and experts find the best athletes at a young age, normally around mid-to-late teens, and do their best job to gain their interest and secure them onto their collegiate team.

11   In high school, Lin failed to receive a single scholarship offer from Division I collegiate basketball programs across America, despite being one of the best basketball players in the state of California. He chose to attend Harvard[9], a school known for its academics rather than sports, where he was guaranteed a spot on the basketball team.

12   "I'm not saying top-5 (basketball player in) state automatically gets you offers[10], but I do think (my ethnicity) did affect the way coaches recruited me," Lin said in an interview with the *San Francisco Chronicle*[11] in December 2008. "I think if I were a different race, I would've been treated differently."[12]

13   Lin starred at Harvard, finishing his four-year career with an astonishing 1,483 points, 487 rebounds, 406 assists, and 225 steals. But excelling at Harvard does not gain the attention of NBA scouts. Lin went undrafted in 2010, instead signing with the Golden State Warriors as a free agent[13]. He received minimal playing time, averaging only 2.6 points per game during the season, leading to his release this past December. He was picked up a few days later by the Houston Rockets[14], but was then released before the start of the season.

14   After a few weeks without a job, he signed a non-guaranteed contract[15] with the New York Knicks. Before nearly getting cut for the third time, he finally received his opportunity to play on 4 February, a 25-point performance against the New Jersey Nets[16] that has now awarded him the chance to start for the foreseeable future.

15   "We should have kept (Lin)," Houston Rockets G. M.[17] Daryl Morey tweeted on 9 February. "Did not know he was this good. Anyone who says they knew misleading U[18]."

16   But how could nobody know? He excelled in high school, dominated at Harvard, and is now breaking records in the NBA.

17　　If not for racial stereotyping, everyone would have known about Jeremy Lin a long time ago. His pure basketball talents that are now being praised by sports experts around the world should have garnered him a Division I scholarship, a draft pick in the NBA draft, and more opportunities to play last season.

18　　But Lin is having the last laugh[19]. The Knicks star has now led his team to a 6-0 record in the past six games, averaging 27 points, eight assists, and four rebounds in that span. He scored the game winning three-point basket on 14 February against the Toronto Raptors[21], and scored 38 points against NBA superstar Kobe Bryant[20] and the Los Angeles Lakers[22] on 10 February.

19　　In only two weeks, Jeremy Lin has not just broken records, sold jerseys, and won games. It's safe to say that he has done something that will forever change the landscape of not only Asian Americans in the NBA, but racial stereotyping in all of sports.

20　　Now that's Lin-sane. (From *The Independent*, February 16, 2012)

New Words

academic /ˌækəˈdemɪk/ *n.* scholars and researchers of a university or a college 学者，研究人员

belt /belt/ *v.* sing loudly and forcefully 呼喊

Caucasian /kɔːˈkeɪzɪən/ *n.* someone from a racial grouping coming from Europe, North Africa, and western Asia; a white person 白种人，高加索人

collegiate /kəˈliːdʒɪət/ *adj.* belonging or relating to a college or to college students 大学的；学院的；大学生的

descent /dɪˈsent/ *n.* a person's family background such as his or her nationality or social status 血统

draft /drɑːft/ *n.* the practice of selecting athletes to serve in a particular team, usu. for a limited period of time 体育选秀；*v.* 选秀

ethnicity /eθˈnɪsəti/ *n.* the state of belonging to a particular ethnic group 种族渊源；种族特点

excel /ɪkˈsel/ *v.* to distinguish oneself, be good at 擅长；善于；突出

garner /ˈɡɑːnə(r)/ *v.* to acquire or deserve by one's efforts or actions 获得，得到

jersey /ˈdʒɜːzɪ/ *n.* a close-fitting pullover shirt, esp. worn by team players in sports 参赛者运动衫

landscape /'lændskeɪp/ *n.* all the features that are important in a particular situation 形势；情形

rebound /rɪ'baʊnd/ *n.* (in basketball) a catch after a shot hits the board behind the basket. (篮球运动中的)篮板球

release /rɪ'liːs/ *n.* the termination of someone's employment (leaving them free to depart) 解约（根据上下文此处意为林成为自由身，可自由交换了）这里与本文的 cut 义同。

G. M. —*abbrev.* general manager(总经理)

scout /skaʊt/ *n.* sb employed to discover and recruit talented persons, esp. in the worlds of entertainment or sports 新秀发现者，星探（*cf.* talent scout)

spot /spɒt/ *n.* a position in the competition, event, TV programme (比赛或电视节目中的)地位；位置

steal /stiːl/ *n.* (篮球)抢断

stereotype /'sterɪətaɪp/ *n.* a fixed general image or set of characteristics that a lot of people believe represent a particular type of person or thing 模式化的形象或特征；固定模式；*v.* 使模式化或定型

versatile /'vɜːsətaɪl/ *adj.* good at doing a lot of things and able to learn new skills quickly and exactly 多才多艺的

Notes

1. The NBA has gone Lin-sane. —NBA 已经热到为林书豪而疯狂的地步。

   a. NBA—*abbrev.* National Basketball Association 美国职业篮球联赛

   b. go Lin-sane—a phrase by the author coined from "go insane (发疯)"

   c. Lin-sane—a coinage by the author from "(Jeremy) Lin" and "insane" "林来疯"

   本文开篇即见典型的报刊语言，作者将林书豪的姓名和 insane (疯狂的)两词巧妙地结合在一起，即兴自造出一个新词 Lin-sane，而隐身于 go Lin-sane 中的词组 go insane 也表现出颇为生动形象的意境，令人耳目一新。即兴造词是新闻报道的一大特点，下文中的 Lin-fectious, Lin-destructible 和 Lin-derella 均为 Jeremy Lin 和肢解后的 infectious(富有感染力的), indestructible(坚不可摧的)和 Cinderella (灰姑娘)等创造的新拼合词，不过就总体而言，这些词大多昙花一现

便寿终正寝。

2. It's been stricken with Lin-fectious love... an unlikely hero.—People from all over the country have been deeply affected by the fans' infectious love towards Jeremy Lin, a hero they never expected, and stunned by his indestructible performance.

  a. stricken—showing the effect of trouble, anxiety, illness etc. (此处比喻人们对林书豪的喜爱近乎狂热,就像患了一场病一样。)

  b. Lin-fectious love—infectious love towards Jeremy Lin

  c. Lin-destructible play—Jeremy Lin's indestructible play

3. New York Knicks point guard... sports' newest Cinderella, or Lin-derella, story.—纽约尼克斯队控球后卫林书豪在NBA世界引起了强烈反响,他克服了重重障碍,演绎了体育界最新版的灰姑娘故事——"林氏灰姑娘"。

  a. New York Knicks—纽约尼克斯队

  b. point guard—(篮球)控球后卫

  c. Cinderella—the main character in a fairy tale 灰姑娘是童话故事《灰姑娘》中的女主人公。此处作者巧妙地把Cinderella拼合为Lin-derella,形象生动地说明林书豪在NBA初期才能被埋没,后来他的成功所带来的轰动效应。

4. ...surpassing Allen Iverson, Michael Jordan, and Shaquille O'Neal for the most ever in that span—... doing better than Allen Iverson, Michael Jordan, and Shaquille O'Neal for the most points that any one player has ever scored during the same period.

  a. Allen Iverson—1975— , an American professional basketball player who was rated the fifth greatest NBA shooting guard(得分后卫)of all time by ESPN(娱乐体育电视网) in 2008. 阿伦·艾弗森,多次入选NBA全明星阵容,曾任美国男篮梦之队队长。

  b. Michael Jordan—1963— , one of the greatest American professional basketball players.

  c. Shaquille O'Neal—1972— , nicknamed "Shaq," one of the greatest NBA players, current analyst on the TV program Inside the NBA "大鲨鱼"沙奎尔·奥尼尔

5. on the bench—sitting on the seats by the court, not playing the game 在替补队员席上

6. Division I collegiate basketball scholarship—美国大学体育总会的一级篮球奖学金

7. NBA draft—an annual event in which the thirty teams from the National Basketball Association (NBA) can draft players who are eligible and wish to join the league. NBA 选秀

   draft *n.* the practice of selecting athletes to serve in a particular team, usu. for a limited period of time 体育选秀; *v.* 选秀 (*cf.* undraft 在选秀中落选)

8. football's next star—a TV program broadcast on Sky1(天空电视台一频道) in the United Kingdom. The show aimed to find a young football player who could be the "next big thing" and reward them with a professional contract at Inter Milan (国际米兰队) in Italy.

9. Harvard—Harvard University 哈佛大学

10. "... gets you offers,..."—此处 offers 为直接宾语, you 为间接宾语, 等于... get offers for you. (给你机会)

11. the *San Francisco Chronicle*—《旧金山纪事报》

12. "I think if I were a different race, I would've been treated differently."此句用虚拟语气,表示他并没有受到这种对待。

13. ... signing with the Golden State Warriors as a free agent.—作为自由球员与金州勇士队签约

    a. the Golden State Warriors—金州勇士队。Golden State 是 California 之别称。

    b. a free agent—a player eligible to sign with any club or franchise, i.e. not under contract to any specific team(可以同任何球队签约的)自由球员

14. He was picked up a few days later by the Houston Rockets,...— He was recruited a few days

    later bythe Houston Rockets,...

    the Houston Rockets—休斯敦火箭队

15. a non-guaranteed contract—非保障性合同。指球队拥有随时解除合同的权利,一旦和球员解除合同,球队不用支付赔偿金,甚至可以不用支付合同期内的剩余工资,连薪水也不会计入球队的薪水空间内。

16. the New Jersey Nets—新泽西网队

17. G. M.—*abbrev.* general manager(总经理)

18. Anyone who says they knew misleading U—U = you 如 Why doesn't she like to call U? 报道性文章的语言不像公文,是非正式用语,随意性大。缩略语多是其一个特点,从本文便可见一斑。(见《导读》四章二节"报刊语言的主要特点"之详解)

19. have the last laugh. —to finally be successful (源自谚语"He laughs best that laughs last.")
20. Toronto Raptors—加拿大多伦多猛龙队
21. Kobe Bryant—1978— , one of the greatest NBA players.
22. the Los Angeles Lakers—洛杉矶湖人队

Questions

1. How does Jeremy Lin become Cinderella or Lin-derella?
2. What has Lin changed in two weeks and what hasn't changed?
3. How does racial stereotyping affect Lin?
4. What does Jeremy mean when Houston Rochets G. M. Daryl Morey tweeted "Anyone who says they knew misleading U"?
5. Do you think Lin breaks the stereotype? Why?

学习方法

英语为何生词多而难记

不少英语学习者都埋怨生词多而难记。这是因为英国在历史上曾遭到多次外族入侵,如英法百年战争。这样,有的外来词就在英语中生根发芽,直接进入或融合到英语里,这也是英语生词多而难记的一个重要原因。读了《基督教科学箴言报》2001年1月2日一篇题为"If you speak English, you're a master of many tongues(语言)"的文章就明白了。它前四段是这么写的:

How many languages do you speak? One, maybe two, you say? Wrong! If you speak English, you use words from at least 35 foreign languages. Want proof? Read the next two sentences out loud:

"Jane saw a baby squirrel eating ketchup(番茄酱) left out after yesterday's barbeque(烧烤). Although she was still wearing her cotton pajamas, she hurried outside to chase the creature away."

There. You just spoke seven languages—counting English!

"Baby" comes from a Dutch word spelled the same way. "Squirrel" is French. "Ketchup" originated in Malay(马来语). "Barbeque" was borrowed from Caribbean Indians(印第安人). "Cotton" was first an Arabic word. And "Pajamas" was taken right from the Urdu language (乌尔都语) of India. Surprised?

全球化后，更多的外来语进入了英语，使其语言更加丰富。此外，英语美语之差异使我们要记忆的词语变得更多，有的词同义异，如 table 作动词就是如此。"黄牛党"英国人说"ticket touts"，而美国人则称"scalpers"，"crosswalk"和"zebra crossing"也是如此。翻开《英汉大词典》的附录一看，词语不同之多令初学者生畏。

尽管如此，刚起步时一定要记忆一定数量的基本词汇，犹如盖房子必须夯实地基一样。掌握两三千词汇后，就可以通过上下文大体猜出某些生词的意思。英文忌重复，跟汉语有时爱重复不大相同。开头遇到生词，不必马上查字典，接下来或许会出现你学过的同义词或反义词，茅塞顿开，再上网或查词典印证，看猜错没有。这样学到的词语就更加牢靠，慢慢举一反三，能力就愈来愈大，语感也随之增强了。（详见《导读》七章二节）

此外，假若我们能多学几门外语，学和记就容易多了。上文中 *The Christian Science Monitor* 的文章便说明了这一点。

Lesson Thirty-nine

课文导读

卡卡是巴西圣保罗队近年来培养出的优秀中场球员,2003年转会AC米兰后曾获得欧冠联赛冠军兼最佳射手、欧洲超级杯冠军、世界杯冠军、欧洲最佳球员、世界最佳球员、欧洲足球先生、世界足球先生等等一连串令人叹为观止的殊荣,他真正实现了荣誉大满贯的"巴西的完美先生"。无论从容貌、球技、教养、风度来看,他都无愧于这些荣誉。卡卡以简练、高速见长,拥有超强的个人盘带能力和速度,准确的传球和远射能力。他似乎天生就有着对战术的领悟力和对赛场的适应力。比赛中,他除了经常助攻队友得分外,还凭借在意甲和欧洲冠军联赛几个关键场次的比赛中技惊四座,远射得分,屡次扮演"单骑救主"的角色,并在队中站稳主力前腰位置,这使其成为任何主帅心目中最理想的球员。然而,成为足球明星对于他来说并不是自然而然的事,读过本文以后我们会对这位足球超级巨星的成长历程有更深的了解,他身上那种不骄不躁的品质也值得我们学习。

Pre-reading Questions

1. Do you like football? Do you often watch football games?
2. Who is your favourite football star? Why do you like him?

Text

Kaka[1]: Brazil's Mr. Perfect

1   Brazil is a conveyor belt[2] that produces brilliant talents. Following in the footsteps of Romario, Rivaldo, Ronaldo, Ronaldinho is Ricardo Izecson Santos Leite.[3]

2   Kaka, as he is better known, is the embodiment of elegance, a player who exudes pure class[4]. His ability on the ball, his ability to

dominate games, to see openings and to make the right decisions—these are all, quite simply, of the highest possible order[5].

3   Kaka's background is far from typical. He hails not from the poverty of the *favelas*[6], but from a middle-class family, with the comforts and educational background that this entails[7]. While his father Bosco, an engineer by profession, has looked after his career and handled all of his contract negotiations, Kaka himself set out a plan[8] for his professional development which he has pursued, irresistibly, with singular determination, leaving little room for chance[9].

4   Kaka is the son-in-law that every mother dreams of. While he never dreamt that he would one day become the best player in the world, he always set out to be number one[10].

5   Born in the capital Brasilia in 1982, Kaka grew up in Sao Paulo after his parents moved there when he was seven. Like all kids of his age, he played football and showed an aptitude for the game early on. However, back then his enthusiasm for the game was nothing beyond the ordinary.[11] It was only when he turned 15 that he decided he wanted to make a career for himself in football, although even then he did not give up his studies.

6   However, three years later, his ambitions almost suffered a fatal blow when he fractured a vertebra in his spine following a swimming pool accident. "At that moment, I realised that I had been saved by the hand of God," he wrote in his diary. Since then, he has been unwavering in his religious faith, and after every latest feat on the football pitch, he never fails to acknowledge his debt to God by raising his arms to the skies.

7   Kaka's professional career has unfolded at a remarkable pace. In 2001, he found himself in the Sao Paulo youth team. By the age of 18 he was already being promoted to the senior team and on 31 January 2002, he made his national team debut for Brazil against Bolivia. By that stage, it was clear that nothing was going to stop him.

8   Three years on, former Sao Paulo and AC Milan[12] star Leonardo[13], who had been following Kaka's development closely, convinced him and his family that he should move to Italy, which he did in the summer of 2003. By this stage, he had already won the FIFA World Cup[14] with Brazil in 2002, and his 48 goals in 131 appearances for Sao Paulo

provided a clear indication of the scale of his talent.

9   Once in Europe, he required no time at all to find his feet.[15] But then Kaka always manages to make even the most difficult challenges appear simple. In the 2003/04 season, he was a revelation, as he helped AC Milan to their 17th Serie A title[16]. Three years later, he had conquered Europe, helping the Rossoneri[17] to the 2006/07 UEFA Champions League[18] crown, and finishing as the tournament's ten-goal top scorer in the process.

Kaka of Brazil raises the FIFA World Player 2007 award during the FIFA World Player of the Year awards ceremony in Zurich Dec. 17, 2007.

10   "He is an extremely calm and composed boy who is never prone to either euphoria or depression," says his coach at AC Milan, Carlo Ancelotti. "He has great inner strength, and there is never any danger of him allowing his success go to his head[19]. He is a great champion."

11   Positioned behind the main striker, in the role of what the Italians call the *trequartista*[20] — part creator, part scorer — Kaka is often the player who conjures the final pass, but equally often he is on hand to apply the finish.[21]

12   However, perhaps the most astonishing thing about the Brazilian is the simplicity of his actions, which are always executed with technical brilliance and total control.[22] His recent goal for Brazil against Peru offers a perfect illustration: after first controlling the ball with his left foot, he delivered a finish with his right that ended up in the top corner of the net.

13 "I'm going through a good period. I enjoy being the link between midfield and attack, bringing the ball forward and taking on[23] defenders. That is the area of the pitch where I prefer to operate," says a smiling Kaka, making it all sound so easy.

14 "He is the complete modern player," says former Brazil left-back Roberto Carlos[24] of his compatriot. "Meanwhile, Barcelona's Edmílson[25] praises Kaka's humility and straightforwardness". He adds that Kaka "has the aura of a leader that should make him the player to captain the Brazil national team at the 2010 and 2014 World Cups." (From FIFA.com[26], November 30, 2007)

New Words

aptitude /'æptɪtjuːd/ n. a natural ability; talent, esp. for learning(天资；才能)

aura /'ɔːrə/ n. a distinctive atmosphere or quality associated with a person or thing(出众的)气质

Bolivia /bə'lɪvɪə/ n. a mountainous country in the western part of South America(玻利维亚)

Brasilia /brə'zɪlɪə/ n. the capital city of Brazil(巴西利亚)

captain /'kæptɪn/ v. to be the leader of

compatriot /kəm'pætrɪət/ n. a fellow country man

composed /kəm'pəʊzd/ adj. free from agitation; calm(镇静的；沉着的)

defender /dɪ'fendə/ n. 防守队员

embodiment /ɪm'bɒdɪmənt/ n. a person, being, or thing expressing a spirit, principle, abstraction, etc.; incarnation(具体表现；体现；化身)

euphoria /juː'fɔːrɪə/ n. a feeling of great (sometimes exaggerated) happiness, confidence, or well-being(心情愉快；情绪高涨、兴奋)

exude /ɪg'zjuːd/ v. to project or display conspicuously or abundantly [充分显露(喜怒)]

favela /fə'velə/ n. a shantytown in or near a city, esp. in Brazil; slum area [(巴西的)棚户区,贫民窟]

feat /fiːt/ n. a notable, esp. courageous, act or deed(功绩；本领)

fracture /'fræktʃə/ v. to cause or to suffer the breaking of a bone, etc. (骨折)

humility /hjuː'mɪlɪtɪ/ n. the quality of not being too proud about yourself(谦逊,谦恭)

irresistible /ˌɪrɪˈzɪstəbl/ *adj.* impossible to resist successfully **irresistibly** *adv.*

left-back /left-bæk/ *n.* 左后卫

midfield /ˈmɪdfiːld/ *n.* 中场

opening /ˈəʊpənɪŋ/ *n.* a favourable opportunity; a chance

Peru /pəˈruː/ *n.* a country on the west coast of S America, north of Bolivia and south of Ecuador (秘鲁)

pitch /pɪtʃ/ *n.* (主英)足球场

prone /prəʊn/ *adj.* having a tendency or inclination; disposed to (有……倾向的;易于……的)

revelation /ˌrevɪˈleɪʃən/ *n.* an often surprising fact (or person) that is made known, esp. one that explains or makes sth clear(水落石出的惊人事实;令人震惊的人物)

Sao Paulo /saʊmˈpaʊləʊ/ *n.* the largest city in SE Brazil and Brazil's financial and industrial centre(圣保罗)

spine /spaɪn/ *n.* 脊柱,脊椎

straightforwardness /ˌstreɪtˈfɔːwədnɪs/ *n.* the quality of being free from crookedness or deceit; honesty

striker /ˈstraɪkə/ *n.* 前锋

unfold /ʌnˈfəʊld/ *v.* to blossom; to develop

unwavering /ʌnˈweɪvərɪŋ/ *adj.* marked by firm determination or resolution; not shakable(坚定的,不动摇的)

vertebra /ˈvɜːtɪbrə/ *n.* 椎骨

Notes

1. Kaka—1982— , his full name is Ricardo Izecson dos Santos Leite, but better known as Kaká. He is a Brazilian midfielder who plays for Italian Serie A club(意甲俱乐部) A. C. Milan and the Brazilian national team. He was the recipient of both the Ballon d'Or(金球奖, 即欧洲足球先生)and FIFA World Player(世界足球先生)of the Year awards in 2007, and was named in the 2008 *Time* 100. Kaka helped AC Milan to the European Champions League title(欧洲冠军联赛冠军)in 2007 as well as the World Club Cup and European Super Cup. 卡卡效力于 AC 米兰俱乐部,是巴西年轻天才中场,特点是带球速度快,得分能力强,远射相当有威胁,他的快速带球吸引对方防守后的突破或分球,以及与舍甫琴科快速行进中的配合,是 AC 米兰最具威力

的进攻手段。卡卡是一个有防守能力的攻击型中场,在巴西国家队中,他被卡雷卡誉为"不可或缺的因子"。
2. conveyor belt——传送带(此处是隐喻的用法,表示巴西源源不断地向世界输送足球天才。)
3. Following in the footsteps of Romario, Rivaldo, Ronaldo, Ronaldinho is Ricardo Izecson Santos Leite.——Ricardo Izecson Santos Leite is following in the footsteps of Romario, Rivaldo, Ronaldo, Ronaldinho.

  a. follow in the footsteps of sb——步某人的后尘,仿效某人;继承某人的事业

  b. Romario——a former Brazilian football center forward who helped the Brazil national team win the 1994 FIFA World Cup. He was selected the FIFA World Player of the Year and won the World Cup Golden Ball in 1994 and named as one of the Top 125 greatest living footballers as part of FIFA's 100th anniversary celebration. 罗马里奥,效力于达伽马俱乐部,曾获世界足球先生、捧起过世界杯。

  c. Rivaldo——regarded as one of the best Brazilian professional football players, currently playing. He most notably played five years with Catalan club FC Barcelona, with whom he won the 1998 and 1999 Spanish La Liga championship and the 1998 Copa del Rey. He was honoured as FIFA World Player of the Year and European Footballer of the Year in 1999. 里瓦尔多,曾效力于西班牙甲级联赛巴塞罗那俱乐部,为队中核心人物。转会西班牙之前曾在科林西安和帕尔梅拉斯队俱乐部效力。

  d. Ronaldo——a Brazilian professional footballer. A member of the Brazilian national team, Ronaldo has played over 100 international matches, and was part of the Brazilian squads that won the 1994 and 2002 World Cups. Ronaldo has won three FIFA World Player of the Year awards (1996, 1997, 2002) and is one of two men to have won the award three times, along with former Real Madrid teammate Zinedine Zidane(齐达内). Ronaldo has been nicknamed "The Phenomenon". 罗纳尔多,职业生涯由巴西俱乐部克鲁塞罗开始,后来从荷兰的埃因霍温队登陆欧洲,后转会至巴塞罗那和国际米兰,后又效力西班牙球队皇家马德里及巴西国家队,为主力前锋。三届世界足球先生得主,代表巴西国家队夺得两次世界杯冠军,一次世界杯亚军。

  e. Ronaldinho——a Brazilian footballer who plays for Serie A side

AC Milan and the Brazil national team. Ronaldinho, meaning "little Ronaldo", is better known in Brazil by the nickname Ronaldinho Gaúcho, in order to distinguish him from Ronaldo, who was already called "Ronaldinho" in Brazil. Among his many achievements and accolades, Ronaldinho is a two-time winner of the FIFA World Player of the Year, European Footballer of the Year and FIFPro(国际职业球员联盟) World Player of the Year awards. He became a Spanish citizen in January 2007. 罗纳尔迪尼奥,通常被叫做"小罗纳尔多",以区别于罗纳尔多。他的超卓球技被大众称为"新一代球王",曾经在 2004 年至 2005 年连续两年获得世界足球先生,2005 年获得欧洲足球先生的殊荣,同年并成为首届世界职业球员协会最佳球员的得主。

4. a player who exudes pure class—an absolutely excellent player

    a. pure—absolute; utter; sheer

    b. class—excellence; exceptional merit

5. these are all, quite simply, of the highest possible order—简言之,所有这些都达到了炉火纯青的地步。

    a. quite simply—frankly; speaking frankly

    b. the highest possible order—the highest class or kind

6. He hails not from the poverty of the *favelas*—He is not a native or poor resident of the slums.

7. with the comforts and educational background that this entails—he has had the comforts and a good education that the middle class family provides.

8. set out a plan—to make a plan

    set out—to design; to plan

9. leaving little room for chance—it means that he plans his own professional development carefully and adheres to it and never allows himself to do anything by chance.

    room—opportunity; occasion

10. he always set out to be number one—he was always determined and attempted to be number one

    set out—to undertake; to attempt

11. However, back then his enthusiasm for the game was nothing beyond the ordinary.—However, at that time his enthusiasm for football was not at all stronger than that of the ordinary children.

12. AC Milan—Associazione Calcio Milan, an Italian professional football club based in Milan, Lombardy. The club was founded in 1899 and has since spent most of its history in the top flight of Italian football. Their home games are played at San Siro(圣西罗球场), also known as the Stadio Giuseppe Meazza. The ground, which is shared with rivals Internazionale (国际米兰), is the largest in Italian football, with total capacity of 82,955.
13. Leonardo—a retired football midfielder, who played for Brazil. He played in the 1994 FIFA World Cup winning side, as well as the runners up(亚军) side in the 1998. 莱昂纳多
14. The FIFA World Cup—an international association football competition contested by the men's national teams of the members of *Fédération Internationale de Football Association* (FIFA), the sport's global governing body. The championship has been awarded every four years since the first tournament in 1930, except in 1942 and 1946, due to World War II.
15. Once in Europe, he required no time at all to find his feet. —As soon as he arrived in Europe, he got used to it at once.

    find one's feet—to get used to a new situation, esp. one that is difficult at first 习惯于新的环境；施展才能
16. Serie A title—意甲冠军

    a. Serie A—Officially known as the Lega Calcio Serie A TIM for sponsorship reasons, Serie A is a professional league competition for football clubs located at the top echelon (级别；阶层) of the Italian football league system. It is widely regarded as one of the elite leagues of the footballing world. Historically, Serie A has produced the highest number of European Cup finalists. In total Italian clubs have reached the final of the competition on a record of twenty-five different occasions, winning the title eleven times. 意大利足球甲级联赛，简称"意甲"，是意大利最高等级的职业足球联赛，由意大利足球协会（Federazione Italiana Giuoco Calcio, FIGC）管理。意甲是世界上水平最高的职业足球联赛之一，其特点为注重防守，并且球星云集，被誉为小世界杯。

    b. title—the championship
17. the Rossoneri—Throughout the entire history of AC Milan, they

have been represented by the colours red and black. The colours were chosen to represent the players' fiery ardour (red) and the opponents' fear to challenge the team (black). Due to Milan's striped red and black shirts, they have gained the nickname Rossoneri. White shorts and black socks are worn as part of the home kit. 红黑军团。在意大利，球迷们称 AC 米兰队为"The Rossoneri", Rosso 是意大利语"红"的意思，而 Neri 就是"黑"。因为米兰队的队服为红黑相间的条纹衫，故有红黑军团的昵称。

18. UEFA Champions League—The Union of European Football Associations is the administrative and controlling body for European football. It is almost always referred to by its acronym UEFA (usu. pronounced /juːˈeifə/). The UEFA Champions League is a seasonal club football competition organised by UEFA since 1992 for the most successful football clubs in Europe. The prize, the European Champion Clubs' Cup (more commonly known as the European Cup), is one of the most prestigious club trophies in the sport. 欧洲冠军杯联赛分组赛阶段有 32 个名额，其中 16 个直接分配给卫冕球队以及 15 支来自欧洲最高排名的联赛冠军及亚军。欧洲足协根据多年欧洲赛事的成绩作统计数据，为欧洲各国联赛订立排名。

19. go to one's head—to make SB conceited or self-important 成功、名利、赞扬等，使某人过于兴奋，冲昏某人的头脑或自满

20. *trequartista*—意大利语，意思是指一个既非中场，又非前锋，有效地串联整队进攻体系的球员。这位置的球员早就存在，但不同年代有不同的称呼。原先，他们被称为内锋或后上中锋(inside forwards or deep-lying centre forwards)。后来又被称为 withdrawn striker (影子前锋)和 playing "in the hole"(意指他们活跃于敌方中场和后防之间)。不论称呼如何，这位置大概是指一个界乎于进攻中场和前锋之间的球员。他必须拥有技术、进攻意识，有为前锋制造得分机会的意识，也有自行射门得分的能力。

21. Kaka is often the player who conjures the final pass, but equally often he is on hand to apply the finish. —他常常是那种能魔术般地传出最后一球的球员，但也常常是随时踢出最后一脚而得分的人。

    a. conjure—to affect or effect (as if) by magical powers(如用魔术般地做成或变出)

    b. on hand—ready (to do sth)

22. the simplicity of his actions, which are always executed with technical brilliance and total control.—他简练的动作总是体现着精湛的技术和完美的控球。
23. take on— to accept as a challenge; contend against
24. Roberto Carlos—a Brazilian football player who played for Spanish club Real Madrid（皇家马德里）for eleven years, winning four leagues, three UEFA Champions League trophies, and two Intercontinental Cups. 罗伯特·卡洛斯
25. Barcelona's Edmílson—a Brazilian football player of Italian descent 巴塞罗那队的埃德密尔逊
26. FIFA.com—国际足联网站

Questions

1. According to the author's opinion, what's the difference between Kaka and other "typical" football players?
2. Why does Kaka always raise his arms to the sky after every latest feat on the pitch?
3. What role does Kaka play in the games? What's his function and characteristics?
4. Please give a brief summary of Kaka's professional career and his achievements.
5. What qualities should we learn from Kaka?

学习方法

名师指点词语记忆法

对未入门者而言，报刊里陌生词语随处可见，是一大拦路虎。如何记忆词汇？英语界前辈李赋宁先生在《英语学习经验谈》一书里作了指导。

"语法知识固然重要，但是词汇知识也同样重要，因为思想和概念首先要通过词来表达。……首先要弄清楚词义，同学们查英汉字典时，往往发现一个词有好几个解释，有时多到十几个解释。如何选择一条最恰当的解释，就是我们在阅读中首先要解决的问题。我们一定要开动脑筋，紧密地结合上下文的意思来寻找一条最合适的解释，这样才能真正培养我们的阅读能力，这样才能把生词透彻理解，牢固地记住。词汇表对初学外语的人是有帮助的，但是我们不应依赖词汇表，我们应该尽早地多利用字

典,尽早地结合上下文来寻找词的恰当的意思和正确的解释,也就是说我们应该尽早地培养我们的独立阅读能力。

"同学们还应该学会逐渐使用以英语解释词义的英语字典。为什么?因为阅读科学文献一定要概念明确。英汉字典往往只给一个汉语译名,这个汉语译名本身的含义可能并不完全相当于原来那个英语单词的词义。因此有时查了英汉字典,仍然感到理解得模模糊糊。至于以英语解释词义的英语字典,所用的方法是给每个词都下一个明确的定义,所以查了这种字典往往理解得更加清楚。

"在查字典时,除了要寻找合适的解释外,还应该注意一下所查的那个词的词源意义。例如,向日葵在英语中俗名是 sunflower(太阳花),但学名是 heliotrope,为希腊文 helios(太阳)+希腊文 tropos(转动)所组成。经常注意词源意义就会增加、扩大我们对于构词法的知识,培养我们分析词义的能力。

"除了词源意义外,在查字典时,我们还应该注意词的搭配,尤其要注意动词和名词的搭配、形容词和名词的搭配、动词和副词的搭配等。例如,meet requirements(满足需要),close attention(密切的注意),talk freely(信口开河)。在阅读时还应该把表示相同的或类似的概念的词和短语都搜集在一起,加以比较,又把表示相反的概念的词和短语搜集在一起,加以对照。这样来理解内容,这样来记生词,效果一定更好。例如,以前学的"The Story of Fire"课文中第一句:Fire could be harnessed and made to work for man. 在这里,动词 harnessed 和短语 made to work 就是表示相同或类似概念的同义词或同义现象,应该搜集在一起,加以比较。同一课也有不少表示相反概念的词和短语:combustible 和 incombustible,materials which burn 和 materials which will not burn 等都应联系起来记。用这样的方法来记单词,才记得多,记得牢。我不赞成同学们把单词抄在生字本或卡片上,孤立地、机械地死背硬记,而是应该把几个词联系起来记。当然在开始的阶段,记单词必须花很大的劳力。每课书上词汇表中有用的词都应有意识地记住。要做到眼到、口到、手到、心到。那就是说把每一个要记住的单词看上几遍,念上几遍,写上几遍,记上几遍。这样机械的死功夫在初学阶段十分必要,到了一年以后就用不着费这样大的气力来死记了。就应该用我上面说的那些办法来更有效地扩大词汇,培养独立阅读的能力。但是即使达到比较熟练的阶段也不能放弃某些较费力的活动,以便达到进一步的准确和熟练程度。例如每日清晨朗读半小时,每日抄写半页课文或资料,每日记住一、两个写得好的句子。基本功要经常地练,不断地练,才能保证外语学得又快又好。

Lesson Forty

课文导读

电视真人秀节目已经风靡世界,是最具竞争优势的收视率争夺者。因为节目和观众互动广泛,极大地满足了观众多方面的心理需求,在电视产业链运营方面具有独特的优势,其社会影响力前所未有。节目的参与者们就像昔日的电影明星一样,为人所崇拜、迷恋和追捧。真人秀所产生的偶像及其迷恋者甚至已经形成了一个个社会交际网。电视真人秀节目的创新引领着电视业的新潮流,改变了电视行业的运作模式。

英国是传统媒体业的鼻祖,其纸介媒体逐步形成了对新闻产业模式的影响并延续至今。今天,它在影视产业新经济中再次抢得先机,世界上许多广受欢迎的电视真人秀节目大多首创于英国。自从1998年英国提出"创意产业"的概念以来,该产业已经逐渐超过其老牌的金融业,跃升为一个有强劲上升趋势的新型经济增长点。在100多个国家的电视台以各种形式演绎创自英国的各类"达人秀"之际,英国正在有步骤、有计划地展开在电视娱乐业称雄世界的宏图。虽然它遭到各国同行的竞争,但是有其政府支持,而且强调创新,优势还是明显的。

Pre-reading Questions

1. What is the reality TV?
2. What kind of reality TV programs do you like best?

Text

The reality-television business: Entertainers to the world

Many of the world's most popular television shows were invented in Britain. But competition is growing.

1 NOT many Britons watch "Who Wants to be a Millionaire?"[1] these days. The quiz show, which routinely drew more than 15m viewers in

the late 1990s, now attracts fewer than 5m. While "Millionaire" is fading in the country that invented it, though, it is thriving elsewhere.

This week Sushil Kumar² won the top prize on the Indian version of the programme. Côte d'Ivoire³ is to make a series. Afghanistan is getting a second one. In all, 84 different versions of the show have been made, shown in 117 countries.

2   Hollywood may create the world's best TV dramas, but Britain dominates the global trade in unscripted programmes—quiz shows, singing competitions and other forms of reality television. "Britain's Got Talent,"⁴ a format created in 2006, has mutated into 44 national versions, including "China's Got Talent" and "Das Supertalent."⁵ There are 22 different versions of "Wife Swap"⁶ and 32 of "Masterchef."⁷ In the first half of this year, Britain supplied 43% of global entertainment formats—more than any other country (see chart).

3   London crawls with programme scouts.⁸ If a show is a hit in Britain—or even if it performs unusually well in its time slot—phones start ringing in production companies' offices. Foreign broadcasters, hungry for proven fare, may hire the producers of a British show to make a version for them. Or they may buy a "bible" that tells them how to clone it for themselves.

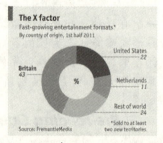

"The risk of putting prime-time entertainment on your schedule has been outsourced to the UK,"⁹ says Tony Cohen, chief executive of FremantleMedia¹⁰, which makes "Got Talent," "Idol" and "X Factor."¹¹

4   Like financial services, television production took off in London as a result of government action. In the early 1990s broadcasters were told to commission at least one-quarter of their programmes from independent producers. In 2004 trade regulations ensured that most rights to television shows are retained by those who make them, not those who broadcast them. Production companies began aggressively

hawking their wares overseas.

5   They are becoming more aggressive, in part because British broadcasters are becoming stingier. PACT[12], a producers' group, and Oliver & Ohlbaum[13], a consultancy, estimate that domestic broadcasters spent £1.51 billion ($2.4 billion) on shows from independent outfits in 2008, but only £1.36 billion in 2010. International revenues have soared from £342m to £590m in the same period. Claire Hungate, chief executive of Shed Media[14], says that 70—80% of that company's profits now come from intellectual property—that is, selling formats and tapes of shows that have already been broadcast, mostly to other countries.

6   Alex Mahon, president of Shine Group[15], points to another reason for British creativity. Many domestic television executives do not prize commercial success. The BBC is funded almost entirely by a licence fee on television-owning households. Channel 4 is funded by advertising but is publicly owned. At such outfits, success is measured largely in terms of creativity and innovation—putting on the show that everyone talks about. In practice, that means they favour short series. British television churns out[16] a lot of ideas.

7   Yet the country's status as the world's pre-eminent inventor of unscripted entertainment is not assured. Other countries have learned how to create reality television formats and are selling them hard. In early October programme buyers at MIPCOM[17], a huge television convention held in France, crowded into a theatre to watch clips of dozens of reality programmes. A Norwegian show followed urban single women as they toured rural villages in search of love. From India came "Crunch," a show in which the walls of a house gradually closed in on contestants.[18]

8   Ever-shrinking commissioning budgets at home are a problem, too. The BBC, which provides a showcase for independent productions as well as creating many of its own, will trim its overall budget by 16% in real terms[19] over the next few years. The rather tacky BBC3[20] will be pruned hard—not a great loss to national culture, maybe, but a problem for producers, since many shows are launched on the channel. Perhaps most dangerously for the independents, ITV[21], Britain's biggest free-to-air commercial broadcaster, aims to produce more of its own

programming.

9   Meanwhile commissioners' tastes are changing. Programmes like "Wife Swap," which involve putting people in contrived situations (and are fairly easy to clone), are falling from favour. The vogue is for gritty, fly-on-the-wall documentaries like "One Born Every Minute" and "24 Hours in A&E".[22] There is a countervailing trend towards what are known as "soft-scripted" shows, which mix acting with real behaviour.[23] "Made in Chelsea" and "The Only Way is Essex" blaze that peculiar trail.[24]

10   These trends do not greatly threaten the largest production companies. Although they are based in London, their operations are increasingly global. Several have been acquired by media conglomerates like Sony[25] and Time Warner[26], making them even more so. Producers with operations in many countries have more opportunities to test new shows and refine old ones. FremantleMedia's new talent show, "Hidden Stars,"[27] was created by the firm's Danish production arm. Britain is still the most-watched market—the crucible of reality formats. But preliminary tests may take place elsewhere.

11   There is, in any case, a way round the problem of British commissioners leaning against conventional reality shows.[28] Producers are turning documentaries and soft-scripted shows into formats, and exporting them. Shine Group's "One Born Every Minute," which began in 2010 as a documentary about a labour ward in Southampton, has already been sold as a format to America, France, Spain and Sweden. In such cases the producers are selling sophisticated technical and editing skills rather than a brand and a formula. With soft-scripted shows, the trick is in casting.

12   The companies that produce and export television formats are scattered around London, in odd places like King's Cross[29] and Primrose Hill[30]. They are less rich than financial-services firms and less appealing to politicians than technology companies. But they have a huge influence on how the world entertains itself. And, in a slow-moving economy, Britain will take all the national champions it can get.
(From *The Economist*, November 5, 2011)

New Words

acquire /əˈkwaɪə(r)/ v. to get sth by buying it

casting /ˈkɑːstɪŋ/ n. the selection of actors or performers for the parts of a presentation 角色分配

clip /klɪp/ n. a short piece of film, TV, or reality TV program 剪辑

commission /kəˈmɪʃn/ v. to ask sb to write an official report, produce a work of art for(委托撰写或制作)(cf. **commissioner**)

conglomerate /kənˈɡlɒmərət/ n. a large firm consisting of several different companies 联合大公司；企业集团

contestant /kənˈtestənt/ n. a person who takes part in a competition or a quiz

contrived /kənˈtraɪvd/ adj. false and deliberate, rather than natural 做作的，不自然的

countervailing /ˈkaʊntəveɪlɪŋ/ adj. having equal power, force or effect

crucible /ˈkruːsɪbl/ n. a melting pot 熔炉

crunch /krʌntʃ/ n. a critical situation that arises because of a shortage of time or money or resources 危急关头

fare /feə(r)/ n. the intellectual food that are regularly consumed, esp. in entertainment 精神食粮

free-to-air /friː tuː eə(r)/ adj. (电视节目和频道)免费接收的

fly-on-the-wall /flaɪ ˈɒnðəwɔːl/ adj. (纪录片)纪实性的，写实的

gritty /ˈɡrɪti/ adj. describing a tough or unpleasant situation in a very realistic way 逼真的，真实的，活生生的

hawk /hɔːk/ v. to sell or offer for sale from place to place 叫卖；兜售

hit /hɪt/ n. sth such as a CD, film, or play that is very popular and successful

labour /ˈleɪbə(r)/ n. the process of giving birth to a baby

mutate /mjuːˈteɪt/ v. to develop into different styles as the result of a change 衍生

Norwegian /nɔːˈwiːdʒən/ adj. belonging or relating to Norway, or to its people, language, or culture 挪威的；挪威人(的)

outsource /ˈaʊtsɔːs/ v. to obtain goods or services from an outside supplier 将……外包；外购

pre-eminent /priːˈemɪnənt, prɪˈemənənt/ adj. more important, powerful or capable than other people or things 卓越的；杰出的；超凡的

prune /pruːn/ v. to cut out unwanted or unnecessary things 精简或除去不需要的部分

retain /rɪˈteɪn/ v. to continue to have 保持；持有

stingy /ˈstɪndʒɪ/ *adj.* not generous, being unwilling to spend money 吝啬的；小气的

tacky /ˈtækɪ/ *adj.* tastelessly showy 低劣的；乏味的

trim /trɪm/ *v.* to cut down on; make a reduction in 削减

unscripted /ʌnˈskrɪptɪd/ *adj.* not finished with or using a script 无脚本的（*cf.* **script** *n.* & *v.*）

vogue /vəʊɡ/ *n.* the popular taste at a given time 流行，时髦

Notes

1. Who Wants to be a Millionaire? —the most internationally popular television franchise of British origin, created in 1998, having aired in more than 100 countries worldwide. In its format, large cash prizes are offered for correctly answering a series of multiple-choice questions of increasing difficulty. The maximum cash prize (in the original British version) is one million pounds. Most international versions offer a top prize of one million units of the local currency; the actual value of the prize obviously varies widely, depending on the value of the currency.《谁会成为百万富翁？》

2. Sushil Kumar—an Indian name 苏希尔·库马尔

3. Côte d'Ivoire—or Ivory Coast, officially the Republic of Côte d'Ivoire, a country in West Africa. 科特迪瓦，旧称"象牙海岸"。

4. Britain's Got Talent—英国达人秀

5. Das Supertalent—（德语）德国达人秀

6. Wife Swap—a British reality television programme, first broadcast in 2003, the final episode was broadcast in December 2009. In the programme, two families, usually from different social classes and lifestyles, swap wives/mothers—and sometimes husbands—for two weeks. In fact, the programme will usually deliberately swap wives with dramatically different lifestyles, such as a messy (邋遢的) wife swapping with a fastidiously (挑剔地) neat one. Despite using a phrase from the swinging (性滥交，交换配偶的) lifestyle, couples participating in the show do not share a bed with the "swapped" spouse while "swapping" homes.《换妻生活》

7. Masterchef—a television cooking game《谁是厨神》

8. London crawls with programme scouts.—There are many scouts searching for reality television programmes in London.

crawl with—to be full of

9. The risk of putting prime-time... outsourced to the UK. —Foreign broadcasters have outsourced the risk of failure in prime-time entertainment to the UK. 国外的电视台把黄金时段娱乐节目的失败风险转包给了英国。

10. FremantleMedia—FremantleMedia, Ltd. is an international television content and production subsidiary（子公司）of Bertelsmann's RTL Group（贝塔斯曼旗下的 RTL 集团）, Europe's largest TV, radio, and production company. Its world headquarters are located in London.

11. "Got Talent," "Idol" and "X Factor"—《达人秀》、《偶像》和《X 音素》
    "X Factor"—a television music competition originated in the United Kingdom, where it was devised（设计）as a replacement for *Pop Idol*. It is now held in various countries. The contestants are aspiring（有志向的）pop singers drawn from public competitive auditions（试听）. The "X Factor" of the title refers to the undefinable（不确定的）"something" that makes for star quality. The prize is usually a recording contract, in addition to the publicity（报道；宣传，推广）that appearance in the later stages of the show itself generates, not only for the winner but also for other highly ranked contestants.

12. PACT—*abbrev.* Producers Alliance for Cinema and Television 英国电影电视联盟

13. Oliver & Ohlbaum—奥利弗和欧哈巴姆联合咨询公司

14. Shed Media—Shed Media Group, a British creator and distributor of television content.

15. Shine Group—a company that includes production companies of scripted and non-scripted television

16. churn out—to produce large quantities of sth very quickly

17. MIPCOM—a TV and entertainment market which is held in the town of Cannes（戛纳）once every year, normally in October 世界视听内容交易会

18. From India came "Crunch"... on contestants. —一部来自印度制作的《危机关头》，真人秀表演者在房子里，里面的墙壁却在移动着，越挤越紧地逐渐挤向表演者。

19. in real terms—accurate, true, by taking account of related price changes

20. BBC3—BBC 3 频道
21. ITV—Independent Television（英国）独立电视集团
22. The vogue is for gritty, fly-on-the-wall documentaries like "One Born Every Minute" and "24 Hours in A&E."—流行的是直面现实、拍摄手法逼真的纪实影片，比如《忙碌的产房》和《急诊室的 24 小时》。

  a. fly-on-the-wall documentaries—documentaries made by filming people as they do the things they normally do, rather than by interviewing them or asking them to talk directly to the camera

  b. One Born Every Minute—a British observational documentary series which shows the day to day activity of a labour ward(产房).

  c. 24 Hours in A&E—a British medical documentary set in King's College Hospital. 91 cameras filmed round the clock for 28 days, 24 hours a day in A&E (Accident and Emergency Room), it offers unprecedented access to one of Britain's busiest A&E departments.

23. There is a countervailing trend... real behaviour.—现在，所谓的"软脚本"（即将表演形式和真实行为糅为一体）节目大有与此势均力敌的趋势。

24. "Made in Chelsea" and "The Only Way is Essex" blaze that peculiar trail.—《切尔西制造》和《埃塞克斯是唯一的生活方式》即此类真人秀的开路先锋，光彩夺目。

  Made in Chelsea—a British BAFTA（英国电影和电视艺术学院）award-winning reality television show, a soap set in the wealthy Chelsea district of London

  The Only Way is Essex—a British BAFTA award-winning reality television show based in Essex, England

  blaze the trail—to lead in forming or finding a new course（开辟道路）

25. Sony—Sony Corporation 索尼公司并购了好莱坞原八大电影公司中的三家（哥伦比亚、米高梅和联艺），因此也成为全世界最大的电影公司。

26. Time Warner—（美国）时代－华纳公司

27. Hidden Stars—one of the new entertainment formats brought to MIPCOM 2011 by FremantleMedia. It is a fresh format that sees friends and family submit performances from singers who would

never normally enter a talent show. Celebrity mentors（名人导师）assess the entries（参赛者）before making secret surprise visits to the unsuspecting singers, who are then invited to audition live on the spot. Each mentor, a star of today, chooses the contestant they think is a star of tomorrow.《挖掘新星》

28. There is... against conventional reality shows.—Some commissioners have their own ideas and do not agree with conventional reality shows, but British producers know how to tackle with the problem. 一些喜欢求新的定制人反对老生常谈的真人秀节目，而英国的节目制作人自有办法对付。
29. King's Cross—an area of central London. The area formerly had a reputation for being a red light district. 国王十字区
30. Primrose Hill—a hill of 256 feet located in London, and also the name given to the surrounding district. The hill has a clear view of central London. 樱草山

Questions

1. Why does the author say "The risk of putting prime-time entertainment on your schedule has been outsourced to the UK?"
2. What are the effects when broadcasters were told to commission at least one-quarter of their programmes from independent producers?
3. What are the reasons for creativity in British programmes?
4. What happens at MIPCOM held in France this year?
5. What kind of challenges does Britain face?

学习方法

词根的重要性

要多快好省学习生词，学了一定数量的词汇后，就应该学点构词法。这里有个公式：Modern English＝Old English＋Middle French，英语与低地德语同属西日耳曼语支，基本词汇相似之处甚多。初学英语时大都比较熟悉，讲法语的诺曼人征服和统治英国约百年（Norman Conquest），英语报刊里大约70％以上词汇都是希腊、拉丁词根加词缀构成的，一度通过法语大量引进，学了构词法可以成百上千记忆猜词，一本万利。这类

构词专著出了一大批,不妨翻翻复旦大学陆国强先生在《现代英语表达与理解》一书中对词根以图表形式作的如下有益的研究:

"英语中不少词是由词根加词缀构成的。词根是词中表示主要意义的成分,而词缀则是表示附加意义或语法意义的成分。如 unacceptable 这一词,其词根是 accept,而 un-和-able 是词缀。英语中词根有不同形式,有的是完整的词,在句中可作为一个独立的单位使用,如 working 中的 work。有的并不是完整的词,而与其他构词成分结合起来构成一个词,如 audience 中 audi 是词根,表示'听'的意思,-ence是名词性词缀。通过语源分析,掌握词根的意义对整个词的理解具有决定性作用。"

见其所列图表:

词根	意义	实例	
agr	farm	agronomy	(农艺学)
aqua	water	aquarium	(水族馆)
anthrop	man	anthropology	(人类学)
astron	star	astronomy	(天文学)
bio	life	biology	(生物学)
capit	head	capitation	(人头税)
celer	speed	celerity	(迅速)
chrome	color	chromosome	(染色体)
chron	time	chronology	(年代学)
crat	rule	autocrat	(专制君主)
dent	tooth	dentist	(牙科医生)
dict	say	diction	(措词)
eu	well, happy	eugenics	(优生学)
frac	break	fracture	(骨折)
gamos	marriage	monogamous	(一夫一妻制的)
ge	earth	geology	(地质学)
greg	group	gregarious	(好群居的)
gress	move forward	progress	(进展)
gyn	women	gynecologist	(妇科医生)
homo	same	homogeneous	(同类的)
hydr	water	dehydrate	(脱水)
ject	throw	eject	(逐出)
junct	join	conjunction	(连接)
loq	speak	loquacious	(饶舌的)
mar	sea	maritime	(海上的)

med	middle	intermediary	（中间的）
meter	measure	thermometer	（温度表）
mit	send	remit	（汇寄）
mono	one	monotony	（单调）
pater	father	paternal	（父方的）
pathos	feeling	pathology	（病理学）
ped	foot	pedal	（踏板）
phobia	fear	hydrophobia	（恐水病）
phone	sound	telephone	（电话）
port	carry	portable	（手提的）
pseudo	false	pseudonym	（假名）
psych	mind	psychic	（心理的）
rect	rule	direct	（指导）
scope	see	telescope	（望远镜）
scrib	write	inscribe	（刻写）
sec	cut	dissect	（解剖）
sequ	follow	sequence	（连续）
spect	look	inspect	（检查）
spir	breathe	respiration	（呼吸）
tact	touch	tactile	（触觉的）
term	end	terminal	（终点）
vid	see	video	（电视的）
voc	call	convocation	（召开）

　　理解词根的含义固然十分重要，但对词缀的意义也不能忽视，特别是一些衍生出新义的词缀必须注意。如 anticulture 反正统或传统文化的/anthero 反对以传统手法塑造主角的。

附 录

I 报刊标题常用词汇
The Vocabulary of Headlines

　　读者一定见过下列这些词汇，但用在标题时，或许不一定知道其中如 accord, bid, gut 和 man 等的意思。事实上，这类短字不但用于标题，正文里也是常用词。对我们而言，记住这些词汇，犹如添砖加瓦，对读报是大有裨益的。

Headline Word	Common Headline Meaning	Example
accord	agreement	Wages **Accord** Reached
aid	to help	Man **Aids** Police
air	to make known	TV **Airs** "Facts" on Arms Delivery
assail	to criticize strongly	Soviets **Assail** US on A-tests
axe	to dismiss from a job to cut, destroy, take away	Governor to **Axe** Aide? Labour **Axes** Colleges in Tory Towns
back	to support	Unions **Back** Peace Move
balk	to refuse to accept	Union **Balks** at Court Order
ban	prohibition	Bus **Ban** on Pupils after Attack on Crew
bar	not to allow, exclude	Club Faces Shutdown for **Barring** Women
bid	attempt offer	New Peace **Bid** in Rhodesia Union Rejects Latest **Bid**
bilk	to cheat	Clerk **Bilks** City of $1 m.
blast *n.* *v.*	explosion; strong criticism to criticize strongly; strike with explosives	Tanker **Blast** near Manila Heagan **Blasts** Democrats
blaze	fire	**Blaze** Destroys Factory
blow	injury/disappointment suffered	Carter Poll **Blow**
boost	help, incentive	Industry Gets **Boost**
cite	to mention	Management **Cites** Labor Unrest for Shutdown
claim	to declare to be true	Man **Claims** Ghost sighting

Headline Word	Common Headline Meaning	Example
claim (claim the life of)	to kill	Bombs **Claim** 40
clash n.	dispute, violent argument Battle	Strikers in **Clash** With Police Marine Dies in **Clash**
v.	to disagree strongly; fight	Mayor **Clashes** with City Council
cool	uninterested; unfriendly	Hanoi **Cool** to Aid Offer
coup	revolution, change in government	Generals Ousted in **Coup**
curb	restraint, limit	New **Curbs** on Immigration
cut	reduction	Big **Cuts** in Air Fares
deadlock	a disagreement that cannot be settled	Jury **Deadlock** in Kidnap Trial
deal	agreement	Pay Pits **Deal** Hope
drive	campaign, effort	Peace **Drive** Succeeds
due	expected	Greek FM **Due** Today
ease	to reduce or loosen	1000 Freed as Poland **Eases** Martial Law
envoy	diplomat	American **Envoy** Taken Hostage
exit	to leave	**Exit** Envoys in Race Storm
eye	to watch with interest	Women's Groups **Eye** Court Vote
eve	the day before	Violence on **Eve** of Independence
fault	to find in the wrong	Study **Faults** Police
feud	dispute; strong disagree-ment	Border **Feud** Danger to Regional Peace
flay	to accuse; criticize strongly	US **Flays** Soviet Block
foe	opponent; enemy	Reagan Talks with Congressional **Foes**
foil	to prevent from succeeding	FBI **Foils** Bid to Hijack Plane to Iran
Gems	jewels	Actress Loses **Gems**
go-ahead	approval	**Go-Ahead** for Dearer Gas
grip	to take hold of	Cholera Fear **Grips** Japan
gunman	man with gun	**Gunman** Raids 3 Banks
gut	to destroy completely by fire	Year's Biggest Fire **Guts** 178 Homes
halt	stop	Channel Tunnel **Halt**
haul	large quantity which has been stolen and later discovered	Cannabis **Haul**
head	to lead, direct	Buchanan to **Head** Peace Mission
head off	to prevent	President **Heads off** Rail Strike

续表

Headline Word	Common Headline Meaning	Example
heist	theft	Jewel **Heist** Foiled
hit	to affect badly	Fuel Strike **Hits** Hospitals
hold	to keep in police control; detain	7 **Hold** for Gambling
ink	to sign	Thailand, Malaysia **Ink** Sea Treaty
jet	aeroplane	Three Killed in **Jet** Plunge
jobless	unemployed	Number of **Jobless** Increases
key	essential, vital, very important	**Key** Witness Dies
kick off	to begin	Fiery Speech **Kicks off** Campaign
lash out	to criticize strongly; accuse	Warsaw Pact **Lashes out** at NATO Missile Plan
laud	to praise	PM **Lauds** Community Spirit
launch	to begin	Police **Launch** Anti-crime Drive
line	position; demand	Israel Softens **Line**
link *v.*	to connect	Fungus **Linked** to Mystery Disease
n.	connection	Mafia **Link** Scandal Breaks
loom	expected in the near future	Treaty Dispute **Looming**
loot *n.*	stolen money or goods	Police Recover **Loot**
v.	to take away of valuable goods unlawfully	Rioters **Loot** Stores
man	representative	Carter **Man** in China
nab	to capture	Gang Leader **Nabbed**
net	to total	Drug Raid **Nets** £1 M
	to capture	Patrol **Nets** 2 Prisoners
nod	approval	Ministry Seeks **Nod** for Oil Saving Plan
ordeal	painful experience, drama	Jail **Ordeal** Ends
office	an important government position	Minister Quits: Tired of **Office**
opt	choose; decide	Swiss **Opt** to Back Tax for Churches
oust	to take power away from, push out, drive out, replace	Voters **Oust** Incumbents Argentina **Ousts** Union Leaders
output	production	Industrial **Output** Increases in Italy
pact	agreement, treaty	Warsaw **Pact** Ends
pay	wages, salary	**Pay** Rise for Miners
pit	coal mine	**Pit** Talks End

Headline Word	Common Headline Meaning	Example
plea	request for help	"Free Children" **Plea**
	a statement in court indicating guilt or innocence	Guilty **Pleas** Expected
pledge	promise	Labour **Pledges** Higher Pensions
plunge	steep fall	Dollar **Plunges**
poised	ready for action	Bolivian Workers **Poised** to Strike
poll	election, public opinion survey	Swedish **Poll** Shows Swing to Right
	voting station	Voters Go to the **Polls** in Japan
post	position in government, business, etc.	Unknown Gets Key Cabinet **Post**
press for	to demand, ask for	Teachers **Press for** Pay Rise
probe *v*.	to investigate	New Vaccine to Be **Probed**
n.	investigation	Mayor Orders Fire **Probe**
prompt	to cause	Court Decision **Prompts** Public Anger
quit	to leave, resign	Will Carter **Quit**?
rage	to burn out of control	Forest Fire **Rages**
raid	attack, robbery	£23 M Drug **Raid**
rap *n*.	accusation; charge	Corruption **Rap** Unfair Says Senator
v.	to criticize	Safety Commission **Raps** Auto Companies.
riddle	mystery	Girl in Shotgun Death **Riddle**
rock	to shock; to surprise	Gov't. Report **Rocks** Stock market
rout	to defeat completely	Rebels **Routed**, Leave 70 Dead
row	a quarrel, argument, dispute	Oil Price **Row** May Bring Down Gov't.
rule	to decide (especially in court)	Court **Rules** Today in Corruption Case
rule out	to not consider as a possibility	Israel **Rules Out** PLO Talks
sack	dismiss from a job	Jail Chief **Sacked**
sack (from "ransack")	to search thoroughly and rob	14 Held for US Embassy **Sacking**
scare	public alarm	Rabies **Scare** Hits Britain
set	decided on, ready	Peace Talks **Set** for April
slay	to kill or murder	2 **Slain** in Family Row
snag	problem; difficulty	Last Minute **Snag** Hits Arms Talks
snub	to pay no attention to	Protestants **Snub** Ulster Peace Bid
soar	to rise rapidly	Inflation Rate **Soars**

续表

Headline Word	Common Headline Meaning	Example
spark	to cause; to lead to action	Frontier Feuding **Sparks** Attack
split	to divide	Nationalisation **Splits** Party at Conference
squeeze	shortage, scarcity	Petrol **Squeeze** Ahead
stalemate	a disagreement that cannot be settled	New Bid to Break Hostage **Stalemate**
stall	making no progress	Peace Effort in Lebanon **Stalled**
stance	attitude; way of thinking	New **Stance** Toward Power Cuts
stem	to prevent or stop	Rainy Season **Stems** Refugee Exit
storm	angry reaction, dispute	MP's Racist Speech **Storm** Grows
strife	conflict	Inter-Union **Strife** Threatens Peace Deal
sway	to influence or persuade	President Fails to **Sway** Union Strike
swindle	an unlawful way of getting money	Stock **Swindle** in NY
switch	change, deviation	Dramatic **Switch** in Incomes Policy Announced
swoop	sudden attack or raid	Drug **Swoop** in Mayfair
talks	discussions	Peace **Talks** Threatened
thwart	to prevent from being successful	Honduras Attack **Thwarted**
ties	relations	Cuba **Ties** Soon?
top	to exceed	Post Office Profits **Top** £40 M
trim	to cut	Senate **Trims** Budget
trigger	to cause	Killing **Triggers** Riot
vie	to compete	Irish Top Ranks **Vie** for Office
void	to determine to be invalid	Voting Law **Voided** by Court
vow	to promise	Woman **Vows** Vengeance
walkout	strike (often unofficial)	Factory **Walkout** Threat over Sacking
wed	to marry	Financier Free to **Wed**
weigh	to consider	Reagan **Weighs** Tax Increase

II 标题自我测试
Self-Tests in Comprehension of Headlines

Below you will find a set of 9 headlines from *Financial Times* and the *Washington Post*. Following these are the articles which appeared with the headlines. Match the headlines and the articles.

1. **Hong Kong's Cheng quits over company disclosure**
2. **Thailand and Vietnam agree to form rice pool**
3. **Rupee sinks against dollar**
4. **Indian workers plan strike**
5. **Kyrgyz Troops Free 4 U.S. Hostages**
6. **U.S. to Close Its Seoul Firing Range**
7. **Colombian Sent to U.S. for Drug Trial**
8. **3 Freed in Philippines, Rebels Say**
9. **Iran seeks foreign tea buyers**

A   **JOLO, Philippines**—Muslim rebels in the southern Philippines apparently released three Malaysian hostages from nearly four months of captivity, but not before bargaining for $1 million more in ransom, negotiators said. Chief negotiator Robert Aventajado said he expects that the Abu Sayyaf rebels will free their remaining 25 hostages, including 12 Westerners, today.

       Aventajado said he received information from another negotiator "that the Malaysian hostages have been released and are now . . . on the way to Jolo." There was no independent confirmation of their release.

Negotiators working for the Malaysians' freedom said they had reached an agreement on the rebels' demand for an additional $1 million ransom payment. An estimated $5.5 million was paid last month to the rebels for the release of six other Malaysians, and a German woman was supposed to cover the three remaining Malaysians, military officials said.

(Associated Press)

B **SEOUL**—The United States has agreed to stop using a firing range in South Korea following complaints from local residents, South Korea's Defense Ministry said.

Anti-U.S. protesters have held rallies demanding the closure of a strafing area and a nearby bombing range since May, when a U.S. Air Force pilot with engine trouble was forced to drop six 500-pound bombs near a village.

Residents said the bombs shattered windows and caused other damage in Maehyang-ri village, on the Yellow Sea southwest of Seoul. They have been demanding compensation and the closure of both the strafing and bombing ranges.

Gen. Lee Han Ho, deputy director of the South Korean air force, said in a news conference that the U.S. air force would close the strafing range and would stop using live bombs at the bombing range. Lee also said approach paths for jets would be moved offshore, residents would be notified of exercises and the special area for emergency bomb drops would be moved 700 yards further offshore.

(Reuters)

C Iran said yesterday it was seeking foreign buyers for more than 77,000 tonnes of surplus tea. The tea had piled up in warehouses over the years and was being withheld from a saturated domestic market, said Mohammad Hassan Ammari Allahyari, a member of the management board of the State Tea Organisation of Iran (STOI). STOI, which once held a monopoly on production and trade, has been largely stripped of its responsibilities under a government plan to liberalise the industry.

Mr Allahyari said the organisation had already exported 20,000 tonnes of tea in the past year. Until recently, STOI bought from farmers and sold in Iran at subsidised prices. The organisation has now pulled out of the tea business.

Mr Allahyari said Iranian traders were interested in buying the surplus at subsidised rates, but STOI planned to sell at market rates and only for export.

Reuters, Tehran

D   Workers at India's two main state-owned telephone companies last night intensified their campaign against liberalisation of the telecommunications industry, which has as part of its final goal privatisation of the two state-owned telephone companies, MTNL and VSNL.

Telephone communications inside the country and abroad have been disrupted by a work to rule since late last week as MTNL employees in particular stepped up their agitation. They now plan to launch a three-day strike from today.

The government of Atal Behari Vaypayee this year opened up national long-distance telephony to private investors and ended VSNL's monopoly on access to international bandwidth links to the internet. The government also recently said that the state monopoly on international calls would end by 2002, two years ahead of schedule. **David Gardner, New Delhi**

E   The Indian rupee sank to an all-time low against the US dollar yesterday after concerns over the rising price of oil, the country's costliest import. Oil prices have touched 10-year highs in recent days. The Nepali rupee, which is fixed against the Indian currency, also fell to a fresh low against the dollar.

The Indian rupee has weakened by about 6.6 per cent since January. The Reserve Bank of India (RBI) tried to calm the markets but as in last month's bout of rupee nervousness, the impact of the central bank's attempts to reassure markets was short-lived. After a brief spurt, the rupee weakened following the RBI's assurances that domestic oil companies' foreign exchanges needs would be fully met. **Khozem Merchant, Bombay**

F   **BISHKEK, Kyrgyzstan**—Government troops battling Islamic fighters have freed four U.S. mountaineers held hostage by rebels in this Central Asian country, a presidential spokesman said.

The spokesman gave no information about the climbers' names, or where or when they were released, and the U.S. Embassy said it had no information. The State Department warned Americans on Thursday to avoid travel to embattled parts of Kyrgyzstan, saying the security situation was "fluid and potentially dangerous."

The rebels are thought to be members of the Islamic Movement of Uzbekistan, which opposes Uzbek President Islam Karimov, who swept across a remote, mountainous area where all three countries share frontiers.

(Reuters)

G   **BOGOTA, Colombia**—The alleged leader of one of Colombia's most powerful drug cartels was sent yesterday to the United States to stand trial, days after drug dealers threatened violence if authorities carried out the extradition.

Security forces escorted Alberto Orlandez Gamboa onto the tarmac at Bogota's international airport, where he boarded a U.S. Drug Enforcement Administration plane, said President Andres Pastrana.

U.S. authorities say Gamboa, 44, is the head of an international drug trafficking and money laundering organization headquartered in Barranquilla on Colombia's Caribbean coast. He faces charges in U.S. District Court in Manhattan that he conspired to import and distribute thousands of pounds of cocaine from Colombia to New York and other U.S. destinations. He is also accused of **smuggling cocaine to Europe and conspiring to launder millions of dollars in drug profits.**

Gamboa is the third Colombian Pastrana has extradited to the United States to face drug charges in the past nine months, following a 10-year moratorium. Gamboa's extradition comes three days after a newspaper ad paid for by a band of drug dealers known as the Our Country Movement threatened to assassinate judges and government officials unless authorities reversed their decision.

Meanwhile, the U.S. government yesterday added two other Colombians to its list of 524 individuals and companies suspected of drug trafficking and banned from doing business in the United States. Arcangel de Jesus Henao Montoya and Juan Carlos Ramirez Abadia are responsible for huge volumes of drugs that have entered the United States, the Treasury Department said.

(Associated Press)

H   Thailand and Vietnam, the world's two largest rice exporters, agreed yesterday to form a limited rice pool that will attempt to support sagging rice prices in key sales. According to a memorandum of understanding signed in Bangkok, each of the two countries will sell 100,000 tonnes of 25 per cent broken rice for $152/tonne, slightly over the current market price.

Niphon Wongtrangan, director of Thailand's Public Warehouse Organisation, said **Manila was expected to buy bulk rice from the newly formed pool.** The Philippines had been hoping to buy 200,000 tonnes of rice from Vietnam at $140/tonne, but Bangkok persuaded Hanoi to form a pool for the sale to stop price-cutting. Mr Niphon said that if successful, the pool sale could be the foundation of an Organisation of Rice Exporting Countries, which he said could work together to support rice prices, just as the Organisation of Petroleum Exporting Countries controls petroleum prices.

However, agricultural analysts said they were sceptical that Thailand and Vietnam – normally competitors in the world rice market – would be able to sustain and deepen their co-operation when it came to sales of higher-quality rice.

The signing of the deal comes at a time when both Thailand and Vietnam are still trying to assess the impact of recent severe flooding in key rice-growing areas. Around 20 per cent of Thailand's rice-growing area has been affected by the floods.

Although both Thailand and Vietnam are estimated to have lost at least 1m tonnes of rice due to the monsoon flooding, Bamroong Krichphaporn, president of the Thai Rice Miller's Association, said he expected only a slight increase in the low market prices for rice, which is in oversupply.

Thailand grows about 22m-23m tonnes of rice annually and sells 6-6.5 tonnes abroad. Vietnam produces an average 33m tonnes of rice a year. **Amy Kazmin, Bangkok** *Additional reporting by Panwadee Uraisin*

I A prominent Hong Kong political party's deputy leader yesterday stepped down from the legislative seat he won in last week's election in response to a public outcry over his failure to disclose ownership of a company to the legislature.

Gary Cheng had also come under fire after a local daily revealed that he passed on confidential government information to a client.

Despite the scandal, Mr Cheng's party, the pro-Beijing Democratic Alliance for the Betterment of Hong Kong, increased its share of the popular vote in last week's election to nearly 30 per cent from 25 per cent in the 1998 election. The party is expected to benefit politically from Mr Cheng's resignation, but observers said it was too early to say that a culture of accountability was taking root in Hong Kong.

Earlier this summer, the head of the local housing authority resigned after revelations of a series of scandals at the authority. Then, this month, the head of the University of Hong Kong resigned following allegations that he sought to interfere with opinion polls conducted by a university professor that tracked the popularity of Hong Kong's chief executive, Tung Chee-hwa, who was hand-picked by Beijing. **Rahul Jacob, Hong Kong**

Key: 1—I, 2—H, 3—E, 4—D, 5—F, 6—B, 7—G, 8—A, 9—C

III 报刊课考试的若干建议
A Brief Introduction to Tests in Reading Comprehension of English Newspapers & Magazines

由高等学校外语专业教学指导委员会英语组 2000 年制定的《高等学校英语专业英语教学大纲》,只将外国报刊选读作为选修课,而六级考试的要求却是"能读懂难度相当于英国[The] *Times* 或[美国][The] *New York Times* 的社论和政论文章",对八级要求"能读懂一般英文报章杂志上的社论和书评"。这么高的要求表明,大纲制定者并未征求报刊教学第一线老师的意见,因而也没有多少学生能达到那么高的水平。

1985 年,编者根据以前出考试题的经验,订出这个外刊选读课考试提纲,供授课教师和读者参考。

1. 考试的目的和要求

考试的目的是使学生通过学习,了解美英的政治、外交、军事、经济、社会、文教和科技概况及当今世界大事,牢牢掌握好有关这方面的核心词语和报刊语言主要特点及读报的核心知识。对美英几大报刊的背景、立场、影响等情况也应有所了解。此外,还要求在阅读理解考试中分析外刊的政治倾向,提高判断能力。

通过 15 或 30 课报刊文选的学习、复习和考试,要求学生大大提高英语报刊阅读理解能力,初步掌握阅读美英报刊必备基本知识,从而为独立阅读打下基础。

2. 考试范围

考试以语言和读报知识基本功为主。具体讲,以课文中出现的政治、经济、外交、军事、文教、宗教、科技、国名、地名等词语为主,如 community, interest, presence, story, the White House, Whitehall, Capitol, Speaker, spokesman, G. N. P., recession, Patriot law/missile, the House of Windsor, Protestant, launch window, Black Africa 等,并了解其中有些词的喻义。学生只要掌握课文内容并将课文后的注释(Notes)、《学习辅导》书里"**Words to Know**"及"新闻写作""语言解说""读报知识"和"学习方法"中介绍的词语和知识掌握好,及格应不成问题。不要求学生去记忆应该在中学或大学一二年级掌握的基本词语,如 byproduct, contract, prolong 等,更不能作为考试范围。阅读理解试题应结合课文中的上述内容,不宜太难。(参见《导读》"语言"和"读报知识")

3. 题型

考试题分三大部分：一是词语翻译：尤其要课文中各种题材如政治、经济、社会、宗教、科技等内容的词语，特别是一讲再讲，仍会混淆的词语。例如：the Capitol（美国国会大厦，喻"国会"）与 capital 和小写的 capitol（州议会大厦，喻"州议会"）不同；the Hill（国会山，也喻"国会"）与 hill 不同；Speaker（议长）与 speaker 和 spokesman（发言人，不用 speaker）不同。同一名词作抽象名词与可数名词时词义不同，如 combat fatigue 与 combat fatigues 不同，democracy 与 a democracy 不同等。此外，学生尚需掌握一些习惯性翻译，如 Secretary of State 译为（美国）"国务卿"，Foreign Secretary（英国）"外交大臣"，Foreign Minister（我国）"外交部长"等。再如 Prime Minister，是王国政府的如英国、荷兰和挪威等按惯例都译为"首相"。但也有例外，如泰国虽为王国，却称"总理"。又如英国外交（和联邦事务）部的"部"，既不是"Ministry"也不是"Department"，而是"Office"。翻译党派也应注意，如德国 Christian Democratic Union 是"**基督教**民主联盟"，而意大利的 Christian Democratic Party 则指"**天主教**民主党"。此外，还应掌握其他一些用作借喻法、提喻法和隐语等的词语。二是选择题：要测试根据上下文判断词义及掌握同义词和反义词等词汇量；三是阅读 passage 或 article 后回答若干问题。passage 或 article 可考虑用要求学生自学的课文。如是课外的，文字应比课文容易些。试题内容与所学课文尽可能有联系。自考生和专科生试题应比在校本科生要浅显些，但第一部分的试题基本相同。

4. 时限

考试时间限定为两小时。考试第一部分的 20—35 个词语翻译需约 20 分钟，第二部分约 40 分钟，第三部分约一小时。

5. 复习方法和建议

复习时一定要读懂课文内容，结合有关文化背景知识重点讲解，使学生掌握上述有关方面的词语，尤其要学会辨析易混淆的词和掌握报刊语言中常见的多义词和喻词。使学生语言和知识双丰收。

以上选自《导读》第七章第五节，部分内容做了修改。

IV 考试样题
Sample Test

Part One (共 30 分)

Translate the following terms into Chinese. (Note: the complete form is REQUIRED if the term is an abbreviation.)

Ⅰ. (共 10 分,每小题 2 分)

1. Yawn
2. GOP
3. NATO
4. CIA
5. FIFA

Ⅱ. (共 20 分,每小题 1 分)

6. The Pulitzer Prize
7. The Pentagon (fig.)
8. Times Square
9. geopolitics
10. Silicon Valley (fig.)
11. guru
12. op-ed
13. classified ads
14. The Ivy League
15. Hispanic
16. The physically challenged
17. the Capitol (fig.)
18. House Speaker
19. the House of Lords/Commons
20. perjury and obstruction of justice
21. the Senate/the House of Representatives
22. checks and balances
23. Attorney General (U.S.)
24. recession
25. private sector

Part Two (共 10 分)

Answer the following questions briefly.

1. List the dominant British newspapers and magazines. (at least three for each)

2. List the four major news agencies in the world.

Part Three (共 10 分, 每小题 2 分)

Paraphrase the underlined parts in the following sentences.

1. Hebert Wang worked for six months at Nortel in Toronto, but he quickly returned to Beijing to found Prient, a start-up that <u>helps old-line companies go online</u>.

2. We're proving that raising standards and <u>holding schools and students accountable for results</u> can lead to dramatic improvements in student achievement.

3. <u>Such frugality seems to run in his circle.</u>

4. The government has also been <u>going after</u> employers who hire undocumented workers.

5. When consumers stop spending, <u>the companies that cater to them idle and lay off</u>.

Part Four: Reading Comprehension (共 40 分)

In this part there are four passages, each of which is followed by several questions. Answer the questions after you finish reading the passages.

Passage One (共 10 分, 每小题 5 分)

The dragon tucks in

Chinese companies are becoming aggressive buyers of overseas assets. It will take longer for them to become smarter ones.

"To spread the 'China Threat' and try to curb China's progress and starve its energy needs is not in the interest of world stability and development. Such attempts are doomed to fail." These feisty words were uttered this week by Zhang Guobao, vice-chairman of China's National Development and Reform Commission, during a visit to an energy conference in New Orleans. He was responding to efforts by American politicians to block an $18.5 billion cash bid made on June

22nd by the China National Offshore Oil Company (CNOOC) for Unocal, a mid-sized American oil firm.

The spat (*verbal fight*) over CNOOC is a symptom of the growing unease felt in developed economies, but especially in America, as more and more Chinese companies have looked abroad for expansion and technological know-how. Just days before the CNOOC bid, Haier, a white-goods maker, bid $2.25 billion for Maytag, a troubled American rival. In May IBM finalised the sale of its personal-computer arm to Lenovo, a deal that also raised political hackles in America.

Americans remember a similar period in the 1980s when Japan was accused of seeking global economic domination as its companies bought everything from Hollywood studios to paintings by Van Gogh. They seem to have forgotten that that threat proved transient, indeed was never really a threat at all. Now comes an increasingly assertive China, its companies flush with cheap cash and its government desperate to maintain its phenomenal economic momentum. As so often when politicians are involved, the truth about the overseas expansion of China's companies is much more complex than hot rhetoric suggests.

Even before the latest row over the CNOOC bid, there were clear signs of China's mounting interest in acquiring real assets abroad aside from oil and gas. The volume of transactions involving a Chinese buyer and an international target has jumped from $2 billion – 3 billion in previous years to almost $23 billion for 2005. Late last year Baosteel, China's largest steelmaker, made a big investment in Brazil, while in 2004 TCL, its leading television producer, bought most of the TV-manufacturing business of France's Thomson plus a mobile handset-making business from Alcatel. Other deals have been less visible, but no less important.

Does this amount to a carefully planned assault on global assets? For all its appearance as a communist-directed monolith, China is ultimately too fragmented for that. Unlike Japan's fabled Ministry of International Trade and Industry in the 1960s and 1970s, China does not have a single agency powerful enough to be an effective co-ordinator. Nevertheless, China's acquisition spree has clear political backing. The leadership in Beijing is determined to create its own set of "global champions"—30 – 50 internationally competitive, yet still state-controlled, firms.

To foster rapid growth and create jobs, China deliberately opened its domestic market to foreign competition relatively early in its economic development. But the quid pro quo (*Latin*: *compensation*) implicit in this strategy was that the government would support, both diplomatically and financially, Chinese companies overseas.

Questions:

1. What are the latest bids made by the Chinese enterprises to purchase overseas assets?

2. Will China succeed in its acquisition of foreign estates in the near future? Why?

Passage Two (共 15 分,每小题 3 分)

America frets as only the rich get richer

"THE top fifth of American households claimed 50.4% of all income last year, the largest slice since the Census Bureau (人口统计局) started tracking the data in 1967." So reported *The Wall Street Journal* just one day before the Commerce Department announced that second-quarter corporate profits were 20.5% higher than a year ago and accounted for 12.2% of gross domestic product (GDP), the highest level in 40 years.

Throw in reports of layoffs at Ford, GM, Intel, and decisions in the nation's boardrooms to reduce the value of workers' pensions while preserving the generous pensions of top executives, and you have some reason to wonder if the famous American dream has turned into a nightmare.

Something is definitely going on that is worrying many observers. Since the 2001 recession year, the economy has grown by almost 12% while the income of the median household — the point at which half of American households have more, and half less — has declined by 0.5%. Last year earnings for full-time workers actually declined — by 1.8% for men, and 1.3% for women.

That said, there is no question that income distribution is becoming a matter of concern — and a political issue — in a country in which calls to man the barricades (防御工事) of the class struggle have historically fallen on deaf ears. When Al Gore played the class card in his 2000 presidential campaign, he was trumped by George Bush's call for tax cuts, even though those reductions benefited wealthy as well as lower-income families.

That was then, and this is now. Centre-left think tanks and opposition politicians are not alone in expressing concern about trends in income distribution. Federal Reserve Board chairman Ben Bernanke recently told a congressional committee: "We want everybody in this society to participate in the American dream. And to the extent that incomes and wealth are spreading apart, I think that is not a good trend."

Two developments are causing observers such as Bernanke some concern. The first is the growing sense that the rich are getting richer, something that nobody save a few hardline lefties ever objected to in America, so long as the poor were also getting richer. Now it seems they aren't. Or, at least, so far in the recent recovery they haven't been.

The second problem relates to the core of the American Dream — social mobility. An oft-told joke in America is that a European (in pre-Thatcher days, we would have said British) worker, seeing his boss drive through the gates in a Rolls-Royce, would want to scratch it, whereas an American worker would think: "Some day I will own one of those".

That worker might be re-examining his position. More and more American workers are coming to believe they and their children are no more likely to rise above their current station than are their European counterparts.

Writing in the *Financial Times*, economics professor Jacques Mistral, of the Conseil d'Analyse Economique and a senior fellow at Harvard's Kennedy School of Government, summaries recent studies as follows: "The situation of a son is more than ever likely to be dictated by his father's social position than by his own merits. If your parents are rich, the likelihood of your being rich is as high as the probability of your being tall if your parents are tall."

So what is going on in America? One thing is huge immigration by poor, unskilled workers. As they enter the workforce, taking on menial jobs at wages too low to attract American workers but a king's ransom by the standards of the clapped-out Mexican economy, they pull average wages down. Some of these workers and their children eventually move up the income ladder, witness the mowers and hoers we know in Colorado who now own their own nurseries. But many never do, partly because, unlike previous waves of immigrants, they return home after accumulating enough money to buy a home or farm or business in their native land.

Another fundamental force at work is globalisation. In recent years more than one billion unskilled, low-paid workers have entered the international workforce — good news for consumers, bad news for Americans sewing shirts and turning out trainers. Meanwhile, globalisation has opened an international market for talented managers, driving up the demand for such executives and, hence, their salaries. The result is downward pressure on wages of the unskilled, upward pressures on executive compensation, and a widening income gap, and one that government-operated retraining programmes have failed to narrow.

All is not lost, however. Ed Lazear, chairman of the president's Council of Economic Advisers, says that hourly earnings have recently begun to grow. Bernanke agrees: "I do think wages will rise. I'm a little surprised they haven't risen more already."

Equally important, Americans are taking steps to reduce the so-called education premium that accounts for some of the increased inequality. Diana Furchtgott-Roth, a colleague at the Hudson Institute since leaving the Labor Department, where she served as chief economist, says: "Our challenge is to get more people to take advantage of educational opportunities ranging from apprenticeships to universities." One million more Americans are now enrolled in institutions offering two-year programmes of advanced education and training than was the case a decade ago.

To borrow from the title of a popular sitcom about the rising black middle class, they will soon be "Movin' on Up".

Irwin Stelzer is a business adviser and director of economic policy studies at the Hudson Institute

Questions:

1. Paraphrase the underlined sentence in the fourth paragraph.

2. The core of the American dream is social mobility. Explain what is social mobility.

3. What is the function of inserting the anecdote about the American worker and European worker in the seventh paragraph?

4. What are the reasons for the problems in America?

5. What measures has America taken to narrow the widening income gap?

Passage Three (共 5 分)

Americans honor parks at Capitol Rotunda

WASHINGTON (AP) — In hushed reverence, Americans paid tribute Monday to Rosa Parks, with more than 30,000 filing silently by her casket in the Capitol Rotunda and a military honor guard saluting the woman whose defiant act on a city bus inspired the modern civil rights movement.

"I rejoice that my country recognizes that this woman changed the course of American history, that this woman became a cure for the cancer of segregation," said the Rev. Vernon Shannon, 68, pastor of John Wesley African-Methodist-Episcopal Zion in Washington, one of many who rose before dawn to see the casket.

Senate Majority Leader Bill Frist, R-Tenn., accompanied new Supreme Court nominee Samuel Alito and his family to the Rotunda, where they paused in silent remembrance. Several senators joined the procession.

Elderly women carrying purses, young couples holding hands and small children in the arms of their parents reverently proceeded around the raised wooden casket. A Capitol Police spokeswoman, Sgt. Jessica Gissubel, said more than 30,000 passed through the Rotunda since Sunday evening, when the viewing began.

Many were overcome by emotion. Monica Grady, 47, of Greenbelt, Md., was moved to tears, she said, that Parks was "so brave at the time without really knowing the consequences" of her actions.

Parks, a former seamstress, became the first woman to lie in honor in the Rotunda, sharing the tribute bestowed upon Abraham Lincoln, John F. Kennedy and other national leaders.

Parks also was being remembered Monday at a memorial service at the Metropolitan A. M. E. Church in Washington and was then to lie in repose at the Charles H. Wright Museum of African American History in Detroit. The program at the Washington memorial service included tributes by Oprah Winfrey, NAACP chairman Julian Bond, Sen. Sam Brownback, R-Kan., and Conyers.

Bush, who presented a wreath but did not speak at the ceremony, issued a proclamation ordering the U.S. flag to be flown at half-staff over all public buildings Wednesday, the day of Parks' funeral and burial in Detroit.

"She was a citizen in the best sense of the word," said Sen. Tom Harkin, D-Iowa. "She caused things to happen in our society that made us a better, more caring, more just society."

Question:

Who was Rosa Parks? And why was she honored by the Americans at Capitol Rotunda at her death?

Passage Four (共 10 分, 每小题 5 分)

Editorial: The Bra Wars

The Bush administration, ignoring the lesson offered by a similarly ill-advised move across the Atlantic, has announced more restrictions on imports of bras and some fabrics made in China. The European Union has shown quite ably just how ridiculous this strategy is. Some 80 million garments have been held up in European ports because of complaints by European textile manufacturers about the flood of cheaper Chinese-made goods since the World Trade Organization abolished the quota system on Jan. 1. Most of those shipments have already been paid for, but arrived after E.U. quotas went into effect. The E.U.'s trade chief, Peter Mandelson, has asked the group's member nations to let the bras and other items in. He recently warned that not doing so could lead to "severe economic pain for many smaller retailers and medium-sized businesses." European officials and China are still negotiating over the quota issue.

The real indication of how bankrupt the restrictions are can be seen in the emptying shelves at stores catering to low-income people. No European products can fill the breach; European manufacturers make high-end lingerie (女贴身内衣), not the cheap stuff.

This isn't the way free trade is supposed to work. For all the talk on both sides of the Atlantic about the benefits of a global market unfettered by protectionism, the wealthy developed countries seem to want free trade only when it benefits their chosen big corporations. Meanwhile, poor consumers suffer the most. The Progressive Policy Institute, a research group in Washington, estimates that shoes and clothing — particularly cheap shoes and cheap clothes — have far higher import duties, relatively speaking, than most other products.

None of this politically expedient protectionism will change a single thing about the way the future is shaping up. Trade experts are unanimous in their belief that China, with its huge modern factories and inexhaustible pool of cheap labor, will continue to dominate the world market for mass-market textiles and apparel. Instead of trying to fight the inevitable, policy leaders in America and Europe should be focusing on developing industries in which their countries can remain competitive and on retraining the textile workers whose jobs migrate. Punishing lower-income consumers in the name of protecting jobs in a dying industry is not the way to go.

Questions:

1. Why did the US and EU exert restrictions on imports of bras and some fabrics made in China?

2. What strategy does the reporter suggest the American and European governments adopt in face of a China which will inevitably dominate the world market for textiles and apparel?

Part Five: Translation (共 10 分)

Saddam verdict may be delayed, prosecutor said

A court trying Saddam Hussein for crimes against humanity could delay its verdict by a few days, the chief prosecutor said on Sunday, in a move that would shift the announcement until after US midterm elections.

The US-backed court had been due to deliver a Verdict on November 5, two days before the US elections in which President George W. Bush's Republicans fear they could lose control of Congress.

The chief prosecutor, Jaafa al-Moussawi, said the Iraqi High Tribunal was still working on the judgment. "We will know a day or two before the trial if they are ready to announce the verdict." Moussawi said.

Saddam could go to the gallows if he is found guilty over his role in the killing of 148 Shi'ite Muslims in the village of Dujail.

参考答案

Part One（共 30 分）

1. Young and Wealthy but normal（年轻而富裕但又节俭[的一代]）
2. Grand Old Party（a nickname for the Republicans）老大党（美国共和党别称）
3. North Atlantic Treaty Organization（北大西洋公约组织）
4. Central Intelligence Agency（中央情报局）
5. Federation Internationale de Football Association（国际足球联合会）
6. 普利策奖
7. 五角大楼；美国国防部
8. 时报广场
9. 地缘政治学
10. 硅谷；高科技集中地
11. 可信赖的顾问、导师
12. 社论对面版，时论专栏版
13. 分类广告
14. 常青藤联合会
15. 居住在美国说西班牙语的拉美人（的）
16. 身体有缺陷者，残疾人
17. 国会或州议会大厦；美国国会或州议会
18. 议长
19. 贵族院（英国上院）/平民院（英国下院）
20. 伪证和妨碍司法执行
21. 参议院/众议院
22. （权力）制衡
23. 司法部长（美国）
24. （经济）衰退
25. 私营部门

Part Two (共 10 分)

1. British newspapers: *The Times*, *The Financial Times*, *The Guardian*, *The Daily Telegraph*

   British magazines: *The Economist*, *The Spectator*, *New Statesman*

2. AP (Associated Press); UPI (United Press International); Reuters; PA (Press Association)

Part Three (共 10 分,每小题 2 分)

1. helps traditional companies advertise or do business through the Internet.
2. making schools and students take the responsibility for results
3. It seems that such frugality is popular among his friends.
4. trying to arrest or punish
5. the companies that provide consumers with what they need now have nothing to do and have to stop their business and dismiss their employees

Part Four (共 40 分)

Passage One (共 10 分,每小题 5 分)

1. CNOOC's $18.5 billion bid for Unocal (aborted); Haier's $2.25 billion bid for Maytag; Lenovo's purchase of IBM personal computer department; Baosteel's investment in Brazil last year; and TCL's purchase of France's Thomson plus a mobile handset-making business from Alcatel.

2. No. China is too fragmented; she does not have a single agency powerful enough to be an effective co-ordinator as Japan did in the 60s and 70s.

Passage Two (共 15 分,每小题 3 分)

1. During the 2000 presidential election the Democratic candidate Al Gore's campaign slogan is social class, while the Republican candidate George W. Bush's is tax cuts. In the end Al Gore was defeated by Bush, even though Bush's tax cut benefited the wealthy more than the middle-lower-income families.

2. Social mobility means that people can move from one social group or status to another, often higher than the original. Or moving upward to a better social group.

3. To explain the American dream, which means that a common citizen can achieve success through hard work.

4. One is the huge immigration by poor, unskilled workers. The other is globalisation which drives up the demand for talented executives and hence their salaries and the consequent downward pressure on wages of the unskilled workers.

5. To provide educational opportunities ranging from apprenticeships to universities.

Passage Three (共 5 分)

Rosa Parks was a black woman who refused to give up her seat for a white man on a city bus in Montgomery in 1955, which touched off the bus boycott and later the civil rights movement in the 1960s in the US.

Passage Four (共 10 分, 每小题 5 分)

1. Because the flood of cheaper Chinese-made goods since the World Trade Organization abolished the quota system on Jan. 1 hurt their textile manufacturers.

2. Instead of trying to fight the inevitable, policy leaders in America and Europe should, instead of practising protectionism, be focusing on developing industries in which their countries can remain competitive and on retraining the textile workers whose jobs migrate.

Part Five (共 10 分)

检察官称,萨达姆判决可能被推迟

正以反人类罪审判萨达姆·侯赛因的法庭首席检察官周日表示,法庭可能推迟几天宣布判决结果。此举意味着宣判将推迟到美国中期选举以后。

这家美国支持的法庭原定的宣判日期是11月5日,也就是美国中期选举前两天。总统乔治·W·布什领导的共和党人担心他们将在此次选举中失去对国会的控制权。

首席检察官贾法尔·穆萨维说,伊拉克高级法庭还在研究如何进行判决。他说:"我们会在审判前一两天获悉他们是否准备宣判。"

如果被判对杜贾尔村148名什叶派穆斯林遇害事件负有罪责,萨达姆可能被判绞刑。

以上试题和答案均由一编委提供。特此说明。